A TIME TO SPEAK

*Controversial Essays
That Can Change Your Life*

Martin Stern

DEVORA
PUBLISHING
NEW YORK◆JERUSALEM◆LONDON

A Time to Speak
Published by Devora Publishing Company
Copyright © 2010 Martin Stern

COVER DESIGN: Benjie Herskowitz
TYPESETTING: Koren Publishing Services
EDITORIAL AND PRODUCTION DIRECTOR: Daniella Barak
EDITOR: Chani Hadad

Soft Cover ISBN: 978-1-936068-15-9

E-MAIL: sales@devorapublishing.com
WEB SITE: www.devorapublishing.com

Distributed by:
Urim Publications
POB 52287
Jerusalem 91521, Israel
Tel: 02.679.7633
Fax: 02.679.7634
urim_pub@netvision.net.il

Lambda Publishers, Inc.
527 Empire Blvd.
Brooklyn, NY 11225, USA
Tel: 718.972.5449
Fax: 781.972.6307
mh@ejudaica.com

www.UrimPublications.com

First edition. Printed in Israel

RABBI MOSHE FEINSTEIN

455 F. D. R. DRIVE

New York, N. Y. 10002

ORegon 7-1222

משה פיינשטיין

ר"ם תפארת ירושלים

בנוא יארק

בע"ה

הנה הקונטרוס על עניני פו"ר שחיברן הרב מ. סטערן שליט"א מאנגלאנד,
היה לפראה עיניו של פרי סבי זצ"ל, אך לא הספיק לחתום על מכתב הסכמה
עד שנסתלק. והזכיר פרי סבי זצ"ל שקונטרוס כזה יכול להיות לחועלה להשריש
יסודי האמונה וזהירות בכמה מדות חשובות כליבם של אחינו בני ישראל,
והביע ברכתו שיצליח הרב המחבר שליט"א לחבר עוד ספרים חשובים.
ועל זה באתי על החתום בערב פסח שנת השמו"ח לכבודו של פרי סבי זצ"ל אלו
סביו.ו של פ"ס זצ"ל. אלו.

מרדכי טענדלר

My late grandfather and teacher, *zts"l*, had the opportunity to look over the booklet on concepts concerning the mitzvah of "Be fruitful and multiply" written by Rabbi M. Stern, *shlit"a*, from England. Unfortunately he was not able to sign his letter of approbation before he passed away, but he wished to have it recognized that this work was valuable in that it would implant fundamentals of the Jewish faith and promote many praiseworthy character traits among our Jewish People. In addition, he wished to convey his blessing to the author, *shlit"a*, that he should publish more such valuable books.

Signed in honor of my grandfather and teacher, *zts"l*,
Erev Pesach 5746

Mordechai Tendler

CONTENTS

PREFACE

In a preface, one can make a few personal remarks that may put the composition of this book into perspective.

When I was a boy, I always found essay writing difficult, which was one reason I gravitated towards mathematics, a subject that did not require that skill. It is rather surprising, then, that I have now been published over 600 times. I remember the difficulty I had with producing my master's thesis and the paper published from it over 40 years ago. In those days before the advent of word processors, writing any lengthy work was a tedious business. Either one had to hire a typist to produce it, which entailed proofreading and consequential retyping, or one tried to type it oneself, with the inevitable errors. In either case, corrections, let alone revisions of the text, meant laboriously retyping the page. I was, therefore, only too happy to take up a post as a lecturer in a college where teaching would be the main duty and I would not be expected to produce any more publications – or so I thought.

It was therefore something of a shock when our college decided to aim for a higher university status and the head of our department called a meeting at which we were all told that we must do research and publish at least one paper a year. Most of my colleagues were in a similar position, with our days being filled with teaching and administrative duties, leaving little time for additional tasks. Furthermore, after 20 years, it was rather difficult suddenly to embark on unfamiliar activity. We were, however, assured that (at least in the first instance) any mathematical publication would be satisfactory and we would not have to make any great advances on the frontiers of knowledge.

I remembered an interesting observation attributed to the Gra (though I have been unable to find any reference to it in his published works) regarding the apparent discrepancy in the value of **pi** as derived from a *pasuk* in *Tanach*. I therefore wrote it up and submitted it to a journal for mathematics teachers, which published it. It was later included in a comprehensive work, *Pi: A Source Book*, published by the prestigious Springer Verlag in 1991. This was the first of several such mathematical curiosities of Jewish interest, some of which I have included in this work. Over the next 10 years and until I retired, I published 35 mathematics papers, though most were concerned with educational topics of little interest to readers of this volume.

About this time, I noticed an article by a certain rabbi who wrote a column in a local Jewish paper. I thought that the article gave an altogether far too lenient ruling on family planning matters, at least in the context of a paper aiming at the not particularly observant public. I felt compelled to respond and this gave rise to a quite heated exchange in the letters column, eventually leading to my production of a short pamphlet on the subject, entitled "Family Planning – A Torah Perspective." I sent it to Rabbi Moshe Feinstein, *zts"l*, who signalled his approval although, as his secretary and grandson, Rabbi Mordechai Tendler, wrote that he passed away before he was able to sign. It was probably the last work he considered before his *petirah*.

About six months later, a letter appeared in another Jewish paper, not known for its sympathy with Orthodoxy, from the co-chairmen of a Masorti (Conservative) synagogue in London giving the misleading impression that it was in fact Orthodox. This was the beginning of a campaign by that movement to expand in England by blurring its theological distinctions with Orthodoxy. I responded and over the years was actively involved in countering their insidious propaganda. I have not included any of these polemics in this volume, but anyone interested can refer to the articles and letters listed at the end of this book. It did, however, lead me to think deeply about the concept of Torah *min hashamayim*, which forms the essential difference between our ideologies, and I have included that article.

I also wrote a Purim parody in the form of a book review to expose the ridiculous excesses of "higher biblical criticism," to which I lay blame for causing the Conservatives to originally break away from Torah Judaism. I enclose it in this volume together with another spoof book review for the amusement of the reader. Incidentally, the wide variety of styles of the different sections would probably lead a textual critic to deduce that they were written by different authors, though they are all my work!

Another topic that interested me was the *Shema*. I noticed that, though it had become de rigueur in many circles to spend a great time over *Shemoneh Esrei*, the *Shema* was said relatively quickly. I often joked that the former was our talking to HKBH, whereas the latter was our listening to Him, and people much prefer to do the former. However, I noticed a few difficulties that I addressed in an article in the *Jewish Tribune* in 1987. Over the years more ideas have come to mind and I have included a much expanded version in this volume. I have also included a few other articles on various liturgical topics that have drawn my interest over the years.

A related topic that drew my attention was the correct pronunciation of our *tefillot* and proper behavior in shul, a few articles of which are also included.

I experimented with various styles and wrote "The *Kiddush* Widow" about the problems of housebound mothers of small children on Shabbat in places where there is no *eiruv*. I was particularly heartened when a lady told me she could hardly believe it had been written by a man, as it described her situation so accurately.

When a friend became an *aveil*, I developed the "Dear Chaim" format, which I found very helpful in allowing me to make comments in a semi-fictional format that I would have had difficulty in addressing directly to the persons concerned. These have appeared in various publications and a selection is included here.

As will be clear to the reader, I tend to be rather controversial, though I hope not offensive, and this is quite intentional since I hope to make the reader think more deeply about the issues discussed.

Over the years, I have learned much from many people and it may be invidious to mention any lest others feel slighted, *chas veshalom*, due to my oversight in omitting their names. I apologize in advance to anyone whom I may have inadvertently overlooked.

First I should like to acknowledge how much I learned from Dayan Gavriel Krausz *shlita*, *Rosh Beit Din* of the Manchester *Beit Din*, who was *rav* of my shul, the *Adass Yeshurun*, for many years, and his successor, Rabbi Yaakov Wreschner *shlita*; their example was an inspiration to many and their departures were a great loss for the shul.

Next I wish to thank Rabbi Simcha Chaim Bamberger *shlita* whose *Daf Hayomi shiur* I have attended for over three cycles and many of whose observations are the source of some of the ideas presented in this volume. Unfortunately, I cannot specify all for they are so many that it is impossible to enumerate them. May he continue to delight the participants in his *shiur* for many cycles to come.

I should also like to thank Rabbi C.A.Z. Halpern of the Beit Din of the Union of Orthodox Hebrew Congregations, London, for his help and encouragement in starting the project that formed the basis of the article reproduced here as Chapter 9, and Rabbi J.

Goldberg of Manchester for the time and effort he put into helping me clarify the *halachic* background of the article.

Many people helped me in the preparation of this book and I should like to thank them all, especially Mr. David Ansbacher, for his assistance in preparing some of the documents, and Mrs. Chani Hadad of Simcha Publishing, for her diligence in harmonizing the various articles that had originally appeared in many different publications that had differing conventions regarding transliteration of Hebrew, spelling, and other stylistic matters, and Ms. Daniella Barak and Ms. Sara Rosenbaum for their help in ironing out all the glitches necessary to bring this book to publication.

Acharon acharon chaviv, I would like to thank my wife, Shoshana, *minashim be'ohel tevorach*, for her patience while I spent so much time closeted with my computer on the preparation of this work. Without her backing I would never have been able to write the many articles of which this book contains a selection, nor the peace of mind necessary for its compilation. *Sheli veshelachem, shelah hu.*

ACKNOWLEDGMENTS

Some sections of this book have appeared previously in various newspapers and journals, though some have been corrected where errors were detected or slightly modified in light of later comments. In particular, I should like to thank the editors of the following for permission to publish articles that appeared in their columns:

Hamaor Magazine, the Journal of the Federation of Synagogues, London: "Making Your Simchah a Simchah for Everyone," "For Everything There Is a Time," and "A Man Does Not Know His Time."

The Jewish Tribune, London: "A Time to Speak," "A King Extolled with Praises," "A Time to Request," "*Kaddish Yosom*," "The *Kiddush* Widow," "*Bera Mezakeh Abba*," "Some Tips on Being *Sheliach Tzibur*," "Shul Etiquette," and "Language and Thought Patterns."

The International Journal for Mathematical Education in Science and Technology, London: "Menstrual Cycle Analysis: a Problem in Pattern Recognition."

Le'ela, Journal of the London School of Jewish Studies: "A Response to the Missionary Menace."

The Mathematical Gazette, Journal of the Mathematical Association, Leicester, UK: "A Remarkable Approximation to Pi," and "Calculations Before Calculators."

Niv HaMidrashia, Tel Aviv: "Some Problems with the Calculation of Sunrise."

Teaching Mathematics and Its Applications, Southend-on-Sea: "It's a Long Long Time from June to September."

Voice Magazine, Journal of the Manchester Beit Din: "Give Honor to the Torah."

Yated Ne'eman, Jerusalem: "*Shorshei Kerem Rosh Nevalim*" and "How to Run a *Minyan*."

CHAPTER ONE:

TORAH MIN HASHAMAYIM

Every day we praise the Almighty, "who has created us for his glory, separating us from those who go astray, and has given us a Torah of truth, implanting within us everlasting life." This faith, as the Rambam puts it, "that the entire Torah which is found in our hands today is that which was given through Moshe Rabbeinu, and is entirely the word of G-d," has sustained and inspired Jews throughout the ages despite the many persecutions to which we have been subjected. That the Torah, as we have it today, was given by the Almighty to the Jewish People at a specific time is agreed by all the classical Jewish philosophers to be one of the fundamental beliefs of Torah Judaism, without which it cannot exist. Whether this belief in itself is a *mitzvah*, as the Rambam holds, or is one of the underlying assumptions upon which Torah Judaism is built, as held by Crescas and Albo, makes little difference to its significance in practice.

While there is some difference of opinion as to whether the whole Torah was given at Sinai or it was given in stages during the forty years' journey through the wilderness, it is a basic belief that its content was an entirely Divine composition and Moshe

Rabbeinu only transmitted it to the Jewish People. The Rambam emphasizes this point very strongly in his formulation of the principle (Introduction to *Perek Chelek*, eighth principal of faith):

> We believe that the entire Torah which is found in our hands today is that which was given through Moshe Rabbeinu and that it is entirely the word of G-d. That is, that it came to Moshe entirely from the Almighty, blessed be He, in a manner which we refer to, for lack of a better description, as speech. Nor is it known to us precisely how this occurred, but only that it was he, Moshe, who received it, and that he was like a scribe, to whom it was dictated […]
>
> The individual who maintains that [any] verses or narratives were written by Moshe himself is regarded by our Sages and our Prophets as the most grievous of apostates, for he believes that the Torah contains essential and non-essential sections […]
>
> And so, too, is the traditional oral interpretation of the Torah [the Oral Law] also the word of G-d. That which we observe today in regard to the form of a *sukkah*…and other *mitzvot* is the very same form which the Almighty, blessed be He, transmitted to Moshe, and which he conveyed to us.

In one of his most important essays on this topic, the Chief Rabbi of the United Kingdom, Dr. Jonathan Sacks, wrote:

> Orthodoxy involves belief in a proposition denied by most non-Orthodox Jews, namely, that the five books of Moses are the unmediated word of G-d. They are, that is to say, revelation. It is in this sense that Conservative Jews often speak of Orthodoxy as fundamentalist […]. The belief in Torah as revelation is not simply *a* fundamental of Jewish faith. It is *the* fundamental of Jewish faith. For were it not for our faith in Torah, how could we arrive at religious certainty about the creation of the world, the meaningfulness of human

existence, the justice of history and the promise of messianic redemption? Our knowledge of these things, fragmentary though it is, is derived from neither logic nor science but from our faith in Torah and its Divine authorship. In this sense, Orthodoxy *is* fundamentalist. ("Fundamentalism Reconsidered," *Leela* 28 (1989) p.9.)

THE PROBLEM FOR "MODERNS"

Few ideas are more profoundly misunderstood than Torah *min hashamayim*, as a result of which many Jews today consider it to be irrational, unhistorical, or even "fundamentalist." Of course it is none of these, but on the contrary, it is an entirely reasonable doctrine and those who hold these erroneous opinions do so out of a wholly misplaced reliance on the results of "modern scholarship." Such "scholarship" is based on a circular argument and once this is realized its results are much less convincing than they appear at first sight.

Modern patterns of thought, especially since the rise of the Enlightenment, have given rise to doubts in the minds of many Jews. The questions they tend to ask are: "When was the Torah written? By whom was it written? Was it written at one time or at various times?" They know that scholars in the nineteenth century and even earlier attempted to answer these questions using evidence from various techniques of textual criticism.

What they do not always realize is that the use of such methods prejudges the issue and decides the outcome in advance. Before the first act of analysis takes place the assumption has already been made that the Torah is not the word of G-d but a human composition, which is as much an article of faith as the Rambam's. Based on this assumption, the only questions to be asked are which men and at what time or times.

The techniques of textual criticism were devised in the Renaissance period to solve the problem of the authorship of various works attributed to the classical authors, some of which were clearly not by the ones to whom they were ascribed. The methods used were generally successful for this purpose though there were always some doubtful cases. We have a similar problem with some works of the *Rishonim*; many readers will be aware that, for example, the Rashba on *Ketubot* is really by the Ramban. The underlying assumption of these techniques is that we are examining the works of human authors. Applying them to the Torah must therefore make the same assumption about its nature, though this is not usually stated by the critics. They are therefore guilty of the logical fallacy known as "poisoning the well." They have removed any supernatural element from the Torah and treat it like any classical text.

Furthermore, an uncritical acceptance of the theories of "higher biblical criticism" is not logically compatible with a traditional Jewish lifestyle, despite assertions to the contrary in certain circles. As Dr. Sacks has written, for Judaism, as opposed to Christianity:

> …the Bible is more central because it represents not just *evidence* of revelation but the *content* of revelation itself. For Judaism, the Torah is not merely a record of events (the Exodus and Sinai), but the constitution of the covenant made on the basis of those events. In it, G-d reveals not only His presence but also His will. What is important to Judaism, therefore, is not only what historically lies behind the text, but the text itself. For this reason, while Protestantism might survive the displacement of the text, Judaism cannot. (*Crisis and Covenant: Jewish Thought after the Holocaust*, Manchester University Press (1992) p. 201.)

CONTENT OR FORM?

The precise nature of the concept of Torah *min hashamayim* does, however, require some closer analysis. There are two ways of understanding it: either that the apparent plain meaning of the text of the Torah is infallibly true, or that the actual text *as written* is in the form designed by the Almighty. It might be argued that the former is implied by the statement *Ein mikra yotsei midei peshuto*, "A biblical statement never loses its literal meaning" (*Shabbat* 63a), yet this cannot always be true since there are many instances where the apparent plain meaning is known to be incorrect. In reality, this view represents the Karaite heresy, which denied the authenticity of the Torah *shebe'al peh*, which the Rambam stated was an intrinsic part of the doctrine. In fact, the Rambam himself considered this literalist approach to be inconsistent with Judaism since he wrote that "Scripture contains nothing that is impossible… and is consistent even with the belief in the eternity of the universe (which he did not in fact accept to be true)" (*Moreh Nevuchim* 2:16), which obviously contradicts the literal meaning of the first chapter of *Bereishit*. He maintains that *where it is not contrary to established facts or traditions* the literal meaning is to be accepted. This opinion is far removed from the literalist opinions put out by present-day Christian fundamentalists. He insists that where an apparent contradiction occurs, the text must be interpreted appropriately to resolve the problem.

So if the Torah's contents, in their literal sense, are not invariably infallible, what does the doctrine of Torah *min hashamayim* really mean? Examination of the Rambam's definition gives us a clue, since he writes, "Moshe…was like a scribe, to whom it was dictated…" as if the Almighty were, so to speak, looking over Moshe's shoulder and instructing him "write this word here… spell it this way…" etc. In other words, it is the form of the text that is crucial.

A closer look at rabbinic sources also leads to this conclusion. For example, there is the principle *Ein mukdam ume'uchar baTorah*, "The Torah is not written chronologically" (*Pesachim* 6b), and its converse, the hermeneutical principle of *hekkesh*, that verses have been written close to one another in order to teach a lesson.

Similarly, the hermeneutical principle of *gezerah shavah*, that a similar word written in two separate verses can be used to link the two, can only have any basis if the Almighty had designed the text with those words in precisely those positions.

We also sometimes find that *Chazal* learn *halachot* from apparently superfluous letters, for example whether it is written *malei* (with a *vav* to signify the vowel *cholam*) or *chaseir* (when it is missing). Even the little "crowns" on certain letters have special significance, which the *Gemara* states contain 'thoughts' of the Almighty that were not even apparent to Moshe Rabbeinu and were left for future generations to discover (*Menachot* 29b). Many of these principles will be applied in upcoming chapters to delve more deeply into the ideas that might be found under the surface in the *Shema*.

Finally, the *Gemara* records (*Shabbat* 88b-89a) that when Moshe went up to receive the Torah, the angelic hosts objected to its being handed over to mere mortals, to which Moshe responded that its commandments had no application to them so it was only fitting for him to bring it down to *B'nei Yisrael*. The obvious problem with this *aggadah* is, "What meaning could the Torah have had for the angels?" One explanation is that they "read" it in a quite different way from us, not as commandments and narratives, but rather as Divine names "written in black fire on white fire" (*Yalkut Shimoni, Yitro* 280).

CHAPTER TWO:

LITURGICAL OBSERVATIONS

INTRODUCTION

There is a story, probably apocryphal, of a Lithuanian *rosh yeshivah* who went to collect funds in the USA shortly after the First World War. On his return to his impoverished *shtetl*, everyone asked him about Jewish life in the *goldene medinah*. His reply, "*Mal'ah ha'aretz chamas*" (Gen. 6:13), literally "The land is full of violence," surprised them. Though they knew that life there was different, they hardly expected that it had degenerated so far and, shocked by his comment, asked him to elaborate. He explained that his comment was not to be taken literally at all but reflected on the low level of Jewish learning. He said, "When I visited the houses of the wealthy Jews in New York, I was at first dazzled by their opulence, but once I had recovered my composure, I noticed one striking fact: the only Jewish books to be seen were *chumashim*, *machzorim* and *siddurim*, whose initial letters spell out the word *chamas*." What had happened to the more assimilated Jews was that their Judaism had been relegated to the synagogue where only such *sefarim* were needed and the age-old tradition of Torah learning had fallen in to desuetude. This state of affairs has unfortunately not changed for the majority over the subsequent decades.

This might not have been quite as disastrous as he assumed if the lack of learning had been replaced by an increase in fervor in prayer, as has happened with the Chassidic movement, but this was not the case. The decline in learning was paralleled by a corresponding decline in attention to prayer. It had become common for people to come late to *shul*, especially on *Shabbat* and *Yom Tov*, and, when there, to engage in idle chatter with their friends. This was not an entirely new phenomenon, having already been noted by the son of the Rambam in Egypt, but, together with the prevailing ignorance of Jewish tradition, precipitated rapid assimilation with increasing intermarriage rates.

The lack of decorum in *shul* gave the various deviationist movements some semblance of truth on which to base their attacks on Torah Judaism and this might explain why they were successful in leading so many Jews astray. This reflects the fact that any heretical movement must have some element of truth in it since something that is evidently totally false must fail to ensnare any but the most gullible. Perhaps this itself is a reflection of the Divine purpose, the *hester panim* under which we live today, since, without such apparent plausibility, we would not have any true freedom of choice and, in consequence, not deserve any reward for our actions.

Unfortunately, *shul* decorum has not improved sufficiently since the days of that *rosh yeshivah*, despite the proliferation of Torah publications in English in recent years, including many modern English translations and other works explaining the meaning of our *tefillot*. On the other hand, there is an evident thirst for spirituality, but this tends to be manifested by an attraction to the occult and Eastern religions, many of which are true *avodah zarah*. This was noted by the late Aryeh Kaplan, who wrote three seminal books on the subject of meditation in Judaism and how this might enhance one's *tefillot*.

On the other hand, there has been a movement in certain

circles to take an extremely long time over the *Shemoneh Esrei*. While this is much to be admired, there may be some disadvantages, as I discuss elsewhere. However, the same degree of concentration is not applied to the *Shema*, which led me to think about some of its deeper meanings. This would appear to contradict the teachings of the *baalei kabbalah* that the *Shema* is associated with the *hitaruta diletata*, arousal from below, which depends on our efforts, whereas the *Shemoneh Esrei* is associated with the *hitaruta dileeila*, arousal from above, which the former induces, the joint effect of which is to provide the conduits for Divine munificence to be opened up. Thus, greater concentration on the *Shema* might seem to be even more important. However, these are somewhat esoteric concepts which we shall not expand on here.

We say the *Shema* every morning and evening as part of the daily prayers and also each night before retiring to sleep. Apart from its full recital, the first verse, which summarizes some of the fundamental principles of Judaism, is also added several times, perhaps most movingly as the climax of the *Ne'ilah* prayer at the end of *Yom Kippur*. It is among the last words uttered by the holy martyrs before making the ultimate sacrifice rather than abjure their faith in the Almighty and His Torah. It is said by children as they gather around an infant boy's crib on the evening before his *brit milah*. As the soul departs in life's final moments, after one hundred and twenty years, the recital of *Shema* forms both a farewell to the present world and an affirmation of faith for a life in the world-to-come.

So important is the *Shema* that, commenting on the words of the *meshuach milchamah* (Deut. 20:3), Rabbi Yochanan said in the name of Rabbi Shimon ben Yochai that even if a person had no other *mitzvah* than the recital of *Shema* morning and evening then he would be saved from all enemies (*Sotah* 42a). The *Yalkut HaGershuni* (ad loc) explains the word *enemies* as referring to the *yetzer hara*, the internal enemy *par excellence*, which is always ready to lead us astray (cf. Gen. 4:7).

In view of this it is not surprising that the *Shulchan Aruch*

(*Orach Chaim* 61) rules that "One should recite the *Kriat Shema* with careful thought, awe, fear, trepidation, and trembling" (*se'if* 1), and "The words *which I command you today* imply that each day one should look upon it as if it has been newly given and not as something that has already been heard many times previously so that they are not dear to one" (*se'if* 2), a warning that is all too apt for passages recited several times a day. The *Mishnah Berurah* (*se'if katan* 4) elaborates that one should read the *Shema,* "like a man reads the decree of the king, with great deliberation, pondering each command separately in order to understand its ramifications."

It then continues in the subsequent paragraphs to rule on many finer details of the recitation, such as separating words that are easily run together (*ibid. se'ifim* 15 – 21), distinguishing hard and soft forms of certain letters or using the incorrect sheva (*se'if* 23). It even rules that one should recite the Shema with its cantillation as found in the Torah (*se'if* 24), though the Rema notes that the general practice is not to be stringent in this matter. However, it will be shown in this article that there are some interesting lessons that may be learned from the way it punctuates the text. There is no mention of the need to avoid putting the stress in a word on the incorrect syllable, the other common source of error, but this is hardly surprising since those using the traditional cantillation would do so automatically.

Unfortunately, placing the stress in the incorrect place can radically alter the meaning when a verb occurs with the *vav ha-hippuch*. Thus, for example, *ve'ahavta* means "and you *shall* love" when stressed on the last syllable, but "and you have loved" when stressed on the penultimate one, implying the exact opposite, that the love of *HaShem* is a historical fact no longer obligatory on us, *rachmana litzlan*.

The *Shema* can be thought of as the initiation of a conversation in which *HaShem* speaks to us, calling out, "Shema, Hear what I have to say to you before you try to ascend any further and speak to Me!" in which every word and phrase is pregnant with meaning. Since the *Shema* consists of sections from the Torah *shebichtav*, the written Torah, it is necessary first to examine precisely what is meant by the concept of Torah *min hashamayim* (see Chapter 1 above) and how it impinges on our understanding of the written text, as opposed to the oral Torah transmitted through the generations by our Sages. Then it will be shown that many interesting lessons can be learned from apparently insignificant orthographic differences. In the next chapter, I have collected various ideas that have occurred to me over the years arising from these textual peculiarities. Wherever possible I have given my source; any others are purely speculative and are presented as such. It is not meant to be in any way exhaustive and there are many more ideas that have been seen in the text by commentators throughout the generations. To paraphrase the *Mishnah's* quotation of the words of the *Kohen Gadol* on *Yom Kippur* (*Yoma* 7:1), "More than I have written here can be read elsewhere."

Before embarking on this topic, I would like to draw the reader's attention to the concept of the *al tikrei*, which I shall use quite frequently. As is well known, in a *sefer* Torah, there are no vowel signs nor, for that matter, is there any punctuation. How the words are read and how they are grouped is based on the Torah *shebe'al peh*, authentic oral tradition. Thus, the sequence *chet, lamed, vet* can be read as *cheilev*, fat, or *chalav*, milk, and the incorrect vocalization can completely change the meaning of a passage with possibly serious *halachic* consequences.

Though the true vocalization and punctuation are fixed, there is a homiletic device known as *al tikrei*, whereby it is not read as in the received text but with a changed vocalization. This is not intended to replace the original, but rather to provide an extra layer of interpretation. A familiar example is that at the end of *Berachot* (64b) on the verse *vechol banayich limudei HaShem verav shalom banayich*, "all your children shall be taught of *HaShem* and great shall be the peace of your children" (Isaiah 45:13), which continues *al tikrei banayich eile bonayich*, "do not read *banayich*, your children but *bonayich*, your builders (i.e., scholars who are the true builders of peace)." Such techniques can suggest allusions in the text as we shall see below.

A further example, in which the punctuation is altered, is found in Sanhedrin (90b) where a suggested homiletic proof that resurrection of the dead is mentioned in the Torah is based on reading *hinecha shochev im avotecha vekam*, "you will lie with your forefathers and rise" (Deut. 31:16), though the last word is clearly separated by an *etnachta* from the first phrase in the Masoretic text.

[Please refer to the appendices at the end of this book for a helpful guide to cantillation signs and the *gematria* systems.]

READING BETWEEN THE LINES OF THE *SHEMA*

The second paragraph of the Shema *(Deut. 11:13–21) forms the basis of this section. A comparison of it with the first paragraph (Deut. 6:4–9) is used to shed light on further important concepts contained in the text, which might escape the reader when reciting it at the usual speed required to keep up with the communal prayers.*

Some of these are shown to be developed in the third paragraph (Num. 15:37–41), even though at first sight its style is quite different and its subject matter unconnected with them. Some of these ideas are further extended by considering the *birchot Kriat Shema* and other places in the liturgy where the *Shema* appears.

The Hidden Light of the *Shema*

There is an interesting custom of touching the *tefillin* at the beginning of the *berachah "yotzer or"* that precedes the recital of the *Shema* in the morning. Since the verses referring to the *tefillin* always mention the *shel yad* before the *shel rosh*, the former is always touched first. However, this might seem somewhat incongruous in this particular instance since the *shel yad*, which is covered, is touched on saying the words *yotzer or*, "who forms light," whereas the *shel rosh*, which is openly visible, is touched on saying *uvorei choshech*, "and creates darkness." It might seem more appropriate for the uncovered one to be associated with light and the covered one with darkness.

There is another problem in the order of Creation that might be seen to shed light on this problem. On the first day, the Almighty commanded *yehi or*, "let there be light" (Gen. 1:3), yet the luminaries were only created on the fourth day (1:14). *Chazal* comment (*Chagigah* 12a) on this anomaly by stating that the primeval light was too bright for Creation to bear and had to be hidden until the end of days when it had reached perfection. This may be the meaning of the sentence used to introduce the *yotzer piyut*: *or olam beotsar chaim, orot me'ofel amar vayehi*, "light eternal is in the store of life, He spoke and out of darkness there was light." With this in mind, the hidden *tefillin shel yad* corresponds very fittingly with the hidden light and, having appreciated this, we might be motivated to look more deeply into the *Shema* and see that there are deeper layers of meaning than appear at first sight.

Incidentally, the *navi Yeshaya* (45:7) would seem to be making a mistake by referring to *yotzer or*, "who forms light," as opposed to *uvorei choshech*, "and creates darkness." We intuitively think of darkness as the absence of light and so would expect the latter to have been created and the former to have been formed by its removal. The current cosmological theory known as the "Big Bang" would, however, fit very well with his terminology. According to it, all matter and energy were originally concentrated in a minute point from which it expanded until the universe as we know it "condensed." Until this expansion had reached a certain critical "size," the gravitational field would have been so strong that, according to the General Theory of Relativity, light would not have been able to escape (like in a "black hole"). Thus, to any observer, everything would have been dark. Only once this critical "size" was reached, could light escape and become visible and so could be said to be formed from the darkness. On the other hand, the *navi* mentions the light before the darkness, which might seem to indicate its prior existence even if this should be invisible to any observer. Whether he really had any of this in mind or *HaShem* had put this formulation in his mouth to indicate such a scenario cannot be determined, but it is an interesting "coincidence" that such an ancient text should agree so well with the latest scientific theory.

The Heart of the Matter

The *Avudraham* (p.77) writes:

> It is said in *Devarim Rabbah*: "Guard my *mitzvot* and live" (Prov. 4:4) – guard the 248 words in *Kriat Shema* and the Holy One, blessed be He, will guard your 248 limbs. However, it will be found to be three words short since in the first paragraph, including *baruch shem kevod malchuto le'olam va'ed*, there are 54 words, in the second 122 words, and in the third 69 words, making a total of 245…Therefore they added *keil melech ne'eman* whose acrostic is *amen* as mentioned in *Massechet Shabbat* 119b.

The passage he quotes does not appear to be in our editions of *Devarim Rabbah*, but a similar passage is found in *Midrash Tanchuma* (*Kedoshim* 6):

> Rav Mani said, 'Do not let the *mitzvah* of *Kriat Shema* be insignificant in your eyes since it contains 248 words, the same number as the limbs of the human body, if one includes *baruch shem*. The Holy One, blessed be He, said *If you will guard what is Mine to recite Kriat Shema properly, then I will guard you*. Therefore David uttered the praise, *Guard me like the apple of Your eye* (Ps. 17:8), to which the Holy One, blessed be He, replied, *Guard my mitzvot and live* (Prov. 4:4).'

The *Avudraham* continues, "They also instituted that the *sheliach tzibur* should repeat the three words *HaShem Elokechem emet* in order to make up the 248 words."

The *Shulchan Aruch* (*Orach Chaim* 61:3) rules accordingly while the Rema (ad loc) adds that one praying alone should say *keil melech ne'emen* as an alternative.

If one examines the *Shema*, one might note that several words are joined by a *makkef* (in most editions of the *siddur*). This occurs 32 times, which is the *gematria* of *lev*, heart. Since words joined by a *makkef* are to a certain extent treated as one word, this reduces the number of words in the *Shema* to 213. Perhaps one can gain an insight from this by observing that this is the *gematria* of the word *yegar*, which is part of the only Aramaic phrase found in the Torah (Gen. 31:47), *yegar sahaduta*, meaning *mound of testimony*. This name was given by *Lavan* while *Ya'akov* called it *gal ed*, which has the same meaning (Rashi *ad loc*). Furthermore, in the Masoretic text, the *ayin* of *shema* and the *dalet* of *echad*, are enlarged, also spelling the word *ed*, as pointed out by the Tur in his commentary. Why the Torah included the Aramaic name given by *Lavan* has always been a mystery. Perhaps it was meant to be a hint to the *Shema* as being a mound of testimony if we only take its message to heart.

In some editions of the *Chumash* there is a further *makkef* joining the words *lo taturu* (Num. 15:39). This makes no difference to the meaning of the verse but changes the cantillation from *kadma ve'azla* to *azla geresh*. In such texts the *makkef* occurs 33 times, which is the *gematria* of *gal*, the Hebrew equivalent of *yegar*. There remain 212 words, which is the *gematria* of *riv*, a dispute, which the mound set up by *Ya'akov* and *Lavan* was meant to resolve.

Justice and Mercy

The first word of the second paragraph, *vehayah*, is a permutation of the letters of the name, *HaShem*, whose *gematria* is twenty six. The introduction to the *Tikkunei Zohar* (9b) points out that there are twelve such permutations and the Arizal noted that the word *chodesh*, month, has *gematria* three hundred and twelve which is twelve times twenty-six. From this he deduced that each of these permutations corresponds to one of the twelve months of the year, as the *B'nei Yissaschar* explains in detail. The regular order corresponds to *Nisan* (*Ma'amarei Chodesh Nisan* 1), whereas that of *vehayah* correspond to *Tishrei* (*Ma'amarei Chodesh Tishrei* 1).

It is interesting to note that permutations of this Divine name occur twelve times in the three paragraphs of the *Shema*, ten in its regular order and twice as *vehayah*. This does not include the one in Deut. 11:17, since it is connected by a *makkef* to the word *af*, and may be considered in this context as a single word of six letters. Alternatively, the latter might be a hint to the intercalated thirteenth month. According to tradition, the wrath (*af*) of *HaShem* is more prevalent in leap years, as is evidenced by the institution of the fasts of *Shovavim Tat* during its extended winter season. Furthermore, the first letters of the three paragraphs of the *Shema* – *shema, vehayah, vayomer* – also total three hundred and twelve, perhaps suggesting a connection between the *Shema* and the months of the year. Incidentally, the name *Elokim* in its various forms appears seven times, corresponding to the seven days of the Creation in which only this name appears.

Along this line of thought, *vehayah* is particularly appropriate to this paragraph since it is concerned with reward and punishment and *Tishrei* is the month in which we are judged.

On the other hand, the first paragraph might be seen as being more inclined to the concept of Divine mercy. Traditionally (*Bereishit Rabbah* 33:4), the Divine names are taken to represent different aspects of G-d's interaction with the world, *HaShem* representing the aspect of mercy and *Elokim* that of strict justice (i.e., paralleling *vehayah*). Its opening words could be understood as suggesting the thought, "Understand O Israel that it is only because you do not see things from *HaShem*'s perspective that you see His acts of kindness to you as being harsh justice, but they are purely acts of kindness since you have no legal claim to anything from Him. Despite your varying perceptions, He is nonetheless one."

In this vein, it might be noted that the concluding word,

echad, has numerical value 13, which is the number of the Divine attributes of mercy (Ex. 34:6–7). Thus the first verse ends with the aspect of mercy to set the tone of the whole paragraph and so corresponds to *Nisan*. This is most appropriate since the Exodus from Egypt took place in *Nisan* and, as *Chazal* tell us (*Midrash Tehillim* 16.5), it was essentially an act of Divine mercy since *B'nei Yisrael* had sunk to such a low spiritual level as to be indistinguishable from the other nations of the world, and had they not been redeemed then, they would have been entirely lost. This might suggest a connection between the first and third paragraphs since the latter contains as its conclusion the *mitzvah* to remember the Exodus.

The third paragraph can also be seen as reconciling the two attributes of justice and mercy in an interesting way. Its final verse has a peculiarity in that at its beginning the Almighty describes Himself as "I am *HaShem* Your G-d" but states that the purpose of the Exodus is that He should be for us "G-d" without the word "*HaShem*," only concluding with a repetition of the first phrase using both terms. This might be explained by reference to *Chazal's* comment (*Bereishit Rabbah* 12:15, *Pesikta Rabbati* 40:3) that originally G-d wished to create the world to run according to the rules of strict justice, but on consideration saw that it would be unable to function under such a regime. Therefore, He tempered His attribute of justice with that of mercy, as alluded to by the double name "*HaShem* your G-d." The purpose of the Exodus, and the subsequent acceptance of the Torah by the Jewish People, was meant to allow a reversion to His original purpose, but He saw that this also would be prevented by the sin of the Golden Calf. However, He wished to indicate His real intention in this verse which, according to this line of thought, may be interpreted to read, "I am HaShem your G-d [who have tempered My control of the world through mitigating My justice with mercy] who has brought you out of the land of Egypt in order to be your G-d [and re-establish My original wish to conduct it through strict justice, which is not possible] I am *HaShem* your G-d [and My mode of control of the world remains as heretofore]." Thus, the three paragraphs can be seen to have an internal connection in that they move from the attribute of mercy to that of justice and finally to their synthesis, without which our world could not continue to exist.

Simchah shel Mitzvah

The teaching of *Chazal* that *kol makom shene'emar "vayehi" tsarah, 'vehayah' simchah*, "Every place where the word *vayehi* is used indicates sadness, whereas the word *vehayah* indicates joy" (*Ruth Rabbah, Pet. 7*), might lead to one to consider why the second paragraph should begin with the word *vehayah*. Since it is known as *kabbalat ol mitzvot* it would seem to suggest that the *mitzvot* themselves are a source of joy since, through their performance, one has the opportunity to increase one's merits. Consequently, the more numerous they are, the greater the joy would be, as Rabbi Chananya ben Akashya says (*Mak. 3:16*), "The Almighty, blessed be He, wished to confer merit upon Israel, therefore He gave them Torah and *mitzvot* in abundance, as it is said, 'It pleased *HaShem* for the sake of its (Israel's) righteousness, that the Torah be expanded and strengthened'" (Is. 42:21).

The Condition for Reward

On a more straightforward level, the first word of the second paragraph, *Vehayah*, can be understood as referring back to the previous verses in the Torah (Deut. 11:1–12), in which the fruitfulness of the land of Israel is linked to its dependence on rain, as opposed to Egypt, which had a ready source of water in the Nile. The former is much less certain and can be seen more clearly as being linked to the bounty of the Almighty, if one does not choose to see it as mere chance. However, the latter option is always available to those who do not wish to see G-d's hand in events. This is essential because if we saw reward and punishment in too obvious a way, we would have no real choice in our actions. We would thus be forced to do right, which would contradict one of the fundamental beliefs of Judaism, robbing us of any moral responsibility.

The next phrase, *im shamoa' tishme'u el mitzvotai*, contains the interesting scriptural use of the infinitive, *shamoa'*, before the finite verb, *tishme'u*, to indicate a continuous action. Chazal often interpret such double forms homiletically to indicate two "listenings" or, perhaps, in this context, listening to two types of *mitzvot*: the *mitzvot 'asei*, positive injunctions, and *mitzvot lo ta'asei*, prohibitions, both of which are described by the Almighty as *mitzvotai*. This dual nature of the *mitzvot* might be seen as being referred to by the subsequent phrases. *Le'ahavah et HaShem elokeychem* might be taken as referring to the negative commandments in line with Hillel's explanation (*Shabbat* 31a) of the command to love one's fellow as oneself as "What is hateful to you, do not do to your fellow," indicating that love in such a context involves the avoidance of transgression. On the other hand, the word *ule'ovdo* has the connotation of a positive action of serving G-d.

Excursus – The *Shema*, a Microcosm of the Torah

We shall develop this idea further below, but before doing so, it is instructive to make a comparison between the wording of our passage with that in the first paragraph of the *Shema* (Deut. 6:4–9). We shall here draw the readers' attention to the seemingly minor differences in phraseology between the two and suggest that they are meant to teach us some important lessons and are not merely the result of the incompetence of some post-exilic redactor trying to harmonize the various documents at his disposal.

In our passage, we have the phrase: *vehayah im shamoa' tishme'u el mitzvotai asher anochi metsaveh etchem hayom*, whereas in the first paragraph we find (6:6): *vehayu hadevarim ha'eleh asher anochi metsavecha hayom al levavecha*.

The first major distinction is that the word *mitzvotai* is replaced by the phrase *hadevarim ha'eleh*. This is in line with the general difference between the two paragraphs that the first deals with general principles, whereas the second is concerned with the specific concept of *mitzvah*. However, the latter phrase might be seen as including the *mitzvot* since it is precisely the same as that used to introduce the Divine utterances at Sinai (Ex. 20:1), which also included both positive and negative commandments. The *Yerushalmi* (*Berachot* 1:5) explains how the *Shema* alludes to all the Ten Commandments and, as Rashi (Ex. 24:12) states, "All the six hundred and thirteen commandments are included in the ten commandments and Rabbeinu Saadiah Gaon explained in the *azharot* he composed which of them are connected to each."

This idea is also found in *BeMidbar Rabbah* (13:17), which states, "You will find six hundred and thirteen letters in the Decalogue from *anochi* to *asher lereiʾecha* (but not including these two words) corresponding to the six hundred and thirteen *mitzvot* and seven extra (in *asher lereiʾecha*) corresponding to the seven days of creation to teach that the whole world was only created by virtue of the Torah."

The Tur (Ex. 20:14) offers an alternative explanation of these extra seven letters as referring to the seven *mitzvot shel benei Noach*. It has been suggested that this may be a misprint and the correct reading should be seven *mitzvot derabbanan*: *hallel, megillah, ner chanukah, ner Shabbat, netilat yadayim, birchot hanehenim* and *eiruv*, which do not depend on any *mitzvot* in the Torah itself. (For a further discussion see *Torah Sheleimah*, vol. 16, pp. 203–213.)

Furthermore, the Decalogue commences with the word *Anochi*, by whose use both our passages may also be making an oblique reference, i.e., that the source of our faith is the Almighty who refers to Himself, as the ultimate "I" upon which everything else depends (cf. Rav S.R. Hirsch's comments *ad loc*). In this context, the word *hayom* might be thought of as alluding to that crucial day when the Almighty revealed Himself at Sinai, which the Torah commands us to remember at all times (Deut. 4:9–10). From this we see that the *Shema* may be seen as implicitly containing all the *mitzvot* of the Torah. Perhaps this is one reason why, according to most customs, its first verse is proclaimed every *Shabbat* and *Yom Tov* when the *sefer* Torah is taken out of the *aron hakodesh*.

Significant Differences in Vocalization

We have pointed out that the general difference between the first two paragraphs is that the first deals with the general principle of *ol malchut shamayim*, the yoke of the Heavenly kingdom, whereas the second is concerned with *ol mitzvot*, the yoke of *mitzvah* observance with its consequent reward and punishment. We might see that this is already hinted at in the vocalization of the two key words at their beginnings, *Shema* and *Shamoa*, both of which consist of the same consonantal "spine."

In the first, the vowels are *sheva* and *patach*. The word *sheva* is related to the word *shav*, meaning nothingness. Perhaps this indicates how we should view ourselves vis-à-vis the Almighty before we endeavor to begin (*patach*) to accept His kingship over us.

In the second, the vowels are *kamatz, cholam* and *patach*. The word *kamatz* means to take a handful and might be seen as a reference to the *mitzvot* as in the *pasuk: chacham leiv yikach mitzvot*, "one with a wise heart grabs *mitzvot*" (Prov. 10:8). Just as the *kometz*, the handful separated and burnt on the *mizbeach*, permits the rest of the *korban minchah* to be enjoyed, so the *mitzvot* allow us to enjoy the benefits of this world.

However, the reward for their observance is not primarily in this world, as Rashi comments on the *pasuk, asher anochi metsavecha hayom la'asotam*, "which I command you to do today"(Deut. 7:11), "to do them today but to receive their reward in the hereafter."

The word *cholam* is related to the word *chalom*, a dream, which might be seen as hinting at this idea, as though this life is but a dream from which we will awaken in the world to come.

Having grasped these lessons, we are then able, as before, to begin (*patach*) and accept the yoke of the *mitzvot*.

Mitzvot or *Minhagim*?

The central difference between Torah world-view and those ideologies that masquerade as "judaisms" lies in the acceptance of the Torah text, as we have it, as being a faithful copy of that revealed by the Almighty to Moshe Rabbeinu. From this follows the characteristic feature of true Torah Judaism that the *mitzvot* consist of acts performed in obedience to G-d's command. For the *ersatz* judaisms, on the other hand, which deny the concept of Torah *miSinai*, *mitzvot* can hardly be more than traditional customs, *minhagim*. The Ktav Sofer notes that if a person performs a *mitzvah* but does not believe that it is Divinely ordained, he is, in reality, a *mumar*, apostate. He derives this idea from the verse in the third paragraph of the *Shema* (Lev. 15:39), *ure'item otam uzechartem et kol mitzvot HaShem ve'asitem otam*, "and you shall see them and remember all the *mitzvot* of *HaShem* to do them." From the order of the terms, he infers that one must always first bear in mind that the *mitzvot* are commandments of *HaShem* and only then perform them. That is why *Chazal* instituted a *berachah* "who has sanctified us with His commandments and commanded us…" before performing a *mitzvah*. He goes on to explain their statement that *Yerushalayim* was only destroyed because people did not make a *berachah* before studying it. They based this lesson on the verse (Jer. 9:12) "For they forsook my Torah and never listened to my voice," which confirms his thesis that the crucial sin was their lack of conviction that the Torah in front of them was, in reality, an accurate transcript of the voice of G-d. Thus, he explains, performing acts that appear to be *mitzvot* without the conviction that they are fulfillment of the Divine imperative is a form of apostasy.

Excursus – *Torah Shebe'al Peh* in the *Shema*

It has been suggested that the letters *bet* and *mem* of the word *bam* in *vedibarta bam* refer to the Torah *shebichtav* and Torah *shebe'al peh*, being the first letters of *bereishit* and *mei'eimatai* with which each begins. This is taken as indicating that these should be the subject of our discourse. Though the former might be possible, it is difficult to accept that the *Shema* should refer to something like the *Mishnah* that was originally not a fixed text. However, one might turn the suggestion round and posit that Rabbi Yehudah HaNasi decided to start the first *Mishnah* with the word *mei'ematai* in order to anchor it in the *Shema*, the reading of which forms its subject. It is even possible that there was a tradition that the Torah *shebe'al peh* should commence with this word.

There is one minor quibble on this suggestion: the word *bam* has a final *mem*, unlike the word *mei'ematai*, which begins with an ordinary one. However, the last word of the *Mishnah*, *shalom*, does end with one. Perhaps this fits even better with the proposed thought, namely that one should think of them, *bam*, from the beginning of the Torah *shebichtav*, *bereishit*, until the end of the Torah *shebe'al peh*, *shalom*. Perhaps there was a tradition that the Torah *shebe'al peh* should end with a final *mem* and Rabbi Yehudah HaNasi chose the word *shalom* for this reason, paralleling the last *berachah* of the *Shemoneh Esrei*.

Also, he called his compilation of the Torah *shebe'al peh* "*Mishnah*," which is derived from the same root as *veshinantam* in our verse, which might add cogency to the suggested connection.

Finally, it might possibly be significant that the *mispar katan* of the word *bam* is six, the number of major sections in the *Mishnah*, and that of the whole phrase apart from the last *mem*, the initial letter of the word *massechta* is sixty, the number into which the *Mishnah* was originally divided. (*Midrash Shir HaShirim Rabbah* 6:14 on *Shir HaShirim* 6:8 "*shishim hemah melachot;*" in our present *Mishnah* there are sixty-three *massechtot* after *massechet Nezikin* was split into the three *Babot* and *Makkot* was separated from *Sanhedrin*.)

The word *Talmud*, used to describe the analysis of the contents of the *Mishnah*, comes from the same root as the word *velimadtem* in the parallel phrase *velimadtem otam et beneychem ledaber bam*, whose *mispar katan* is seventy. This might be a hint to the seventy elders (Num. 11:16) who were to form the final arbiters as to whether any particular *halachah*, derived by such reasoning, were authentic (*Sanhedrin* 86b ff).

Furthermore, this number seventy is represented by the letter *ayin*, meaning an eye, which is related to the word *iyyein*, to study in depth, which is the purpose of *Talmud*.

It might be noted, in this context, that the parallel passage to the one quoted above from *BeMidbar Rabbah* adds: "and all of them were given to Moshe at Sinai among which are statutes and judgements, Torah and *Mishnah*, *Talmud* and *Aggadah*" (18:17).

This seems to imply that the whole Torah, both written and oral, are contained in the Decalogue which, we have seen, is itself contained in the *Shema*.

Excursus – *Shema* and *Kedushah*

It is, therefore, not surprising that *Chazal* (*Menachot* 99b) tell us that we can fulfill the *mitzvah* of *talmud torah* through its twice daily recital, but that this *halachah* should not be repeated in front of an *am ha'aretz*. The reason for this qualification might be that the latter would only say the words without thinking and thereby not fulfill his obligation which depends on *iyun*, pondering its deeper meaning (Rashi *ad loc*). They even say (*Chullin* 91b) that its proper recital makes one more beloved to the Almighty than the angels who are only permitted to utter His name after three words (*kadosh, kadosh, kadosh*), whereas we can do so after only two (*Shema Yisrael*). Perhaps one reason why *Chazal* included the *kedushah* in the first blessing before *Kriat Shema* each morning was as a courtesy to them.

Conversely, they may have had a similar motivation for including the first verse and last phrases of the *Shema* in the *kedushah* in *chazarat hashatz* in *Mussaf* on *Shabbat* and *Yom Tov*. In view of this, it is perhaps significant that the numerical value of the word *Shema*, 410, is identical to that of *kadosh*, possibly hinting that its recital with a proper understanding of its message can raise us to a higher level of sanctity.

Interestingly, in *birchat kriat Shema*, the angelic doxology is introduced by the phrase "and they all take upon themselves the yoke of the kingdom of heaven one from another…and call out in awe." Thus it forms a precise analogue of our acceptance of the yoke of the kingdom of heaven with the recital of the *Shema*.

Excursus – *Shema* and *Shemoneh Esrei*

Interestingly, *Shomer Yisrael*, said after *Tachanun*, which itself follows, and in some sense forms the climax of, the *Shemoneh Esrei*, also has the same quotes and concludes that without the merit of the *Shema*, "we do not know what to do." However, in it, *Shema* precedes *Kedushah*. This perhaps parallels the fact that *Shema* itself precedes *Shemoneh Esrei* in the *seder hatefillah*.

This connection with *Shema* is reinforced in the extended version for Mondays and Thursdays, *Vehu Rachum*, which culminates with the plea: "Be gracious to a people who in constant love proclaim the unity of Your name, saying *Shema Yisrael...*"

Furthermore, the *Raya Mehemna* (255b) links the number eighteen of the *berachot* that *Anshei Kenesset Hagedolah* composed to the eighteen times the Divine names are used in the *Shema*; *HaShem* eleven times and *Elokim* seven times with various prefixes and pronominal suffixes. Perhaps the nineteenth *berachah*, *Birchat Haminim*, introduced after the *churban*, corresponds to the one occurrence of the word *elohim* in the meaning of pagan deities which we hope will also be "uprooted, smashed, cast down and humbled speedily in our days." Presumably this extra *berachah* will no longer be needed in the messianic era when "false gods will be exterminated and the world will be perfected under the rule of the Almighty, all mankind calling on His name." Similarly, the seven times the name *Elokim* is used might correspond to the seven *berachot* on *Shabbat* since that name is used exclusively in the creation narrative that culminates in the *Shabbat*.

There are, however, some important differences between *Shema* and *Shemoneh Esrei*; for example, the former should be said audibly, and the first verse even in a loud voice, in order to improve concentration (*Orach Chaim* 61:4, *cf. Kitzur Shulchan Aruch* 17:5), whereas the latter should be said in at most an undertone (*ibid.* 101:2). This might reflect that, in a sense, the difference between them is that in the latter we are talking to the Almighty and presenting our requests to Him, whereas in the former we are being called upon to listen to His requests of us. We need to hear what He has to say, but He can hear even our inner thoughts, as the prophet Isaiah says (65:27), "Before they call, I will answer; while they are still speaking, I will hear." By contrast, the prophets of the *ba'al* "called out with a loud cry...but there was no reply" for which *Eliyahu Hanavi* mocked them saying that perhaps the *ba'al* was asleep or otherwise occupied (1 Kings 18:28–9).

From this we can also appreciate why *Chazal* arranged the *Shema* to be said before the *Shemoneh Esrei* since a precondition for the Almighty to hear us is that we should first listen to Him.

Another difference is that other people are not permitted to pass in front of someone reciting *Shemoneh Esrei*, nor sit within four *amot*, approximately six feet, of them, restrictions which do not apply to someone saying the *Shema*. This can cause problems where someone recites *Shemoneh Esrei* at considerably greater length than others, or in a place near an exit which others may need to use. Thus, one wishing to expand his *Shemoneh Esrei* would be well advised to choose his place carefully so as to avoid inconveniencing other people. These considerations would not apply to the *Shema* and one could put as much time into it without such worries. The only point that would have to be considered is the necessity to finish in time to be able to start one's *Shemoneh Esrei* with the congregation so as to fulfill the *mitzvah* of *tefillah betzibur*. This can always be achieved by starting earlier and letting the congregation "catch up" with oneself. As the *ba'alei mussar* comment, one should not be *frum* at other people's expense.

Singular or Plural – The Individual or the People

A further difference between the first two paragraphs of *Shema* is that the first is in the singular whereas the second is almost entirely phrased in the plural. This might indicate that, when it comes to fundamental principles of the Torah, each individual has to come to his or her own understanding of his or her relationship to the Almighty. We each have our own special place in G-d's scheme for the world and no one can fulfill the role designated for someone else. On the other hand, as regards commandments, we are addressed as a group to indicate that we are in a sense all responsible for each other and, therefore, we must view our fellow's transgression as our own, to some extent, unless we have done our utmost to dissuade him from straying from the Divine will.

It might be noted, in this context, that the first letters of the words of the first verse of the *Shema* consist of *shin, alef* (twice) and *yod* (three times), which spell the word *ish*, man. The repetition of the *alef*, which has numerical value one, might be seen as indicating that each individual should listen to G-d's message. The initial letters of the last two words are *alef* and *yod* which, together with the initial *shin* of *Shema*, make the word *ish*, and the same is true of the penultimate pair. This might be seen as forming the phrase *ish ish*, the one *shin* being used twice to bind the two words *ish* together into one unit, meaning "every person individually" as opposed to a group (*Pesachim* 66b), which conveys the same message. The last two letters of the word *Shema* form the word *am*, people, in reverse order, possibly hinting at the communal nature of our obligations. The letters of the words *ish ish* are separated like isolated individuals, whereas the letters of *am* are in close juxtaposition, as if to indicate that the people are joined together as a single unit.

Furthermore, the third *yod*, which has the numerical value of ten, hints at the size of an *edah*, the smallest group that can be considered a public unit in its own right for matters of *kedushah*. Thus, we might see both the individual and collective covenant alluded to twice in this verse.

Incidentally, the letters of *am* together with this extra *yod* at the beginning of *Yisrael* form an anagram of *ami*, my people, perhaps hinting to the verse, "and who is like your people Israel…" (1 Chron. 17:21), of the Almighty's *tefillin* (*Berachot* 6a). It also continues the thought in the conclusion of the second *berachah* immediately preceding the morning *Kriat Shema, habocher be'amo*

Yisrael beʾahavah, "who has chosen His people Israel in love." These contents of G-d's *tefillin* reciprocate our duty to love Him, which is the message contained in ours.

To Include the Sages?

The next phrase, *leʾahava et HaShem Elokeychem uleʾovdo bechol levavechem uvechol nafshechem,* also shows some tantalizing differences from its parallel in the first paragraph (6:5), *veʾahavta et HaShem Elokeycha bechol levavecha uvechol nafshecha uvechol meʾodecha.*

In these passages we find the usually untranslated word *et,* which indicates the direct object of the verb, in this case the Divine name. Is it possible that this is another case that alludes to Rabbi Akiva's homiletic explanation (*Pesachim* 22b) based on its alternative meaning of *with,* that it is to include love of the Sages who transmit His will to us, together with our love of the Almighty? Presumably Shimon Haʾamsoni (*ibid.*) also expounded on it similarly in this verse, since he only gave up this mode of exposition when he found difficulty with its use in Deut. 6:13 eight verses later. Why he should have had no difficulty associating the Sages with love of the Almighty, as opposed to reverence towards Him, requires further consideration.

Creation from Nothing

Alternatively, one might note that the word *et* has no independent meaning and is only used to indicate that the following word is the object of the verb. Indeed, it is not always used and so there might be some significance attached to its inclusion, which was the basis of Shimon Haʾamsoni's attempted exegesis.

In the *Shema,* it is attached everywhere by a *makkef* to the word it qualifies, except for this one case in the first paragraph where, surprisingly, it is even separated from it by a *tippecha.*

In the first verse of the Torah, it also is found free-standing, but there it is attached to the qualified words, *hashamayim… haʾaretz,* by a *merecha.* This seemingly meaningless word, however, consists of an *alef* and a *tav*, the first and last letters of the alphabet, which might indicate there the inclusion of everything from beginning to end. Another way of putting this concept is that the totality of existence has come to be from nothingness.

It might also be noticed that the *mispar katan* of the word *et* is five, which might be a hint at the five books of which the Torah is composed. This might be linked to the Vilna Gaon's contention that absolutely everything in existence is referred to in the Torah *shebichtav*, the only problem being to discover the connection.

The use of *et* in the first paragraph of the *Shema* might be a subtle way of suggesting that *HaShem Elokeycha* is to be seen in His role as Creator of everything, yet is separate from, and indeed transcends, His creation. On the other hand, the second paragraph, where it is joined to *HaShem Elokeychem*, indicates His intimate connection with His creation. Furthermore, the second paragraph, which is concerned with the reward for doing *mitzvot*, is more related to His immanence, since they are concrete actions that connect us to Him. On the other hand, the first paragraph is more concerned with the general and abstract *mitzvah* of loving *HaShem* which, despite our longing for Him, must make us realize His transcendent nature. Thus, we can see in these two verses a reference to the apparent paradox of Divine transcendence and immanence that can only be reconciled by the concept that creation exists in G-d rather than that He is in it.

Furthermore, the word *et* can be vocalized as *ot*, meaning *sign*, though that word itself is never found spelled defectively anywhere in *Tanach*. However, it is spelled defectively in the derivative forms, *haot* three times (Ex. 3:12 4:8, 8:19) and *laot* once (Ex. 12:13), all in the Exodus narrative, the remembrance of which is one of the *mitzvot* included in the *Shema*. On the other hand, the plural is found several times in this defective spelling, as is the word with pronominal suffixes. So one might understand the word *et* homiletically as indicating a sign. Thinking along these lines, one might possibly read one such passage (Ex. 4:8) as, "It shall be if they do not believe you and do not listen to the voice of the first *et*, they will believe the voice of the latter *et*," understanding the first as referring to the first verse in the Torah and the latter to our verse in the first paragraph of the *Shema*.

The Problem of the Missing *Etim*

After discussing the possible significance of the word *et*, it might be interesting to consider why it is not used consistently to mark the direct object of the verb.

When the latter is a pronoun, there are two possible constructions – most commonly, as a suffix to the verb and, less usually, as a freestanding word formed by adding the appropriate pronominal suffix to the word *et*. The former is found four times, three in the first paragraph, in the words *metsavecha*, *ukeshartam* and *uchetavtam*, and once in the second paragraph where the last of these is repeated.

The latter is used six times, three in the second paragraph and three in the third. In four of these cases, the verb is in the second person plural which, in all but three places in the whole of *Tanach* (Num. 20:5, 21:5 and Zech. 7:5, in conjunction with other verbs), only the freestanding object construction is used. Furthermore, *metsaveh* is only found with a second person singular object as in the first paragraph, *metsavecha* and no other, though parallel forms are found with other verbs, e.g., *menachemchem* (Is. 51:12).

This leaves only *hotseti etchem*, which requires consideration since, though *hotsetichem* is not found, several other forms do occur: *hotsetiha* (Zech. 5:4), *hotsetim* (Ez. 20:14), *vehotsetim* (Ez. 34:13), and, more significantly, *hotseticha* (Gen. 15:7, Ex. 20:2, Deut. 5:6), twice, as with our verse, in reference to *Yetziat Mitzraim*; perhaps the anomaly here is meant specifically to attract our attention.

When the direct object is a noun, it is normally marked as such by a preceding *et* when it follows directly after the verb, but this is omitted in four places in the *Shema*, all in the verses concerning reward and punishment in the second paragraph: *venatati metar…, ve'asafta deganecha…, venatati esev…,* and *va'avad'tem elohim…* These form an uninterrupted sequence of direct objects, all those preceding and following them being marked by the word *et.*

One might note that these consist of three verses referring to the actual rewards and one to the conditions for punishment. However, in the verses detailing the condition for reward and the punishments themselves, the regular marker, *et,* appears.

One might possibly interpret this anomaly along similar lines to Rabbi Akiva (above) that the presence of the word *et* is meant to associate someone or something with the object of the verb and, conversely, its absence indicates a lack of such association.

In our case, this additional person might be ourselves and be meant to suggest that while we are personally responsible for satisfying the conditions for reward, the latter are a manifestation of Divine beneficence. On the other hand, the Almighty considers our tendency to disobey as being essentially foreign to our basic nature and therefore omits the inclusive particle. However, once we have done so, the actual sequence of punishments is, so to speak, brought about by ourselves despite His wish not to do so. Thus, the *et* is reintroduced. This might be seen as reflecting the warning (Deut. 31:18), *va'Anochi haster astir panai bayom hahu,* "I will certainly hide My face on that day," a concept that will be elaborated below.

And All Your Possessions…

Another difference between the two paragraphs of the *Shema* is that *uvechol me'odecha* in the first is not paralleled by *uvechol me'odeichem* in the second. One way to explain this can be derived from the *Mishnah* (*Berachot* 9:5), which expounds this phrase as follows:

> A person is obliged to praise G-d for the bad just as he praises Him for the good, as it says, "And you shall love *HaShem* your G-d with all your heart and with all your soul and with all

your resources": "with all your heart" means with both your inclinations, i.e., with the good inclination and with the evil inclination (based homiletically on the spelling of the word *levavecha* with a double *bet*, rather than the more usual *libecha* with only one); "and with all your soul" means even if He takes your life; "and with all your resources" means "with all your wealth."

From this *Mishnah* we see that we are obligated to undergo martyrdom rather than deny our love of the Almighty. Normally, this would not be required if we were asked to transgress a *mitzvah*, apart from the three cardinal sins, unless our action was meant to be a demonstration of our apostasy, or in public. Clearly the *Mishnah* implies that such a denial is equivalent to apostasy.

On the other hand, this explanation of *uvechol me'odecha* as indicating that we must be willing to give up all our wealth is not true when it comes to doing a *mitzvah*. While it would hold for the avoidance of a transgression, we have a general principle that we do not have to spend more than a fifth of our assets in order to fulfill a positive commandment (*Shulchan Aruch, Orach Chaim* 656:1, *Rema* and *Mish. Ber. ad loc*). Thus, it would be inappropriate to have the phrase *uvechol me'odeichem* in the second paragraph.

Alternatively, one could interpret this verse homiletically as referring to our obligation to recite the *Shema* in all situations in line with the comment in the *Mishnah* (*Berachot* 54a) that the word *me'od* in *uvechol me'odecha* (Deut 6:5) can be taken to be derived from the word *midah*, measure. From this association it interprets *uvechol me'odecha* to signify *bechol midah umidah shehu moded lecha hevey modeh lo*, "with whatever measure he measures out to you, thank Him."

Excursus – The Patriarchs and the *Shema*

The Tur (*ad loc*) finds an interesting allusion in this verse to the patriarchs: "The word *ve'ahavta* is an anagram of *ha'avot*, the patriarchs: *bechol levavecha* refers to *Avraham* of whom it is said (Neh. 9:8) "and you found his heart (*levavo*) faithful before You"; *uvechol nafshecha* refers to *Yitzhak* who was prepared to give up his life for *HaShem* (at the *Akeidah*); *uvechol me'odecha* refers to *Ya'akov*, of whom it is written (Gen. 28:22) 'and whatever You give me, I shall surely tithe to You.'"

Chazal in various places (*Pesachim* 56a, *Devarim Rabbah* 2:25) also root the *Shema* in the lives of the patriarchs. Perhaps the most striking is the incident when *Ya'akov* wished to bless his sons on his deathbed:

> *Ya'akov* wished to reveal the end of days to his sons but the Divine presence was withdrawn from him. He said 'Perhaps, G-d forbid, there is some flaw in my children, like *Avraham* from whom issued *Yishmael*, or *Yitzhak* from whom issued *Eisav*.' His sons replied to him, 'Hear *Yisrael*, *HaShem* is our G-d, *HaShem* is one. Just as in your heart there is only one (G-d), so in our hearts there is only one (G-d).' At that, our father *Ya'akov* responded: *Baruch shem kevod malchuto le'olam va'ed*, 'Blessed is the name of His glorious kingdom for all eternity.'

From this, the *Rabbanan* deduce that we interpolate *Ya'akov's* response into our recital of the *Shema*. However, since it is not included explicitly in the text of the Torah, we say it in an undertone (*ibid.*).

Though *Kriat Shema* is called *kabbalat ol malchut shamayim*, accepting the yoke of the kingdom of heaven, this response is the only place a word related to kingship is explicitly found in it. Also, when this pseudo-verse is included, the word *melech* is "coded" with a letter gap of thirty-five in the text from the *mem* of *shema*, the *lamed* of *malchuto* and the final *chaf* of *bechol-levavecha*. Furthermore, the final *chaf* is the seventieth letter after the initial *mem*, and we have seen above the significance of the number seventy. Also, these three words form the phrase *shema malchuto bechol-levavecha*, which could be translated as "understand His kingship with all your heart," indicating this very *mitzvah*. While finding such a short word is not statistically significant, its location with this gap at the very beginning of the *Shema* and its use of the word *malchuto*, not in the text as written in the Torah, might be suggestive.

In another passage (*Sotah* 17a, *Chullin* 89a), *Rava* connects *Avraham* with two of the *mitzvot* mentioned in the *Shema*: "As a reward for *Avraham* saying (to the king of *S'dom*) (Gen. 14:23), 'If (I shall take anything which is yours even) so much as a thread or a shoe strap …,' his descendants were privileged to perform two *mitzvot*, the blue thread (in the *tzitzit*) and the strap of the *tefillin*."

On the other hand, we find in *Seder Eliyahu Rabbah* (24:16) that *tzitzit* are associated with *Ya'akov*: "It says, 'They shall make themselves *tzitzit* on the corners of their garments for all generations, *ledorotam*' – do not read *ledorotam* but *ledor tam* and the word *tam* refers to *Ya'akov* as it says (Gen. 25:27) *veYa'akov ish tam*."

Perhaps one could say that the three paragraphs of the *shema* themselves correspond to the three patriarchs. The first paragraph might be seen to correspond to *Avraham*, who first recognized the existence and unity of G-d; the second to *Yitzhak*, who was prepared to give his life to do His will; and the third to *Ya'akov*, whom the above *midrash* associates with the *mitzvah* of *tzitzit*. Furthermore, *Avraham* is the paradigm of the quality of love, *chessed*, whereas *Yitzhak* is that of justice, *din*; *Ya'akov* represents their synthesis, which is truth, *emet*. Similarly, the first paragraph emphasizes the love of *HaShem* and the second reward and punishment. Finally, at the conclusion of his prophecy, *Michah* (7:20) says, *titen emet leYa'akov chessed leAvraham*, which perhaps gives an additional insight into why the word *emet* is appended to the last paragraph in the *Shema*'s twice-daily recital.

From all this, it is hardly any wonder that *Chazal* included in the morning prayers the passage from the *Seder Eliyahu Rabbah*

(21:5), in which we invoke the memory of the patriarchs as a reason why we are obligated to recite the *Shema*:

> A person should always be G-d-fearing [...] and proclaim 'Master of the worlds, not in the merit of our righteousness do we cast our supplications before You [...] but we are Your people, the members of Your covenant, children of *Avraham* who loved You, to whom You swore at Mount Moriah; the offspring of *Yitzhak*, his only son, whom he bound on the altar; the community of *Yaakov*, Your firstborn son [...]. Therefore we are obliged to thank You [...]. We are fortunate that we rise early and stay late, evening and morning, and proclaim twice daily, '*shema Yisrael...*'

This passage concludes, interestingly, with the blessing to be said before martyrdom, "who sanctifies Your name in public," for which the *Akeidat Yitzhak* has always been seen as the prototype.

Excursus – *Kaddish* and the *Shema*

It is interesting to note that the *Targum Yerushalmi* (to Gen. 49:2) includes the conversation between *Yaakov* and his sons mentioned above and translates, *Baruch shem kevod malchuto leolam vaed*, as *Yehei shemeih rabba mevarach lealmei almin*. This declaration is essentially the one that forms the core of the *Kaddish*, about which the *Gemara* (*Shabbat* 119b) says, "Anyone who answers '*Amen, yehei shemeih rabba* [...] with all his strength, any evil decree against him is torn up."

Excursus – A Hint to the Primacy of Moshe Rabbeinu's Prophecy in the *Shema*

There is an alternative explanation of the origin of the added verse, *Baruch shem kevod malchuto leolam vaed*, given in *Devarim Rabbah* (2:25):

When Moshe Rabbeinu ascended on high (to receive the Torah), he heard the ministering angels saying to *HaKadosh baruch Hu, 'Baruch shem kevod malchuto le'olam va'ed,'* and he brought this down to *Yisrael*. So why do they not say it in public? *Rabbi Assi* said, 'To what may this be compared? To one who has stolen a piece of jewelry from the royal palace and given it to his wife, but telling her only to wear it in the house.'

The *Midrash* (*ibid.*) continues to explain that this is the reason why we only say it aloud on *Yom Kippur,* "when we are clear of sin like the ministering angels."

This *midrash* is very perplexing since other prophets were also privileged to hear an angelic doxology. *Yeshaya* describes his vision of the angels praising the Almighty (ch. 6) and quoted their praise as: *kadosh, kadosh, kadosh* [...]. Similarly *Yechezkel* had a vision, which he described in even greater detail (ch. 1), but found no problem in recording what he heard (3:13): *Baruch kevod HaShem mimekomo.*

Furthermore, we repeat both these verses in the *kedushah* that is inserted in every *chazarat hashatz,* as well as in the *berachah, yotzer or,* every morning and the *kedushah desidra,* which is said at least once every day. Clearly these two angelic statements must be of a more exoteric nature than the one that Moshe Rabbeinu "stole."

Thus, one might understand that Moshe Rabbeinu had the ability to grasp something of much deeper significance than the other prophets from his encounter with the heavenly hosts, showing that his level of prophecy was qualitatively on a much higher level, as *Chazal* (*Yevamot* 49b) put it: "All the other prophets only saw their prophecy as through a cloudy glass, whereas Moshe Rabbeinu saw his as through a clear glass." The *Shema* can, therefore, be seen as reminding us every day of the primacy of his prophetic message and confirming that "there will never arise again in *Yisrael* a prophet like Moshe who experienced *HaShem* face to face" (Deut. 34:10).

Excursus – Remembering the *Beit HaMikdash* in the *Shema*

We saw above that *Devarim Rabbah* (2:25) describes the declaration, *Baruch shem kevod malchuto le'olam va'ed*, as "a piece of jewelry stolen from the royal palace…only to be worn in the house."

The following *baraita* (*Ta'anit* 16b) provides another nuance of meaning for this *midrash*, explaining that it was said in place of *amen* as the answer to every *berachah* said in the *Beit HaMikdash*.

> With regard to what was it said (that the congregation answers *amen*)? In the provinces (i.e., outside the *Beit HaMikdash*), but it was not so in the *Beit HaMikdash* because we do not respond *amen* there. From where do we derive that we do not respond *amen* in the *Beit HaMikdash*? As it says (Neh. 9:5): 'Rise up and bless *HaShem* our G-d from the world to the world, and let them bless the name of Your glory exalted above every blessing and praise […].' But in the *Beit HaMikdash*, what does (the *sheliach tzibur*) say? (He concludes each *berachah*) 'Blessed is *HaShem* G-d of Israel from the world to the world. Blessed is *HaShem* […],' and the people respond, *Baruch shem kevod malchuto le'olam va'ed*. (*cf.* Rashi *ad loc* and also *Yoma* 69b and *Berachot* 54a)

Since there is no hint that this response was said quietly, it is clear that it was said aloud in the same manner as we say *amen* after a *berachah*. That we say it in an undertone perhaps reflects that the angels were angry that Moshe Rabbeinu had 'stolen' it. This is similar to their objection to his receiving the Torah: "What is man that You remember him, or the son of man that you notice him?" (Ps. 8:5), and their subsequent discomfiture at his hands (*Shabbat* 88b). On the other hand, the Almighty is happy with this praise (*Berachot* 3a), obviously not viewing it as "stolen goods", and therefore permits its open use in His house.

As we have seen above, we are to say the Aramaic version aloud, but this is no contradiction since the angels do not understand Aramaic and we can therefore safely do so (*Shabbat* 12b).

Thus, our saying it in an undertone in the *Shema* may be seen as both a remembrance of the *Beit HaMikdash* and an affirmation of our hope for the time when it will be rebuilt, speedily in our days, when we will once again be able to declare it with all our strength.

The Reward for Compliance

Having analyzed the Almighty's requirements of us, the text proceeds to detail the reward for their fulfillment.

We might note that all these rewards are phrased by G-d in the first person, "*I shall provide rain for your land in its proper time,*" indicating that the Almighty promises to intervene directly in the course of nature to ensure that the rains come when needed. This is in striking contrast to the punishments, where He is referred to more indirectly. Also, unlike the latter, the verb, "I shall give," is linked to its object, "rain for your land," by the *te'amim*.

What is even more surprising is that we are informed that immediately after He has sent the rains, *ve'asafta deganecha vetiroshecha veyitsharecha*, as if we would not have to wait months for it to grow.

It is also significant that in these verses our ownership of the various items is recognized as *artzechem*, "*your* land," *deganecha*, "*your* grain," etc.; again, this contrasts with the punishments, as if our right to any material possessions is contingent on our observing the *mitzvot*.

Both Man and Beast You Save, *HaShem*!

The next verse continues, *venatati eisev besadecha livhemtecha*, but surprisingly concludes, *ve'achalta vesava'ta*, "and you will eat and be satisfied," rather than *ve'achlu vesav'eu*. The *Gemara* (*Gittin*

62a) deduces from this strange wording that we are obliged to feed our domestic animals before we are permitted to eat. On a more allegorical level, this also might allude to the need to feed our own animal nature before being able to be satisfied in a more spiritual sense. Man may not live by bread alone (Deut. 8:3), but where there is no bread, there is no Torah (Av. 3:17), emphasizing that the Torah is given for man to live by it (Lev. 18:5), not to die as a result of its observance (Yoma 85b).

Incidentally, the letters of *esev* (grass) at the beginning of the verse are an anagram of the root *sava'* (satisfy), of the last word, *vesava'ata*, the only difference being that the *ayin*, which has the meaning *eye*, is transferred from its beginning to its end. Perhaps this might be a hint to the essential difference between us and animals; their eye is only on what is in front of them on which they can feed, whereas we should be able to recognize in retrospect the ultimate source of our sustenance.

The remaining letters of these words form the root *siv*, to become old, which is the ultimate reward in this world for the *mitzvot* (Deut. 11:21). In this connection it might be noted that moving the point of the *sin* in the root *sava'* produces the root *shava'*, meaning *to swear*, which is also used in this verse in its *nifal* form, the *kal* never being used in *Tanach*. Since the *nifal* usually connotes a passive or reflexive form of the basic meaning, this usage raises a problem since, in this case, it is clearly used for the direct action, "which *HaShem* swore [...]." Perhaps this indicates a fundamental difference between the Torah viewpoint and that of Western civilization in the concept of oath-taking, in that the person swearing an oath is considered as, in some sense, not taking a direct action but rather responding to the one to whom the oath is being made. From this perspective, the final promise of the Almighty may be understood as contingent on our acceptance of our obligation to listen to Him, with which this paragraph commences.

If a similar repointing is applied to *siv*, the letters form the root *shuv*, to return (to *HaShem*), which is, perhaps, the underlying message of this paragraph of the *Shema*.

Lifnim Mishurat Hadin

What is much more surprising is the comment in the *Gemara* (*Berachot* 35b):

> Rabbi Chanina bar Pappa contrasted [two verses. In one verse (Hosea 2:11)] it is written 'and I will take back My grain in its time…' and [in another (Deut.11:14)] 'and you will gather your grain…' He resolves the apparent problem by stating that 'there is no contradiction [since the latter refers] to a time when Israel does not do the will of G-d, whereas [the former refers] to a time when they fulfill His will, as we learn from a *Baraita* [which states that]…at a time when Israel do the will of G-d their work is done by others, as it is stated (Isaiah 61:5): 'and strangers shall arise and shepherd your flocks…,' but at a time that Israel does not do G-d's will they have to do their own work as it is written, 'and you will gather your grain…,' and not only that, but they will have to do the work of others, as it says (Deut. 28:48) 'and you will serve your enemies.'

It would appear that the *Gemara* contradicts the plain meaning of our verse as specifying the reward for keeping G-d's *mitzvot*. There have been many suggestions for resolving this difficulty, but we might find one that follows from the comment above on the omission of the phrase *uvechol me'odeichem* paralleling *uvechol me'odecha* of the first paragraph of the *Shema*. We suggested this was because a positive commandment did not require the sacrifice of all one's wealth. However, our unwillingness to do so might be considered, at a higher level (*lifnim mishurat hadin*) not to be fulfilling G-d's will in the most perfect way.

Furthermore, since we are unwilling to transcend the minimal requirements of the Torah, we are comparable to our cattle, who cannot transcend their physical nature. They completely fulfill their purpose in the world, whereas we, through our ability to make a choice to act beyond G-d's minimal requirements, do not. Perhaps this concept is also hinted at in the following verse, where our right to "eat and be satisfied" must be preceded by our giving our cattle their fodder.

Yoreh umalkosh – an Apparent Redundancy

Having specified that He will give us *metar artsechem be'ito*, the rain of your land at its (correct) time, the words *yoreh umalkosh* would appear to be superfluous since these are precisely the two seasonal rains mentioned previously. Since we know that the Torah does not use any unnecessary words, there must be some additional message that is alluded to by their use.

According to Rashi, the word *yoreh* comes from the root *resh vav hei*, meaning *saturate*, because this rain saturates the parched land and enables the seeds to germinate. On the other hand, Redak (*Sefer HaSheroshim*) derives it from the root *yod resh hei*, with the same meaning. This latter root has a second meaning, *teach*, from which the word Torah itself is derived, as Redak points out. The word *yoreh*, as a verb, from this source is also found, as in, "To whom shall He teach knowledge (*yoreh de'ah*)?" (Isaiah 28:9). From this comes the traditional formula, *yoreh yoreh*, by which permission is given to a scholar to decide *halachic* questions.

The word *malkosh* is an anagram of the word *shekalum*, meaning *they shall weigh them up*. Similarly, a *halachic* discussion is referred to as a *shakla vetarya*, literally *weighing and shaking*. This might be seen as an oblique hint to the process by which a scholar comes to deliver a *halachic* judgement, alluded to by the word *yoreh*.

Furthermore, the *mispar katan* of *malkosh* (19) is equal to that of *iyun*, in-depth examination, which is the purpose of the *shakla vetarya*. On the other hand, the *mispar katan* of *yoreh* (14) is one less than that of *psak*. While there is a principle in *gematria* calculation that one may add the *kollel*, i.e., one for the word itself, which would allow the equality of the two, this might indicate that *psak* alone is deficient without prior *iyun*.

Thus, these two apparently redundant words might suggest

a further, more spiritual, reward for listening to *HaShem* that we should merit to understand better His Torah through penetrating arguments resulting in a correct *halachic* decision. Furthermore, the word *malkosh*, hinting at the to and fro of *halachic* debate, needs its letters to be rearranged, whereas *yoreh*, hinting at a clear decision, does not.

There is one apparent difficulty with these suggested allusions, namely that the word *yoreh* means the earlier rain and *malkosh* the later one, whereas the concepts associated with them are the final *psak* and the preliminary discussion respectively. However, this may itself be an allusion to the fact that at Sinai, the Jewish People said *na'aseh venishma*, putting the acceptance of the practical implementation of the Divine commandments, "we shall do," before their detailed study, "we shall hear."

An alternative solution to this difficulty may be that it is often best for a *psak* to be given first and the reasoning behind it only later. There is a story that when Rav Chaim Brisker once had a *sha'alah*, he sent it to Rav Yitzhak Elchanan with the request that he only give him the *psak* without any explanation because he was sure that if the reasoning were given he would examine it with his critical acumen and pull it to pieces. He wanted to avoid this temptation since he held that a rav has *siyata dishmaya* when issuing a *psak* that should not be subject to such *iyun* by others.

Interestingly, if we replace each letter of *malkosh* by the one following it in the alphabet we obtain the letters of the word *nirmezet*, meaning *that which is hinted at*, with only the order of the *resh* and *mem* reversed. Similarly, if we replace them by the preceding letters we obtain an anagram of the word *letsorkah*, meaning *for its purpose*. Perhaps this is to show us that apparently redundant words are there for the specific purpose of hinting at other concepts apart from their straightforward meaning. This brings to mind the words of the Psalm (139:4–6), "For a word is not yet on my tongue but You knew it all. Before and behind You formed me and laid Your hand upon me. It is beyond my knowledge; exalted, I cannot grasp it."

Self-effacement That Brings to Divine Favor

One might develop this anagrammatic approach to the final phrase of this verse "*ve'asafta deganecha vetiroshecha veyitsharecha.*" The first word comes from the root *asaf* which is the anagram of *efes*, nothingness, from which a verbal form *ve'afasta* could be derived with a possible meaning "and you will be nothing." The second word, *deganecha*, is an anagram of *negdecha*, next to you, or, in this context, compared to yourself. The final words, *vetiroshecha veyitsharecha*, are anagrams of *yesharetucha* (*cf.* Num. 18:2) meaning, "he will serve you" (i.e., do your wishes) and *veyirtsecha* (*cf.* 2Sam. 24:23 where the *he* is omitted through elision) meaning, "and he will show you favor," respectively. Thus, this phrase might be used to suggest the thought that "if you will be as nothing in your own eyes, He will do your wishes and show you favor."

A Deeper Significance of "Grain, Wine, and Oil"

An alternative explanation of the terms "*deganecha vetiroshecha veyitsharecha*" might be as hints to the different aspects of the Torah. *Tehillim* 104: 15 speaks of "wine that makes man's heart rejoice, oil that makes his face shine and bread that strengthens a man's heart." From this, one might take the word *deganecha*, grain from which bread, the staple of physical life, is made, as representing the basic foundation of our spiritual sustenance, the written Torah. Similarly, the word, *vetiroshecha*, wine, represents the oral tradition which, with its argumentation, develops the written Torah and applies it to new situations. As *Chazal* put it, "there is no greater joy than the resolution of Torah problems." One might speculate that the word *deganecha*, grain, rather than *lachmecha*, bread, is used here to emphasize that, though the Torah *shebichtav* contains the basis of revelation, it is still in an unfinished state, requiring the Torah *sheb'al peh* to bring it into a form in which it can be applied in practice. Finally, the word *veyitsharecha*, oil, might represent the more esoteric aspects of our tradition, which can lead to a more refined spiritual illumination.

Also, it might be significant that the acronym of the three

words *deganecha vetiroshecha veyitsharecha* is *dati*, My law. This might lead us to the thought that though the Torah *shebichtav* and the Torah *sheb'al peh* form the *dat*, law, it requires the *kabbalah*, esoteric Torah, to make it truly *dati*, My (G-d's) law.

Admonition against Transgression

Arriving to the admonition and punishment, we find a striking difference from the rewards for compliance with G-d's will. Unlike the latter, it seems as if the Torah goes out of its way to introduce delays. In the admonition there are five stages to the warning, all separated by disjunctive accents:

(i)   *hishameru lachem*, guard yourselves
(ii) *pen yifteh levavechem*, lest you heart be seduced
(iii) *vesartem*, and you turn astray
(iv) *va'avadtem elohim acherim*, and serve other gods
(v)   *vehishtachavitem lahem*, and bow down to them

Even within each stage it seems as if the Torah hesitates to suggest that we might go astray. Though in the first phrase the words are joined by a *munach*, in the second they are separated by a *tippecha*, as if it were saying, "lest there be seduced, G-d forbid, your heart." Similarly, in the fourth phrase the verb is separated from its object by a *pashta*, as if the Torah is hoping to be able to avoid even having to mention the possibility that we might actually come to serve idols. Up to this stage, the warnings refer to attitudes rather than actual acts, as though the Torah is putting off the evil moment when it must do so. When this becomes inevitable at the fifth stage, it again separates the verb from its object, this time with a *tippecha*, as if the Torah hopes to avoid having to warn against bowing down to idols.

The Punishment for Transgression

Paralleling the five-fold nature of the warning, we can discern five stages in the punishment, also separated by disjunctive accents:

(i)   *vecharah af HaShem bachem*, and the wrath of *HaShem* blaze against you

(ii) *ve'atsar et hashamayim*, and He will restrain the heavens

(iii) *velo yihyeh matar*, and there will be no rain

(iv) *vehadamah lo titen et yevulah*, and the land will not yield its produce

(v)   *va'avadtem meherah mei'al ha'aretz hatovah asher HaShem noten lachem.*

Unlike the verses detailing with reward, this verse is phrased impersonally as if to indicate that G-d punishes by withdrawing His active providence and leaving us to the ordinary processes of nature. Furthermore, there is the same apparent hesitation as in the warnings. Thus, the first stage is not phrased as "I shall be angry with you," paralleling "I shall provide rain for your land in its proper time," but rather "then the anger of *HaShem* will blaze against you," as if the anger were, so to speak, separated from the essence of the Almighty. Furthermore, the name *HaShem*, referring to His mercy, is used rather than the apparently more appropriate *Elokim*, and the object "against you" is separated from its verb by the *te'amim* as if it were an afterthought which the Torah did not really wish to include. The second stage, "and He will shut up the heavens," is also tentative. Even the next phrase, "and there will be no rain," allows room for Divine mercy since it might imply that rain be withheld but some other source of water might still be forthcoming. Even the fourth phrase, "and the soil will not yield its produce," leaves open the possibility that somehow there might be some other source of sustenance (cf. *Or HaChaim ad loc*). It is only at the final stage, when all the disasters have not led us to return to the fulfillment of G-d's will, that the fateful words literally meaning "and you will speedily be destroyed" are uttered. However, they are modified to exile by *mei'al ha'aretz hatovah*, so as to mean "and you will speedily be removed from the good land."

Parenthetically, the *Shulchan Aruch* (*Orach Chaim* 61,19)

notes that one should make a short pause between words *vecharah* and *af* lest we appear to say *"vecharaf HaShem"* suggesting cursing *HaShem, r"l.*

Life and Death in the *Shema*

The *Shulchan Aruch* cautions us (*Orach Chaim* 61:21) to be particularly careful to make a break between words ending in a *mem* when followed by words commencing with an *alef* to avoid appearing to enunciate the words *met, motam* or *moto*, connoting death.

It is interesting to note that this phenomenon is not found in the first paragraph at all, and four times in each of the second and third. Moreover, its first occurrence is immediately after the section concerning punishments where we find *vesamtem et, ukeshartem otam, velimadetam otam,* and *otam et.* Perhaps one might infer that this is a further warning of the punishment for idolatry which consists of the four components against which this paragraph warns us:

(i)   *pen yifteh levavechem,* lest you heart be seduced
(ii)   *vesartem,* and you turn astray
(iii) *va'avadtem elohim acherim,* and serve other gods
(iv)   *vehishtachavitem lahem,* and bow down to them

Corresponding to these four occurrences in the second paragraph, there are four in the third, *ure'item oto, uzechartem et, va'asitem otam* and *va'asitem et.* One might notice instructive parallels between them:

(i)   *vesamtem et* corresponding to *ure'item oto,* that which we place we must look at,
(ii)   *ukeshartem otam* corresponding to *uzechartem et,* that which we tie (*tefillin*) should make us remember,
(iii) *velimadetam otam* corresponding to *va'asitem otam,* that which we teach should lead to correct action, *otam et*

corresponding to *va'asitem et*, the latter lesson is here repeated to emphasize that it applies both to the one who teaches and the one who is taught.

Furthermore, the fourfold use of words connoting death might be a reference to the four forms of death imposed by the courts: stoning, burning, decapitation and strangulation.

It might be significant that the word *met* consists of the two letters *mem* and *tav*, which each have a *mispar katan* of four, though their ordinary *gematria* is not. The word *met* itself appears four times in our list and the derived forms also four times in all, *moto* once and *motam* three times.

The *Shulchan Aruch* also warns (*Orach Chaim* 61:20) us to be careful to separate words where the first ends with the same letter as the second commences. Interestingly, this also happens eight times in the *Shema*: a *lamed* on four occasions, a *mem* on two and a *bet* and a *peh* on one occasion each. Of these, it might be significant that the *gematria* of *peh* is eighty, as is also that of the two *mems* (40+40), the normal lifespan of a strong human being (Ps. 90:10). Furthermore, the four *lameds* (30 each) have a total of one hundred and twenty, the traditional maximum lifespan.

Once again we see the pattern of two sets of four, which might be significant. The name of the letter *lamed* connotes the concept of *learn*, or, in the *piel*, *teach*, which might be an indication to us that we should delve more deeply into this phenomenon. The other group, *bet*, *peh* and *mem*, seems at first sight to be less connected until one notices that they are the three labial consonants, formed with the lips. Also, the first two have two pronunciations, one plosive and the other fricative, both of which appear in this context. Thus, all the labial phonemes of the Hebrew language are represented in this group. Perhaps this is meant to draw our attention to the lips and might allude to the verse *borei niv sefatayim, shalom shalom larachok velakarov* [...], "He creates the *fruit of the lips*, peace peace to him who is far off and to him who is near [...]" (Is. 57:19). In this connection one might note that the word *peh* means *mouth*, the main source of speech, which is one of the main distinctions between man and other animals.

So these two types of mistake against which we are warned seem to put before us the alternatives of life and death.

Excursus – The Importance of Care in Distinguishing Similar Sounding Letters

It is interesting to note that the punishment "and you will speedily be destroyed" uses the word *va'avadtem* spelled with an *alef* which may be seen as paralleling the phrase "and serve other gods" which uses the word *va'avadtem* spelled with an *ayin*. The difference between the pronunciations of these letters is very slight yet the difference in meaning is profound; perhaps this particular choice of words is meant to draw our attention to the care needed in the enunciation of the words of the *Shema*.

If the word *Shema* itself is pronounced with an *alef* instead of an *ayin*, the resulting meaning of the first verse is radically changed and would then mean "Perhaps, Israel, *HaShem* is our G-d, (perhaps) He is one" which is the complete antithesis of its true meaning, and its replacement by an agnosticism.

If the reverse change is made in the phrase *Kriat haTorah*, its meaning changes from "reading the Torah" to "tearing up the Torah," *chas veshalom*, something just as horrifying to any committed Jew. Yet the latter perhaps describes accurately the methods of the so-called Bible critics in their search for separate human "source documents" for the Torah, that have been used by modern heretical movements to justify their denial of Torah Judaism.

The consequence of such misreadings might be that instead of *HaShem* having redeemed the Jewish People, *ga'al Yisrael*, as we say in the blessing after *Kriat Shema*, He might also change the *alef* to an *ayin* as in *vega'alah nafshi etchem*, "and My spirit will reject you" (Lev. 26:30), *rachmana litzlan*.

Thus, apparently minor changes in the reading that might pass almost unnoticed can be crucial to the meaning of a passage. The *Shulchan Aruch* (*Orach Chaim* 61:16) warns that one should take care to pronounce the words *nishba' HaShem* separately so that the former should not sound as if it ended with a *hei* instead of an *ayin*, which would change the meaning from "which *HaShem* promised" to "which *HaShem* was taken prisoner." This is, of course, difficult for Ashkenazim who cannot pronounce an *ayin* at all. Similarly, the ruling that one should extend the pronunciation of the *dalet* of *echad* (*se'if* 6) is almost impossible for most communities, who do not distinguish between the plosive (*degushah*) and fricative (*rafui*) forms of this letter.

Later (*se'if* 17), it rules that one must be careful to voice the *zayin* of *tizkeru* and *uzechartem* so that it should not sound like a *sin*, implying that we only keep His commandments in order to receive a reward. Even more so, it should not be sounded as a *shin* implying a call to drunkenness or, even worse, with the *kaf* replaced by a *kuf*, which would give it the meaning "in order that you may lie," which is utterly heretical.

What has always surprised me is that there is no similar warning to be careful about the *zayin* in the word *zonim*, going astray, which would be misread *sonim*, suggesting enmity either to the *mitzvot*, *r"l*, or to those whose practice of them differs in some way from our own (a fault that is not entirely unknown in ostensibly "frum" people), the antithesis of the commands in the first two paragraphs *ve'ahavta et HaShem* [...] and "*le'ahava et HaShem* [...].

From these examples we see that insufficient care can make the difference between us loving (*ohev*) *HaShem* and hating (*oyev*) Him, so that our words change from His being much praised (*mehullal meod*) to much profaned (*mechullal meod*), *chas veshalom*.

Excursus – Past and Future

Not only can carelessness in pronouncing letters change the meaning of a word, but even putting the stress on the wrong syllable can radically alter its meaning. This is particularly significant in verbs with the *vav hahippuch*, which changes the tense, as opposed to the *vav hachibbur*, which does not. For example, the word *ve'ahavta*, which when stressed *milra*, on the last syllable, as in the *Shema*, means "and you shall love" in the future, which is essentially a command, whereas if stressed *mil'eil*, on the penultimate syllable, means "and you have loved," something that has already happened in the past.

This stress change is so important that it overrides the otherwise universal rule of *nesog achor*, whereby the stress is thrown back when the following word is stressed on the first syllable, and not separted from it by a disjunctive, so as to avoid, wherever possible, two successive stressed syllables, e.g., the phrase (Ex. 20:23) *elohei chesef veilohei zahav*, where the first *elohei* is *mil'eil* whereas the second is *milra*. An example of this *ve'ahavta lo* occurs in Lev. 19:34, but this exceptional situation does not occur in the *Shema*, where all such words are separated by disjunctive signs, for example, in the phrase *venatati esev* where the word *venatati* is marked with a *tevir*.

The one word where this stress shift rule seems to be broken, *vesavata*, has the stress on the penultimate syllable for a completely different reason, that it is a pausal form where the stress is always thrown back, even where otherwise the *vav hahippuch* would have shifted it forward; it still means "and you will be satisfied." So we see that there is a hierarchy of priorities in the rules regarding the stress shift which might be seen as a parallel to the ethical and *halachic* problems we meet in everyday life. Clearly this is something over which great care must be taken.

Excursus – Weekdays, *Shabbat* and *Yom Tov*

On *Shabbat*, in this *berachah*, the first paragraph *hameir la'aretz* is replaced by an expanded version *hakol yoducha*, which adds a few sentences at the beginning and end. Interestingly, the Ashkenazim, unlike the Sefardim and Teimanim, omit the *pasuk* (Ps. 104:24): *Mah rabu ma'asecha HaShem, kulam bechochmah asita mal'ah ha'aretz kinyanecha.* Presumably this is because it was perceived as referring to the six days of creation, but this reason is slightly far-fetched since our sense of wonder is not lessened on *Shabbat*, as witnessed by its inclusion by most other groups. Nonetheless, this custom certainly is quite ancient and is found in the *Machzor Vitry* compiled by Simchah of Vitry, a pupil of Rashi. On the other hand, the *Kol Bo* (s.122), a compilation of laws and customs by an anonymous Ashkenazi writer, probably of the 13th century school of *Maharam Rottenburg*, has the intriguing comment that *hakol yoducha* has 113 words. If one counts those in the Ashkenazi version, one finds that it only has 104 but, were the missing *pasuk* of 10 words included, the difference is more easily explained since it is quite possible that the *Kol Bo's* version omitted one word, possibly the somewhat meaningless *selah*.

Also the *piyut*, *Keil Baruch*, which has an *aleph-bet* acrostic based on its words, is replaced by the much longer *piyut*, *Keil Adon*, where the acrostic is based on the first words of each phrase. Neither of these changed versions, however, refers directly to the *Shabbat*, but they are followed by a paragraph specifically referring to it, *LaKeil Asher Shavat*, before returning to the regular formulation *Titbarach Tsureinu*.

There is another interesting difference in the customs of the Ashkenazim and Sefardim regarding what should be done on a *Yom Tov* that falls on a weekday. The former use the usual weekday formulation whereas the latter use the one for *Shabbat*, only omitting the section, *LaKeil Asher Shavat*, referring specifically to it, recommencing at its end, *Shimcha HaShem Elokeinu Yitkadash*. I have not found any discussion as to the underlying reason for this difference but would speculate that Ashkenazim view the expanded version as being in its entirety *Shabbat*-specific, whereas the Sefardim regard it as reflecting the greater leisure on that day. Since this reason applies equally on *Yom Tov*, perhaps the latter use it even when *Yom Tov* does not fall on *Shabbat*, only omitting the words that actually refer to *HaShem's* resting from creation.

When or How

The phrase, *beshivtecha beveitecha uvelechtecha vaderech*

uveshochbecha uvekumecha, which appears in both Deut. 6:7 and 11:19, also bears further analysis. The *Gemara* (*Berachot* 15a) derives from the use of the pronominal suffix "**your** sitting…**your** walking" that this excludes someone who is busy doing some other *mitzvah*, since the Torah could have written *shevet* and *lechet*.

The last two words, *uveshochbecha uvekumecha*, form the basis of the dispute between *Beit Hillel* and *Beit Shammai* (*Berachot* 10b). The latter take them as an instruction as to the manner in which the *Shema* is to be recited, reclining in the evening and standing in the morning. The former observe the juxtaposition of the words *uvelechtecha vaderech* to argue that the recitation is to be done *kedarko*, "in its natural manner" and these words refer instead to the times of recitation. Thus, *Beit Hillel* translates them as "at the time you lie down and the time you arise."

The *Mishnah* (ibid.) tells that Rabbi Tarfon tried to follow both opinions and was thereby put in danger because of bandits, commenting that he deserved even to lose his life because he went against the ruling of *Beit Hillel*. This seems at first sight a somewhat strange comment until one realizes that *Beit Shammai's* interpretation excludes the use of these words to indicate the time of recitation. Since wherever there is a dispute between *Beit Hillel* and *Beit Shammai* we follow the former and ignore the latter's ruling, it follows that Rabbi Tarfon was, in effect, acting like a *zakein mamre* who would be liable to the death penalty (Deut. 17:12).

Finally, the order of the words *uveshochbecha uvekumecha* raises a problem as to why we are instructed first with respect to the time we lie down and only afterwards when we arise. While it might be argued that this parallels the order in creation, in which night preceded day, this is hardly satisfactory here since our activities start when we get up in the morning and finish when we go to sleep. Perhaps the Torah is hinting to us that our going to sleep should also be for the purpose of waking up in good time fully refreshed in order to fulfill the will of the Almighty and that we should not stay up so late that we cannot do so.

Exile and Redemption

There is another problem with the phrase *beshivtecha beveitecha uvelechtecha vaderech*, namely that it contrasts sitting *beveitecha*, in *your* house, with walking *vaderech*, on *the* way. This might hint at a distinction between when the Jewish People is settled in its own land with the open manifestation of the Divine presence in the Holy Temple, the quintessential *beveitecha*, a time when it is easy to acknowledge the yoke of the kingdom of heaven, and the time of exile, *vaderech*, on an alien road, i.e., a time of Divine self-concealment, when this is more difficult.

The words *uveshochbecha uvekumecha* could be considered to continue this theme and be interpreted as instructing the acknowledgement of the Almighty at the time "when you lie down" from the pressures of a *churban*, when everything seems to be falling apart (note that *shachav* is an anagram of *kavush*, pressed or defeated), and perhaps even more significantly "when you get up" at the time of the messianic *geulah* (cf. Isaiah 60:1 et al.) when it will be easy to forget more mundane obligations in the excitement of the situation. The experiences of recent times with the Holocaust and the foundation of the State of Israel perhaps show how easy it is to get carried away by such climacteric events.

The Four Stages of Existence

An alternative way of understandng the phrases *beshivtecha beveitecha uvelechtecha vaderech uveshochbecha uvekumecha* is as referring to the obligation to instuct one's children during four stages of their existence.

The first, *beshivtecha beveitecha*, might be understood to refer to the period before birth when the as-yet unborn child is taught the whole Torah by an angel in its mother's womb (*Niddah* 30b). This idea that the unborn child is aware of Torah values may be reflected in the *Midrash* (Gen. R. 63:6), which states that when *Rivkah* was pregnant with twins, of which she was unaware, she noticed that the child moved as if to be born whenever she passed a *Beit Hamidrash* and also when she passed a *Beit Avodah Zarah*. She asked the meaning of this apparently self-contadictory tendency and was informed that she was carrying twins, one of which would be *tzaddik* and the other a *rasha*.

In fact, according to the *Gemara* (*Yevamot* 62a, *Avodah Zarah* 5a, *Niddah* 13b and Rashi *ad loc*), the soul even pre-exists conception. It informs us that the souls of all who are to be born into this world originate from beneath the *kissei hakavod*, so that might be seen as the soul's natural home, *beveitecha*.

Having emerged from the womb, the person must make his way in this world, to which the phrase *uvelechtecha vaderech* naturally applies. This might have been the motivation for the mother of Rabbi Yehoshua ben Chananiah in going every day to the *Beit Hamidrash* while pregnant with him to ask those learning there to pray for her unborn child to grow up to be a *talmid chacham*, and then later taking him there in his carriage to hear the Torah being learned, even though at that stage he could not follow the discussions, so that he should become accustomed from infancy to the sound of *limud haTorah* (Yer. *Yevamot* 1.6).

After the completion of his lifespan, the person passes on to the next world, the body lying in the grave, *uveshochbecha*, to be followed eventually by life in the eschatological era of *Mashiach*, alluded to by the word *uvekumecha*, which might be understood as referring to his rising from the grave in the end of days.

Forging an Eternal Link

There is yet another way of understanding the phrases *uvelechtecha vaderech uveshochbecha* as referring to the outcome of one's teaching one's children. As a result of it, they should continue in the true Torah way not only in your lifetime, *uvelechtecha vaderech*, but even after you have passed away, *uveshochbecha*, so that at the time of *techiat hameitim*, *uvekumecha*, you will have the satisfaction of knowing that you managed to forge a firm link in the *masorah* of *Klal Yisrael*.

Tefillin and *Mezuzah* – the Visible Symbols

This line of thought can be extended to give a further insight into the four physical symbols commanded in both paragraphs: the *tefillin shel yad, tefillin shel rosh, mezuzah* on one's door, and the *mezuzah* on one's gate. The main problem to be guarded against in the time of the Temple when everything seemed to be going well was to attribute success to one's own endeavors: *kochi ve'otzem yadi asah li et hachayil hazeh*, "this wealth has come to me through *my* power and the strength of *my* hand" (Deut. 8:17). To counteract this "strength of our hands" we require the "sign on our hands" of the *tefillin shel yad*. This line of thought also gives a reason why the *tefillin* are to be bound specifically on the arm rather than any other part of the body.

In both paragraphs of the *Shema* the command is "to tie them as a sign," whereas in the other two verses where *tefillin* are mentioned (Ex. 13:9 and 16), it is stated "and it shall be a sign." In the latter, the purpose of the *tefillin* is stated to be to remind us of the strong arm with which the Almighty took us out of Egypt, i.e., His *hashgachah* of which we need to be constantly aware. In our paragraphs, however, the act of tying is emphasized since, as the *Mesillat Yesharim* (ch. 7) observes, "external actions stir up internal feelings" and the love of G-d and His commandments require daily reinforcement.

On the other hand, during the exile, it is easy to imagine that all is lost and so we require the *tefillin shel rosh*, placed over the brain to impress on our minds the closeness of the Almighty despite His concealment. The *shel yad* is a message to each individual and is therefore covered (*Menachot* 34b based on Ex. 13:9), whereas the *shel rosh* has to be displayed publicly to indicate our confidence that His concealment does not imply that He has abandoned us. This message is implicit in the words of Rabbi Eliezer the Great (*Menachot* 35b et al.) who interprets the verse (Deut. 28:10), "And all the peoples of the earth will *see* that the name of the Almighty is called upon you and they will fear you" as a reference to the *tefillin shel rosh* which must therefore be visible to all.

Thus, the *halachah* that one must have the *tefillin shel yad* in place prior to donning the *tefillin shel rosh* might be taken to suggest that a condition for the peoples of the earth to see that the name of the Almighty is called upon us and, thereby, to fear us, is that we should first realize that any success we may have is not a result of our power or the strength of our hands, but rather through our adherence to the will of the Almighty.

It might be worth noting that the verse concerning the *mezuzah* has its major division, by a *tippecha*, which is a *melech,* after the word *beitecha*, your homes, separating it from *uvisharecha*, your gates, whereas the natural point to divide the verse would seem to be at *uchetavtam*, which only bears a *tevir* which is a *mishneh*, a lesser pause; if the major division had been at *uchetavtam*, a *zakef gadol* would have been more appropriate. This seems to hint at a significant distinction between the two types of *mezuzah*. Perhaps they can be seen as referring to the times of destruction and redemption respectively. In the former case, the last to be destroyed will be our private dwellings, opening up our private domain to the hostile world, which we therefore mark with a *mezuzah* on its doorpost. With the messianic redemption, on the other hand, we will once again have our own cities to whose gates we will be able to affix a *mezuzah*, a time when (Isaiah 60:10–11): "Aliens will rebuild your walls, their kings will wait upon you [...] your gates will always stay open [...] to let in the wealth of nations, with their kings in procession."

On the doors of our homes, it bears a message of hope that the destruction will only be temporary and that we can look forward to a better future. On our gates, it is a reminder not to be carried away by the excitement of messianic expectations, and to hold fast to the Almighty and His *mitzvot*, even when we seem to witness a radical change in our circumstances.

Some Further Comparisons
between the First and Second Paragraphs

There are still some differences between the two passages that require explanation. In our passage we have *velimadetem otam et beneichem*, whereas in the first paragraph we have *veshinantam levanecha*. The latter verb might be translated *and you shall repeat* or *you shall inculcate,* as opposed to the former, which carries more clearly the meaning of teaching. Alternatively, the two words might be thought of as referring to two different aspects of teaching with *veshinantam* emphasizing the idea of teaching the subject manner, as opposed to *velimadetem*, which emphasizes the teaching of the children. Perhaps this can be explained by noting once again that the first paragraph is in the singular, addressed to each individual, and the second in the plural, speaking to the community as a whole. Though any particular person may lack pedagogic skills, the community will have in it those able to teach effectively. Thus, the individual can only be told to repeat the Torah to his children and to inculcate it by example, whereas the community can set up educational institutions where all children, even those whose fathers cannot do so personally, can be taught. Some commentators suggest that the word *veshinantam* might be related to the word *shein*, tooth, to emphasize the incisive nature of Torah learning.

A further difference in this matter of *Talmud Torah* is that the first paragraph states, *veshinantam levanecha vedibarta bam*, but the second, *velimadtem otam et beneichem ledaber bam*. Thus, the first paragraph, by stating "*you* shall talk of them," seems to emphasize that the person performing this *mitzvah* should do so everywhere and at all times. On the other hand, the second paragraph, by using the words "you will teach them to your sons so that *they* will talk about them," seems to be discussing the learning outcome.

This difference would also seem to be backed by the different *te'amim* used. In the first passage, the main pause, signified by the *tippecha*, is on the word *vedibarta*, signifying that it is connected to the previous words, i.e., the teacher, whereas in the second, it is on the word *beneichem*, separating it from *ledaber bam*, suggesting that it goes on those taught.

This might also be hinted at by the fact that the word *veshinantam* takes the indirect object, *levanecha*, whereas *velimadtem* takes the direct object, *et beneichem*, i.e., repeating the lesson by being a role model to them is something *we* do, as opposed to teaching which has the hoped for outcome that *they* will carry on the tradition.

A slightly more homiletic explanation might be that the usually untranslated word *et* might here have its other connotation of *with*, suggesting that the phrase means "and you shall teach them together with your sons," which also implies that the "talking about them" applies to both the parent and child.

This passage might also be teaching that the only effective way of teaching is when one's conduct *beshivtecha beveitecha uvelechtecha vaderech uveshochbecha uvekumecha* is a consistent example of the lesson to be imparted. Put another way, our children will learn more from what we do than from what we tell them

According to this interpretation, it appears as though G-d is assuring us that whatever our present backsliding, we will eventually return to His ways. Put another way, this means that the continuity of Jewish People as a whole is guaranteed, even if a large proportion of individual Jews may appear to have abandoned the Torah and assimilated into their non-Jewish environment. In our times, the truth of this is demonstrated by the *Ba'al Teshuvah* movement, the like of which has never been seen before; even grandchildren of those who actively campaigned to eradicate Torah are today learning in *kollelim*.

Educational Method in the *Shema*

Following on from the latter point, one might note is that in the first paragraph the word "your sons" is the indirect object *levanecha*, whereas in the second paragraph it is the direct object *et beneichem*. This might be an indication of how one should approach the training of the young. The first paragraph is concerned basically with abstract concepts such as the unity of *HaShem* and our more spiritual obligations such as to love Him. Though one is obliged to teach these even to small children, even among the first verses they learn to repeat, one cannot expect them to fully understand their meaning until they reach a higher level of maturity; hence the use of the verb *veshinantam*, "you shall *repeat*," and the indirect object *levanecha*. On the other hand, when it comes to actually doing *mitzvot*, we should teach them, *velimadtem*, "you shall *teach*," i.e., explain the practical details of their performance even if they cannot yet grasp their underlying concepts; for example, we put *tzitzit* on a boy when he is very young even though he really has no idea what they signify. This shows that the mechanical performance of *mitzvot* should be introduced at a very early age so that when the child becomes mature they are second nature to him. This might be the significance of the use of the direct object, *et beneichem*, putting it, so to speak, in apposition with the word *otam*, them, i.e., the *mitzvot*, meaning that the *mitzvot* should become an integral part of the personality of our children. This might be seen as a source in the Torah for the advice (*Mishlei* 22:6), *Chanoch lana'ar al pi darko, gam ki zakin lo yasur mimenah*, "teach the youth according to his capability, when he matures he will certainly not turn aside from it."

Divine Confidence in Us

The next three verses (Deut. 11:18–20) mention the *mitzvot* of *talmud Torah*, *tefillin* and *mezuzah*, and repeat those in the first paragraph (Deut. 6:8–9), with minor changes in wording. The *Gemara* (*Menachot* 36a–37b) deduces many *halachic* consequences from the differences in the order of these *mitzvot*.

However, we might take a slightly different approach by translating the verbs in the future tense in the verses in the first paragraph as commands, while understanding those in the second as statements about our reaction to the previously enumerated rewards and, more specifically, punishments. Thus, we might translate *vesamtem et devarai eileh al levavechem ve'al nafshechem* as, "and you will place these words […]" rather than "place these words […]!"

If we develop this idea further, we can see this return as comprising several steps, each following logically from the previous one. Having taken to heart the punishments, the first outward manifestation is *ukeshartem otam le'ot al yedchem*, that we tie the *tefillin shel yad*, which are not visible to others, to our arms. Only after this do we have the confidence, *vehayu letotafot beyn einechem*, to place the *tefillin shel rosh* that others can see.

However, it would at this stage appear that we are only prepared to do so in the privacy of our homes, at most in front of our children. Their curiosity leads us to the next stage, *velimadetem otam et beneichem*, in which we teach them G-d's will, initially *ledaber beshivtecha beveitecha*, to talk of them privately at home and only subsequently, as our confidence increases, *uvelechtecha vaderech*, in the public domain and at all times *uveshochbecha uvekumecha*. Finally we feel able to advertise our adherence to *HaShem* completely publicly with *uchetavtam al mezuzot beitecha uvish'arecha*. This emphasis on our adherence to the principles and practices of the Torah, both in private and in public, is also its answer to the motto of the *maskilim*, "Be a Jew in your home but a man in the street."

Tefillin – Principles and Practices

The main purpose of the *tefillin* is as a sign and reminder. For this purpose there is an interesting difference between the first paragraph, which is primarily concerned with basic principles and attitudes to *HaShem*, and the second, which is primarily concerned with *mitzvot* and their observance. In the first, the verse *veshinantam* comes before *ukeshartam*, hinting that principles need to be inculcated before there is any use for remembering them. On the other hand, in the second paragraph, the verse *ukeshartem otam*, preceded by *vesamtem*, comes before *velimadetem*, hinting that observance of *mitzvot* in practice comes before learning their underlying reasons or, as the Ramchal puts it in his *Messilat Yesharim*, "external practices arouse internal fervor."

It is custom to touch the *tefillin* at certain points during *davening*, one of which is during the recitation of *yotzer or uvorei choshech* at the beginning of the first *berachah* before *kriat shema*, first the "hidden" *shel yad* and later the "visible" *shel rosh*. While this is based on their order in the *pesukim* in which the commandment appears, it would seem to go against the Ramchal's paradigm. Perhaps this can be explained by seeing this touching as itself the external practice and it is primarily to remind the worshipper that its purpose is to "arouse internal fervor" that it is done first.

It also seems somewhat paradoxical that the "hidden" *shel yad* should be associated with *or*, light, whereas the "visible" *shel rosh* is associated with *choshech*, darkness. This might also be explained as an indication that from a Divine perspective what we perceive as light and darkness may not be the ultimate reality as the *pasuk* (ultimately derived from *Yeshaya* 45:7) itself implies by describing darkness as having been created *ex nihilo*, whereas light is merely formed from some pre-existing entity.

Tefillin – the Sign of Truth

In the first paragraph of the *shema* we find the phrase *ukeshartam leot al yadecha*, the verb including its object as a suffix, whereas in the second this form is not used, but rather the object, *otam*, appears as a separate word. This contrast also is seen between *veshinantam* in the first and *velimadtem otam* in the second paragraph. One might have expected to find *ukeshartum* and *velimadtum*, but this form of the verb is not found anywhere in *Tanach* though, apart from feminine forms, almost every combination of subject and object suffixes appear. Furthermore, there is always a danger that the two words might be slurred into each other and result in one saying *motam*, their death, something that the *Shulchan Aruch* (*Orach Chaim* 61:21) specifically warns against, as it does in the much more serious case (*se'if* 19) not to read *vecharah af* as *vecharaf*, so that the phrase could mean "he will revile *HaShem* among you," *chas veshalom*. Furthermore, these pairs of words are all linked together by the *te'amim*, making it even more difficult to avoid these errors.

Perhaps the difference in such similar passages as we have here is meant to draw our attention to this omission. One possible reason is that the word *otam*, when spelled defectively, is an anagram of the word *emet*, truth. Its repeated use in place of the abbreviated form is meant to teach us that the *Tanach*, where the defective spelling overwhelmingly predominates in this particular form of the verb, reflects the idea that *HaShem's* revelation contains the essence of truth, as *Chazal* express the thought (*Shab.* 55b), "truth is the seal of the Holy One, blessed be He" and who "is close [...] to all who call on Him in truth" (Ps. 145:18). Thus, the *Tanach* has His seal imprinted throughout if we only choose to see it there.

Conversely, the very word, *motam*, with its connotation of death against the saying of which the *Shulchan Aruch* warns us, might also be seen as a warning of the consequence of not adhering to the path of truth laid out for us by the Almighty in His Torah.

Mezuzah – Echo of Creation or Portent of *Mashiach*?

We noted above that the *te'amim* on the verses referring to the *mezuzah, tevir, merecha, tippecha, sof pasuk*, are not what one would have expected from the natural sense of the verse in a short *pasuk* of only 4 words (*al* and *mezuzot* are connected by a *makef* and are therefore treated as one word). A *zakef gadol* would seem to have been more appropriate than the *tevir*. (This occurs in Num. 31:33, 34, and 44, that are of the same length). Perhaps one might suggest that the traditional sequence of *te'amim* is meant to recall, subliminally, the verse *vayechulu hashamayim veha'aretz vechol tzeva'am*, "thus the heavens and the earth were completed, together with all their host," to which it fits entirely naturally. There would then be an allusion in the *Shema* to G-d's creation of the world. That this is not entirely without foundation can be seen from the tradition that the name *shin dalet yod*, which connotes His role as creator (*Chagigah* 12b), should be written on the reverse of the *mezuzah*.

Another verse in which this sequence of *te'amim* occurs is *vataharena shtei bnot Lot meiavihen*, "and the daughters of Lot became pregnant from their father" (Gen. 19:36). The nations of Moav and Ammon, from whom *Mashiach* is descended, through Ruth (Moav), the grandmother of King David, and Na'amah (Ammon), the mother of Rechav'am, arose as a result of this incident. Thus, one might find here a portent of the ultimate completion of creation with its perfection when *Mashiach* eventually comes.

Blessings and Curses

Finally, there is a typographical difference between the corresponding passages in the two paragraphs that merits consideration. In the second paragraph we find the words *letotafot* and *mezuzot* each spelled with an extra *vav*, which is missing in the first paragraph. It is difficult to explain this discrepancy, which makes no difference to the meanings of the words, so without some authentic tradition, the following must be seen as merely tentative.

Shortly after the second paragraph of the *Shema*, we find (Deut. 11:26–32) the commandment to announce the blessings and curses consequent on keeping G-d's commandments, on Mount Gerizim and Mount Eval respectively. This complements the theme of our passage by publicizing its message. Later (Deut. 27) the details of this ceremony are specified, it being the first *mitzvah* to be performed by the *B'nei Yisrael* on entering the land (Joshua 8:30–35) after the conquest of Jericho and Ai. In this ceremony, six tribes were to stand on Mount Gerizim and the remaining six on Mount Eval. If we note that the letter *vav* has the numerical value six, it is possible to suggest that these two *vavs* might be hinting at this very division of the blessings and curses. Possibly the one in *letotafot*, coming immediately after the passage dealing with

63

punishments, refers to the curses and that in *mezuzot*, preceding the verse, "So that your days and the days of your children may be prolonged [...]," to the blessings. Furthermore, it is much more common for people to be jolted out of their complacency and return to *HaShem* when disaster strikes than as a result of exceptional good fortune. Also the *tefillin* are attached to our person, perhaps reflecting the greater deterrent effect of fear of punishment, whereas the *mezuzah* is fixed to our home, with its blessings, which protects us from the outside world and its trials.

That the commandment of *Talmud Torah* is sandwiched between them may also be significant, hinting that specifically this *mitzvah* has the power to transform curses into blessings. This transformative property of the Torah is also alluded to by the *Gemara* (*Kiddushin* 30b), basing itself on a verse in the second paragraph (Deut. 11:18): "The Rabbis taught in a *Baraita*, 'vesamtem – sam tam' – the Torah is compared to a life-giving medicine (*sam*) [...]. The Holy One, blessed be He, said to Israel, 'I have created the evil inclination and I have created the Torah as its antidote. If you involve yourselves with Torah you will not be delivered into its hand.'"

In this context, it might be significant that a *mizbeach* was to be built on Mount Eval (Deut. 27:4), rather than on Mount Gerizim, to show that the curses had a positive purpose to educate the Jewish People to avoid transgression rather than being purely for retribution. Perhaps this is also a lesson for future generations, that we should not misinterpret our persecutions as showing that *HaShem* is a G-d of vengeance, but remember that His mercy extends to thousands of generations unlike His punishment, which is only carried forward at most four, and then only if they continue in their fathers' evil ways (*son'ai*) (Ex. 34:7).

This concept might even be seen in the spelling of these words. The word *totafot*, whose extra *vav* we suggested might allude to the curses, could have had yet another extra *vav* to make it fully *malei*, unlike the word *mezuzot*, which has two. Perhaps this also alludes to the "deficient" nature of the curses in that *HaShem* does not wish to punish us and only does so to the minimal extent, as opposed to blessings that He wishes to bestow on us fully. This might be a source for the advice of *Chazal*, that one should push away wrongdoers with one's left hand but at the same time draw them close with one's right (*Sotah* 43a, B.M. 53a, *Y. San.* 87a).

Eretz or *Adamah*?

In the second paragraph, the words *eretz* and *adamah* are used alternately, apparently both referring to *Eretz Yisrael*, with no obvious reason for using one rather than the other. Thus, we find *venatati matar-artsechem be'ito* (14), *veha'adamah lo titen et yevulah* (17), *va'avadtem meherah me'al ha'aretz hatovah* (ibid.) and *lema'an yirbu yemechem […] al ha'adamah* (21). Though this alternating pattern is continued in the final phrase *kimei shamayim al ha'aretz*, the word there refers to the whole world and not to *Eretz Yisrael* specifically.

HaRav S.R. Hirsch states that the word *adamah* is related to the root *dum*, meaning *still* as in *vayidom Aharon* (Lev. 10:3) and, perhaps, this idea might help us solve our problem. By analogy one might relate the word *eretz* to the root *rutz*, meaning *run*, which has almost the opposite connotation. Thus the two words could be thought to suggest how the land might relate to us in two contrasting ways; when we obey *HaShem*'s will, it *runs* to reward us, whereas when we do otherwise, it remains *still* and does not "give its produce," though it still wishes, so to speak, to *run* to "do good." However, the ultimate reward will be that we shall 'have our days […] extended' on the land, which will then remain *still* and thus we will have eternal tranquility on it.

The Ultimate Rewards

The rewards and punishments mentioned in our passage are of an essentially this-worldly nature, being tied to the success or failure of the harvest. Even the last verse only promises longevity as a reward for keeping the *mitzvot*. Yet often people who appear righteous suffer while those who appear wicked seem to prosper.

Many thinkers over the centuries have tried to find some solution to this problem but are forced to the conclusion that this is only possible in some future existence.

The *Gemara* (*Sanhedrin* 90b) notes that in the final verse of the paragraph, the text states that the Almighty has sworn to give the Land of Israel to our fathers by writing *lahem*, to them, rather than *lachem*, to you. Since our ancestors have long passed away, this is taken as a proof of the resurrection of the dead; otherwise the Almighty would not be able to fulfill His promise. Thus, there is an eschatological allusion implicit in our text. This may also be hinted by the words *uveshochbecha uvekumecha*, which might be translated in this context as "when you lie down (in the grave) and when you get up (at the time of the resurrection of the dead)."

Furthermore, the messianic concept is also hinted at in the first verse of the first paragraph of the *Shema* (Deut. 6:4) where the *ayin* of *shema* and the *dalet* of *echad* are enlarged, spelling the word *ed*, meaning a witness. Thus, our recitation of the *Shema* is an act of witness to all the world of the fundamental principle of our religion, G-d's unity (*Rokeach, Kol Bo, Avudarham,* cf. *Berachot* 13b). The significance of this act of witness is emphasized by the prophet Isaiah in several passages:

- You are My witnesses, says *HaShem*, and My servant whom I have chosen in order that you should consider and believe in Me and understand that I am He and beside Me there no god was formed and after Me none shall exist. (43:10)
- I have made you a witness to the peoples, a prince and commander of peoples. So you shall call a nation you do not know, and a nation that does not know you shall run to you, for the sake of *HaShem* your G-d, the Holy One of Israel who has glorified you. (55:4–5)

The latter idea, that we are to be instrumental in the universal recognition of G-d, is also hinted at by the enlarged *ayin*, which has numerical value seventy, the traditional number of nations in the world (cf. Tur *ad loc*). At the end of his *Mishneh Torah* (*Hil. Melachim* 12:5), the Rambam quotes the Prophet Isaiah, who saw this as the ultimate purpose of creation when he prophesied:

> They will not do evil nor destroy in all My holy mountain, for the world will be filled with the knowledge of *HaShem* as the waters cover the sea (11:9).

"In those days ten men from all the languages of the nations will take hold of the corner of a Jew's cloak [the word used, *kanaf*, might allude to the *tzitzit* commanded in the third paragraph of the *Shema*] and say, 'We will go with you because we have heard that G-d is with you'" (Zech. 8:23), with the result that "*HaShem* will be King over all the world – on that day *HaShem* will be one and His name one" (14:9), that is, as Rashi observes (Deut. 6:4), that in the future He will not merely be *Elokenu*, our G-d, but the one G-d of all nations, leading to the fulfillment of His promise: "And I shall bring them to My holy mountain, and I shall gladden them in My house of prayer; their offerings and their sacrifices will find favor on My altar, because My house will be called a house of prayer for all nations" (Isaiah 56:7).

Only in those messianic times will it be possible to see our present existence in its proper perspective, and only then will we be able understand G-d's true justice. Until then we can only trust that all that happens does happen for the ultimate good, as it says (*Berachot* 60b), "To tell Your kindness in the dawn (the time of messianic redemption when we shall see it clearly) and Your faithfulness by night (in our present circumstances when we must take it on trust)" (Ps. 92:3, Rashi ad loc).

While examining the two words *shema* and *echad*, one might note that not only do their final letters spell out the word *ed*, but their initial letters spell out, in reverse order, the word *eish*, fire, and their middle letters *cham*, hot, perhaps hinting that only if we are hot as fire in our devotion to *HaShem* will we be able to bring this influence to bear on the nations of the world in order to achieve His ultimate purpose.

Perhaps the association of the *Shema* with this messianic hope is the reason why Ashkenazim, following the *Seder Rav Amram Gaon*, include the apparently anomalous plea each morning, "May You shine a new light on Zion and may we all speedily merit its light," at the end of *birchat yotzer or*, the praise of *HaShem* as the creator of the luminaries.

Excursus – The Seven Heavens and the Earth

Having pointed out the significance of the letters in the first *pasuk*, *Shema*, we might consider in more detail those in its last word, *echad*. The first letter, *alef*, has *gematria* one, the same as the word's meaning, while the last, *dalet*, has *gematria* four corresponding to four points of the compass, representing His control of the whole world. The second, *chet*, has gematria eight, traditionally referring to the whole universe consisting of seven heavens and the earth. Each of the heavens corresponds to one of the brightest objects visible in the sky: the sun, moon and the five planets that can be seen with the naked eye. As Rabbi Ya'akov Emden points out in his commentary on the *siddur* (p. 227 of the corrected edition), these are alluded to in *birchat yotzer or*: the Sun (*po'eil gevurot* cf. *Teh.* 19.6), Moon (*oseh chadashot*, referring to its waxing and waning, thereby fixing the months, *chodoshim*), Mars (*Ma'adim*, the bloody one, *ba'al michamot*), Jupiter (*Tzedek*, justice, *zorei'a tsedakot*), Mercury (*Kochav*, the messenger, *matzmiach yeshuot* cf. Num. 24:17), Venus (*Nogah*, *borei refuot* cf. *Chab.* 3:4) and Saturn (*Shabta'i*, which "rules over *Shabbat*, *nora tehillot*" cf. Ps. 92:1). To these we might add the Earth as being indicated by the last phrase, *adon hanifla'ot*, as the arena in which *HaShem* performs His wonderous actions.

Incidentally, each of these is associated with a day of the week, after which the day is named: Sunday (SUN's day), Monday (MOON's day), Tuesday, in French Mardi (MARS' day),

Wednesday, in French Mercredi (MERCURY's day), Thursday, in French Jeudi (JUPITER's day, the ending piter merely meaning father), Friday, in French Vendredi (VENUS's day), Saturday (SATURN's day). It might be noted that *Chazal* reversed the daily order of Mercury and Jupiter in the *berachah*, but no obvious explanation springs to mind. One might speculate that planting, *zorei'a*, had to precede sprouting, *matzmiach*, and that justice, *tzedakot*, precedes salvation, *yeshuot*, as is implied by the *navi* Yeshaya (1:27): *Tzion bamishpat tipadeh veshaveyah bitzdakah,* "Zion shall be redeemed through justice."

There is a second set of eight expressions in the next *berachah*, *Ahavah Rabbah,* which might be seen as mirroring these, each representing a further spiritual ascent corresponding to the various heavenly bodies, just as that *berachah* refers to the *Torah*, the spiritual equivalent of the material universe referred to in the first one. To show the parallelism we might set the two in parallel columns:

Lehavin	*po'eil gevurot*
ulehaskil	*oseh chadashot*
lishmo'a	*ba'al michamot*
lilmod	*zorei'a tzedakot*
ulelameid	*matzmiach yeshuot*
lishmor	*borei refuot*
vela'asot	*nora tehillot*
ulekayeim	*adon hanifla'ot*

The first term, *lehavin*, might be seen as referring to the description of *Yissachar* (1 Chron. 12:32) as being *"yod'ei vinah la'ittim,"* knowing the understanding of times," traditionally interpreted as their calendrical expertise, since time is controlled by the sun.

The second term, *lehaskil*, might be seen as referring to the ability to combine the lunar months with the solar year, as the *Gemara* (*Shab.* 75a) states to be the meaning of Moshe Rabbeinu's words (Deut. 4:6) that "this is your wisdom and understanding in the eyes of the nations."

The third term, *lishmo'a*, might be seen as referring to hearing the sound of war (cf. Ex. 32:17).

The fourth term, *lilmod*, might be seen as continuing this concept in line with the words of the *navi Yeshaya* (2:4), that in the messianic era, a time of universal justice, no one will learn war any more, whereas the fifth term, *lelameid*, might also be an echo of a similar prophecy of the *navi Yirmiyahu* of these latter days (31:34) when it will no longer be necessary for each person to instruct his fellow in the ways of *HaShem* since everyone will be aware of them resulting in *HaShem* pardoning all wrongdoings.

The sixth term, *lishmor*, can be seen as referring to the commandment (Deut. 4:15) to carefully guard one's health.

The seventh term, *la'asot*, can be seen as referring to the *Shabbat*. In its first mention, there is the commandment (Gen. 2:3) to be an active party in the act of creation.

Finally the last term, *lekayeim*, might be a reference to the fact that the world only continues to exist through the will of *HaShem* and what appears to us as the workings of "laws of nature" are really miracles performed by Him. As *Chazal* put it in the *berachah* of *Modim*, we thank Him for, "His miracles that are performed for us each day and wondrous and beneficent deeds every instant, evening, morning and noon."

It may not be too farfetched to suggest that this parallelism might reflect the mystical ascent to the highest spheres through these different ways of apprehending and implementing the Divinely revealed *divrei Torah*, also alluded to by the eight words in the angelic doxology heard by the prophet *Yeshaya* (6:3, *kol ha'aretz* being joined by a *makkef* and therefore treated as one word).

Some Perspectives on *Tzitzit*

From the above discussion, it should be apparent that many nuances of meaning become apparent when one compares the texts of the first and second paragraphs of the *Shema*. On consideration, one might see that some of them are developed in the third paragraph.

It starts with one possible parallel, the *mitzvah* of *tzitzit* which, like *tefillin* and *mezuzah*, are meant to remind us of our duties to the Almighty. Unlike *tefillin*, which have a degree of sanctity that precludes wearing them in certain circumstances, and the *mezuzah*, which is fixed to the doorpost, *tzitzit* can be worn everywhere and so provide a constant and visible reminder, their effectiveness for which is graphically illustrated by the incident described in *Menachot* 44a.

A further parallel between the *mitzvot* of *tzitzit* and *tefillin* might be seen in the former's purpose of preventing us from going astray after our hearts and our eyes. In this context, the heart might be understood as an allusion to the *tefillin shel yad* which, as the meditation prior to putting on the *tefillin* puts it: "He has commanded us to lay the *tefillin* on the hand as a memorial of His outstretched arm, opposite the heart, to subdue the longings and designs of the heart to His service." The eyes are even more clearly an allusion to the *tefillin shel rosh* that are to be placed between the eyes. Furthermore, the word *tzitzit* might suggest the word *tzitz*, the plate worn by the *kohen gadol* on his forehead, which was engraved with the words "*kodesh laShem*."

Perhaps this relative lack of sanctity is hinted at by the indirect way this *mitzvah* is commanded, at four degrees remove, "And the Almighty *said* to Moshe *to say* 'speak to the Children of Israel and *say* to them that they should make *tzitzit*,'" in contrast with the peremptory, "*bind them* as a sign on your hand [...] *write them* on the doorposts of your house!"

Another way of understanding the *mitzvah* of *tzitzit* might be suggested by the *berachah* before the morning recital of the *Shema*. The custom is to gather the four *tzitziyot* as one says "bring us in peace from the four corners (*kanfot*) of the world," indicating a parallel between the *tzitzit* and the Jewish People and later, while reciting the third paragraph, to kiss them each time the word *tzitzit* is said. It is interesting to note that it is in the absolute form at the first and third times but in the construct the second (*tzitzit hakanaf*), depending on the subsequent word. Even though the two grammatically different forms are spelled identically, this dependence is indicated by the *te'amim*. Because of this it is not proper to kiss them until the end of the phrase in that case, something not widely known.

One might possibly learn from the sequence of first making "*tzitzit* on the corners," followed by putting a thread of blue on the "*tzitzit* of the corners" and finally that they should be "*tzitzit*" to be seen, the idea that we must first attach ourselves to the Almighty, who promises to cover us with the corner of His garment, so to speak, as a sign of His everlasting covenant with us (Ezekiel 16:8). Only once we are firmly attached to Him can we have any absolute value in our own right and be seen to be the messengers of His will.

The custom is to hold the *tzitzit* until one reaches the word *la'ad*, forever, in the *berachah* after the morning *Shema*, after which they are kissed and released. This word could be vocalized to read *le'ed*, for a witness, developing the above idea that we should be the evidence of the truth of the concepts contained in the *Shema* (Isaiah 43:10). Interestingly, this is done at the second time the word *la'ad* appears in this paragraph, which might be a hint that "by the word of two witnesses…shall a matter be confirmed" (Deut. 15:19).

Following this line of thought, one might see a similar hint in the conclusion of the *hashkivenu* blessing after the recital of the evening *Shema*. The words *shomer amo yisrael la'ad*, meaning "who protects His people Israel for ever," might be read as, "who protects His people as a witness." That this formula is changed on *Shabbat* and *Yom Tov*, omitting *la'ad*, fits in with their special nature as witness to Him.

There appears to be some redundancy in the third paragraph. First it states that the purpose of the *tzitzit* is "that you shall see it and remember all the commandments of the Almighty and do them and not go astray after [the desires of] your heart or [what] your eyes [see]" (v. 39), but continues, "In order that you shall remember and do all My commandments and [thereby] be holy to your G-d" (v. 40), apparently merely paraphrasing the previous verse.

On closer consideration we might see that this is not so. In the first verse the purpose of the *tzitzit* is phrased in a negative way, as a means of avoiding temptation. The second could be understood as developing this further by using such avoidance of transgression, rather than seeing the *tzitzit per se*, as leading us to raise ourselves spiritually to a higher level of holiness.

This idea might be reinforced by noting that the first verse refers indirectly to "the commandments of the Almighty," which is changed in the second to "My commandments," showing a more intimate connection between the *mitzvot* and their commander. Since we are expected, so to speak, to try to emulate Him, the two verses correspond to our internalization of His will so that the heteronomous commandments of the Almighty become our own autonomous actions.

The *Frum Yetzer Hara*

In the third paragraph, the purpose of the *tzitzit* is stated to be *ure'item oto uzechartem et kol mitzvot HaShem va'asitem otam*, "and you shall look at it and remember all the commandments of *HaShem* and do them," in order that *velo taturu acharei levavechem ve'acharei einiechem asher atem zonim achareihem*, "you will not go astray after your hearts or your eyes after which you [tend to] stray." *Chazal (Ber.* 12b) interpret this as follows:

> *acharei levavechem*' refers to heresy as it says 'the fool says in his heart (*belibo*) there is no G-d' (Ps. 14:1), *ve'acharei einiechem* refers to immorality as it says, 'and *Shimshon* said to his father, get that woman for me because she is attractive

in my eyes (*be'einai*)' (Judges 14:3), *atem zonim* refers to idolatry as it says, 'and they went (*veyiznu*) astray after idols' (Judges 8:33).

However, we might suggest that *acharei levavechem* might parallel the terminology in the first two paragraphs, *bechol levavecha* and *bechol levavechem*. There we queried the use of the form *levavecha* with a double *bet* rather than *bechol libecha* with only one, which the *Mishnah* expounds as meaning "with both your inclinations, i.e., with the good inclination and with the evil inclination" (*Berachot* 9:5).

One might suggest that here also the double *bet* refers to both, i.e., that the *tzitzit* should protect us from both our evil inclination and our good one. This latter rather surprising concept can be thought of as referring to the so-called *frum yetzer hara* that tries to persuade us that certain actions are good traits though they might not be in the particular circumstance in which it would have us perform them. One example is learning Torah, which is generally a full-time duty, during *chazarat hashatz* when we are supposed to be concentrating on what is being said. Though this might be basically permitted, it can lead less educated people to think that *chazarat hashatz* is not so terribly important and thereby come to converse at that time, a sin which the *Shulchan Aruch* (*Orach Chaim* 124:7) describes as greater than one can bear. Another is being particular careful in one's *davening* and thereby taking much longer than everyone else, again an admirable trait, though a side effect might be that those in one's vicinity, who might be tired, are precluded from sitting down, a case of where *bein adam laMakom* might conflict with *bein adam lechaveiro*.

Perhaps this is also implied by the the double *bet* form used in *pen yifteh levavechem*, "lest your hearts be enticed" in the second paragraph since it is the common failing of human nature known as "cognitive dissonance" to be blind to those aspects of one's actions that do not fit in with one's inner motivation, thereby following what one perceives to be one's good inclination even in situations where there might be less than good consequences.

Tzitzit – the Double Reminder

There is a strange duplication in the third paragraph in that it first states *ure'item otam uzechartem et kol mitzvot HaShem*, "and when you see them you shall remember and do all of *HaShem*'s *mitzvot*," and then *lema'an tizkeru va'asitem et kol mitzvotai*, "in order that you shall remember and do all My *mitzvot*" seems the same. What is meant by remembering in order to remember? Perhaps one might be able to resolve this by understanding the first *pasuk* as a command to remember and do the *mitzvot* of *HaShem* in order "not to turn away after the inclinations of our hearts or eyes," as the *pasuk* concludes, i.e., to follow His directives as opposed to our own personal whims. As a result, we may come to the higher level of seeing the performance of *mitzvot* as, in a sense, coming closer to the Divine (*mitzvotai* as opposed to *mitzvot HaShem*) which would motivate us to a greater striving for their perfect performance (*lifnim mishurat hadin*) and so become *kedoshim*, sanctified, in the sense that we are restrained even in those matters which, though strictly speaking permitted according to the letter of the law, offend against its spirit. As the Ramban puts it, we should avoid being a *naval birshut haTorah*, a rogue within the strict parameters of the Torah.

Joining Redemption to Prayer

In the second paragraph, the ultimate reward is stated to be the eternal possession of the Holy Land, the essential precursor of whose first occupation was the Exodus from Egypt, whose memory is commanded in the third. According to the *Mishnah* (*Berachot* 12b), this is the main reason for its daily recital.

It is further explained there that this *mitzvah* to remember the Exodus will also be operative in the messianic era referred to at the end of the second paragraph, notwithstanding the prophecy:

Therefore the days will come says *HaShem* when they will no longer say '*HaShem*, Who brought the Children of Israel out of the land of Egypt, lives.' Rather [it will be said] '*HaShem*, Who brought the Children of Israel from the lands of the north and from the lands where He has scattered them, lives.' I will bring them again into the land and they shall dwell on their land (Jeremiah 23:7–8).

Though the *Mishnah* quotes these verses, we find them repeated (ibid. 16:14–15) with a few differences, the only one of major significance being that "and they shall dwell on their land" is replaced by "I will cause them to dwell on their land which I gave to their fathers," echoing even more strikingly that of the second paragraph.

We might notice that this final verse in the *Shema*, during which we are commanded to remember the Exodus, "I am *HaShem* your G-d who has taken you out of the land of Egypt," also gives the reason that He did so "in order that I should be your G-d." The mere Exodus would have been pointless without this acceptance of the Divine sovereignty. This is paralleled at the beginning of the Exodus narrative where Moshe Rabbeinu is told to say to Pharaoh not merely "Let My people go" but rather, "Let My people go *so that they may serve Me*" (Ex. 7:26), something so easily overlooked in our secular age.

It is customary to add the word *emet* which is really the first word of the blessing after *Shema*, to the end of the last paragraph. The *sheliach tzibur* repeats *HaShem Elokechem emet* to affirm that the *Shema* contains the ultimate truth.

The Fifteen Steps

One might note that once the word *emet* is appended to the *Shema* there are fifteen adjectival descriptions left at the beginning of the concluding morning *berachah*. Perhaps *Chazal* chose this number once again to parallel the fifteen steps that went up from the *ezrat nashim* to the *azarah*, in order to teach us that only after we have listened to what *HaShem* has to tell us can we ascend to speak to Him and present our own petitions, which might be seen as corresponding to the *vidui* recited at the time of making *semichah* on our *korban*.

It is interesting to note that after this list of fifteen attributes come the words *hadavar hazeh*. The word *devir*, which is another name for the Holy of Holies, has the same root letters as *davar*, so this phrase may be seen as reinforcing the thought.

Thus, the last paragraph of the *Shema*, in alluding to the Exodus, is, by implication, returning to the theme of the ultimate redemption. Having internalized a firm trust in its eventual realization, we are then allowed to address the Almighty with our own prayers, which the *Gemara* (*Berachot* 9b, 42a et al.) commands us to do without delay.

The number fifteen is itself significant, being the numerical value of *Kah*, one of the Divine names and might be seen as hinting to the verse "Trust in *HaShem* for ever and ever, because *HaShem* through His name *Kah* is an everlasting stronghold" (Isaiah 26:4), included in the *Kedushah deSidra* said each day.

Divine Kingship

Incidentally, each of these fifteen adjectival descriptions begins with the letter *vav*, whose numerical value is six, making a total of ninety, the *gematria* of *melech*, king. This might be seen as significant when one considers that the *Shema* is an acknowledgement that the Almighty is the King of all creation, which is the reason its first verse concludes the ten verses of kingship in the *mussaf* on *Rosh HaShanah*. This intimate connection is emphasized by the inclusion in the *Shema* of the *mitzvah* of remembering the Exodus from Egypt, the culmination of which was the crossing of the *Yam Suf*. After this event, the *B'nei Yisrael* concluded their song of praise to *HaShem* with the declaration that "*HaShem* will reign for all eternity" (Ex. 15:19), which itself is the first of these kingship verses.

Furthermore, the *berachah* following the *Shema* develops

this theme of the Exodus and also contains this verse, showing its intimate association with the *Shema* itself. Similarly, the daily recitation of *Pesukei deZimra*, which immediately precedes the morning *Shema*, concludes with this paean followed by three of the kingship verses. In some rites, these are followed by the first verse of the *Shema*, thus reciprocating this connection.

A Further Four Steps

Having drawn our attention to the word *emet* by separating it from its natural position at the beginning of *emet veyatsiv* and joining it to the end of the third paragraph of the *Shema*, it might be significant that *Chazal* included four sentences beginning with *emet* in this *berachah*, before summarizing the main events in *Yetziat Mitzraim*:

1. *Emet, Elokei 'olam…*
2. *Emet sheAtah Hu HaShem…*
3. *Emet Atah Hu Adon leamecha…*
4. *Emet Atah Hu rishon…*

One might suggest that these correspond to the four steps leading from the *Ezrat Yisrael* to the *Ezrat Kohanim*, continuing the ascent we noted previously; it was from these steps that the *Levi'im* sang when the offerings were brought. Furthermore, we noted above that the word *emet* appears coded in anagrammatic form in the *Shema* itself: three times as *otam* and once as *atem*, i.e., a total of four times, which might be seen to correspond to these four "truth statements."

Having ascended these four steps, one would have reached the base of the steps leading up to the *ulam*, the antechamber of the *Beit haMikdash* proper.

There is a further occurrence of the word *emet* not at the beginning of a sentence: *emet ve'emunah chok velo ya'avor*, "true and trustworthy a statute that will never pass away." This instance might correspond to the word *emet*, which, as we noted above, was detached from the *berachah* and appended to the third paragraph of the *Shema*, and might thereby be seen as expanding and explaining its significance. This would then be similar to the initial words of the corresponding *berachah* in the evening, *emet ve'emunah kol zot vekayam aleinu*, "true and trustworthy is all this and established for us."

An alternative symbolism of the number four might be the four worlds noted previously. With this in mind, the word *emet* becomes particularly significant since *Chazal* teach that *emet* is the seal of the Almighty (*Shabbat* 55a), which might indicate that it "seals" the connection between the worlds.

The Waters of Truth

A further observation on the word *emet* is that it consists of the letters *alef* and *tav* with the letter *mem* between them. The former are the first and last, respectively, in the alphabet and, therefore, represent the totality of creation, yet they spell *et*, a word which is meaningless in itself, as we have seen above. The name of the letter, *mem*, is related to the word *mayim*, waters, and its insertion might be connected to the primeval state when "the earth was without form and void and the spirit of G-d hovered over the waters."

This relationship of the word *emet* to *mayim* may be of particular significance in this *berachah*, which is concerned with the events associated with *Yetziat Mitzraim* and, in particular, at the *Yam Suf*, where the pursuing Egyptians were drowned in the returning waters.

Why Do We Repeat "*Ani HaShem Elokechem*"?

In the final *pasuk* of the third paragraph we find the phrase *Ani HaShem Elokechem* repeated. While it makes perfect sense to say, "I am *HaShem* your G-d who took you out of the land of Egypt," it is strange to find the first three words repeated. Perhaps one might explain this as a reference to the work we must do on ourselves in recognizing *HaShem*. As the joke would have it, taking the *Benei Yisrael* out of Egypt was accomplished in seven days, but it took forty years of wandering in the *midbar* to take Egypt out of the *Benei Yisrael*! Thus, the repetition of *Ani HaShem Elokechem*, with no action performed, might be meant as an instruction to us to internalize our relationship to *HaShem* so that we can remove the *tuma* of Egypt from ourselves.

This line of thinking suggests a possible further reason for adding the word *emet* at the end of this *pasuk*. It might be viewed as an acronym for *et-eretz Mitzraim totziu*, "you shall remove the land of Egypt (from yourselves)," suggesting that the whole *pasuk* should be understood to mean, "I am *HaShem* your G-d who took you out of the land of Egypt to be your G-d – I am *HaShem* your G-d (who commands you to) remove the (influence of the) land of Egypt (from yourselves)."

Some Further Thoughts on "These Words"

We noted above that the word *davar* has the same root letters as the word *devir*. The *devir*, or as it is usually called, the *kodesh kodashim*, was the innermost part of the Temple which was never entered except by the *Kohen Gadol* on *Yom Kippur* and, in the first *Beit HaMikdash*, only contained the *aron*, which housed the second *luchot* (Ex. 34:1), on which were inscribed the ten utterances of the Almighty at Sinai, together with the fragments of the first ones which Moshe Rabbeinu had smashed (Ex. 32:19). (It was empty in the second *Beit HaMikdash*.)

It might be worth noting in this context that the word *devir* only differs by having the additional letter *yod*, whose numerical value is ten. When the *yod* is removed the word could be read as *dever*, pestilence, primarily cattle disease (Ex. 9:3–6). Perhaps one might see this as a hint that if we ignore the ten utterances, which implicitly include all of the Torah, we are liable to suffer illness on the level of all animal life. Also, the word *dever* is an anagram for one of the other plagues brought on Egypt prior to the Exodus, *barad*, hail (Ex. 9:18–26), which destroyed all vegetation in the fields. Interestingly, in connection with these two plagues, unlike the preceding ones, the Torah tells us explicitly that the animals and crops of the *Benei Yisrael* were not affected, demonstrating clearly that they were Divine interventions in nature and not mere fortuitous occurrences.

The Torah was given in the *midbar,* wilderness, and this word also has the same root letters as *davar* but with an extra initial *mem,* which has numerical value forty. Perhaps this hints to the forty years spent by the *Benei Yisrael* wandering in the *midbar* before entering *Eretz Yisrael.*

Another word with the same root letters is *devorah,* a bee, which has an extra final *hei,* with numerical value five (in Isaiah 7:18 it also has an extra *vav*). In *Midrash Shocher Tov* 1, we find the proverb, "Say to the bee: I wish for neither your honey nor your sting." Thus, the bee represents the concept of reward (honey) and punishment (sting), associated with our compliance, or otherwise, with the precepts of the Torah. The extra *hei* might hint to the five levels of soul: *nefesh, ruach, neshamah, yechidah,* and *chayah,* and the effects of a person's *mitzvot* on them.

With a different vocalization, *devorah* can be read as *doverah,* a raft, (1 Kings 5:23) which can save the life of someone lost in the water. Perhaps this could be seen as a hint that the concepts contained in the *Shema* can be a life raft to us in this world and help to save us from "drowning" in its distractions.

These words are formed from the root *davar* by adding the extra letters *yod, mem,* and *hei* respectively. When all three are added we obtain the word *hadevarim* as in the phrase *hadevarim haeileh,* these words, used in the first paragraph of the *Shema,* which perhaps gives some further insights into its deeper significance.

Furthermore, one might note that the word *darbon,* a goad, comes from the root *darav* which is also an anagram of *davar* and "the words of the wise are like goads" (Ecc. 12:11), which should lead us to "fear G-d and keep His commandments for this is the whole purpose of man" (*ibid.* 12:13). In contrast, the word *revid,* a necklace, has root letters *ravad,* another anagram of *davar,* but is a symbol of almost regal status (Gen. 41:42), perhaps alluding to those who take to heart the message of the *Shema.*

Conclusion

The *Avudarham* (p.80) notes that the word *shema* might be taken as an acronym in several ways, deriving the message: "*Se'u marom 'eineychem*, 'raise your eyes on high and see' (Isaiah 40:26). Who? *Shakai melech 'olam*, 'the Creator, King of the universe.' When? *Shacharit, minchah 'arvit*, 'morning, afternoon and evening.' If you do this you will be accepting on yourself the yoke of the kingdom of heaven, *'ol malchut shamayim*, which is an acronym of *shema* in reverse order."

Since there are traditionally seventy interpretations of the Torah (*BeMidbar Rabbah* 13:15), one might suggest yet another: *Shema, listen* to what the Almighty is commanding you, *makir, recognize* it as the Almighty's command to you, *'iyen, examine carefully* His message.

Furthermore, when read in the reverse order, the enlarged *ayin* and *dalet* in this verse read *da*, meaning "know," implying that we are commanded to know with complete certainty the truths contained in the *Shema*. Thus, the Rambam writes, as the first *mitzvah* of his *Mishneh Torah*, that "the foundation of foundations and the pillar of wisdom is to *know* the existence of the Creator" (*Hilchot Yesodei HaTorah* 1:1).

In a similar vein, the word *shamo'a* at the beginning of the second paragraph, which is spelled precisely the same as *shema*, could be considered a reverse acronym for *'ol mitzvot Shakai*, indicating that we should accept the *yoke* of the *commandments* of the *Creator*, which forms the content of that paragraph.

Similarly, the numerical values of the letters of the word *echad* might be seen as an acknowledgement that the Almighty is *alef*, one, *chet*, eight, ruler of the seven heavens and the earth, and *dalet*, four, whose power is over the four corners of the world (*Shulchan Aruch Harav* 61:6). On the other hand, one should take to heart what the *Ba'alei Mussar* say that it is all very well to recognize His rule over the universe, but one must not exclude Him from one's own private domain, i.e., oneself.

I have presented only a few ideas that might be derived from the *Shema*, but it should be clear that a careful reading reveals many profound concepts that are so easily missed because we are so used to its daily recital that we often do so by rote.

In certain circles it is seen as a sign of piety to recite the *Shemoneh Esrei* with great deliberation, and at considerable length, much more than is given to the *Shema*. Hopefully some of the thoughts presented here will help restore the balance so that we should merit that He instill in our hearts the ability to understand and discern; listen, learn and teach; keep, perform and establish all the words of His Torah, and that He should enlighten our eyes so that we can appreciate the many levels of meaning therein when we declare "Understand O Israel, *HaShem* (the all-merciful Lord of the universe, essence of existence) is our G-d (the all-powerful judge who can do anything and controls the world and runs it according to His will yet, nonetheless, looks after each one of us individually), *HaShem* is one, unique and indivisible (besides Whom nothing else really exists)."

AN OVERVIEW OF THE SHEMONEH ESREI

Having listened to the words of the Almighty in the *Shema*, one is prepared to present one's own requests in the form established by the *Anshei Knesset HaGedolah*: the *Shemoneh Esrei*. Since he is speaking to the Almighty, he should consider it as if He were standing directly in front of him and, thereby, be filled with an appropriate sense of awe at the Divine presence. Needless to say, complete concentration on what one is saying is necessary though, recognizing human weakness, *Chazal* decided to restrict this requirement in its full severity to the first paragraph in the first instance. The deeper significance of this restriction will be explored further below.

The *Shemoneh Esrei* can be thought of as being composed of three parts, the first three *berachot*, which are praises of the Almighty, the intermediate twelve (now thirteen) which contain our personal requests, and the last three, in which the communal aspect is paramount. Of these, the first set has the same wording in all current rites, whereas the remainder have minor textual variations (which do not affect their basic meaning). We will first examine the internal structure of the former and then look at how they include hidden intentions that set up the necessary "conduits" for the Divine beneficence to "percolate" down to answer us. Having done so, we will turn to the remainder and try to find the reasons for this variability.

The Daily *Tefillot*

Though the *Shemoneh Esrei* was composed by the *Anshei Knesset HaGedolah*, the concept of three *tefillot* each day is much more ancient (*Berachot* 26b). According to one opinion, they correspond to the main parts of the sacrificial cult: *shacharit* to the *tamid shel shachar*, the morning offering, *minchah* to the *tamid shel bein ha'arbaim*, that of the afternoon, and *ma'ariv* to the burning on the altar of the elevated portions of the sacrifices, which could take place at night.

According to the other opinion, their provenance was even more ancient, going back to the *Avot*, the Patriarchs: *Avraham* instituted *shacharit*, as it says "And *Avraham* got up early in the morning" (Gen. 19:27), *Yitzhak* instituted *minchah*, as it says "And *Yitzhak* went to meditate in the field towards evening" (Gen. 24:63), and *Ya'akov* instituted *ma'ariv*, as it says, "And he arrived (or rather 'pleaded', cf. Jer. 7:16) at the place and remained there because the sun had set" (Gen. 28:11). It is interesting to note that these times of prayer are alluded to in their very names, in which the second letter forms the first letter of its time: *Avraham* – *boker* (morning), *Yitzhak* – *tzaharaim* (afternoon), *Ya'akov* – *erev* (evening).

Quite apart from their association with the times of the *tefillot*, there is an ancient tradition associating them with the first three *berachot* of the *Shemoneh Esrei*, the first concluding *Magen Avraham*, the second *Mechayeh Meitim* (an allusion to the *akeidah* (Gen. 22) in which *Yitzhak*, according to one *midrash* (*Pirkei de-Rabbi Eliezer* 31), actually died and then was brought back to life), and the third *HaKel HaKadosh*, to which the angelic doxology, the *kedushah*, is added, referring to *Ya'akov*'s dream vision of a ladder with angels ascending and descending (Gen. 28:12). These ideas are developed further in many of the *kerovot* (*piyutim* – poetic insertions in the *Shemoneh Esrei*).

Though this is not mentioned in the sources, it is possible that the *Anshei Knesset HaGedolah* decided to have twelve petitions to correspond to the twelve tribes and a final three alluding to the verse, "And I brought you out of the land of Egypt…and sent before you Moshe, Aharon, and Miriam" (Micah 6:4).

Some Further Thoughts on the First Paragraph of the Shemoneh Esrei

In his article "The First Paragraph of the Shemoneh Esrei" (*Tradition*, vol. 38, no. 2, Summer 2004), Rabbi Hillel Goldberg points out some remarkable numerical patterns in its construction. His article prompted me to put down some thoughts that had occurred to me over the years, which form the basis of this article. In particular, he draws attention to a pattern of threes that seems fundamental, though on some minor points I would disagree as to his precise construction of them, as I will explain below.

There appears, however, to be a pattern of four unifying these triads, which he seems not to have noticed, representing the "four worlds" through which the Kabbalah traces the "percolation" of Divine beneficence from the essentially unknowable *Ein Sof* down to ourselves: *olam ha'atzilut, olam haberiah, olam hayetzirah, olam ha'asiah*. Each world represents the same concepts, but, as one progresses downwards, in an attenuated form. An analogy that might explain this is to think of a pile of paper with clear writing on the top sheet. On the second one there will be an impression that is still readable, whereas the third can only be read with difficulty. On the fourth, the impression, though still there, is almost invisible and will only be readable by someone who is aware of its existence and examines it with the utmost care and concentration.

Rav Chaim of Volozhin, *zt"l*, wrote (*Nefesh Hachayim Sha'ar*

2:10) that the *Anshei Knesset HaGedolah* hid within *Shemoneh Esrei* the greatest esoteric secrets of the Torah, including the secrets of Creation and the mysteries of the Heavenly realm (*Pirkei haMerkavah*). The Kabbalah teaches that there is an intrinsic tension between *gevurah*, power (equivalent to *din*, justice), and *chessed* (or *rachamim*), mercy, in the universe, the former being represented as the left and the latter the right in the scheme of *Sefirot*, emanations of the Divine.

These may be thought of as representing a "thesis" and "antithesis" in the Divine scheme, which are reconciled in a 'synthesis', which combines the two in a harmonious manner, as in Rabbi Goldberg's scheme. However, what appears as a synthesis in one "world" is only the beginning of a fresh division in the next. Thus, the Divine influence is seen as coming from the *Ein Sof* through such a three-stage process in each of the "worlds." That *chessed* should represent the thesis and *din* the antithesis might seem surprising since the Midrash (*Ber. R.* 12:15) states that the Almighty originally intended to create the world according to *din* and only later changed the blueprint to *rachamim* when He realized, so to speak, that the former would be incapable of continued existence. However, Rashi, in his comment on *Bereishit* 1, points out that *hikdim midat rachamim*, He made *rachamim* precede *din*, which makes it the thesis.

A careful examination of the first paragraph of the *Shemoneh Esrei* seems to reveal evidence of this structure in which each of these 'worlds' is represented. In the diagram (Fig. 1), the main body of this paragraph has been set out to show this structure, as will be explained. (In order to avoid writing Divine names, throughout this article, the letter *hei* has been replaced by a *dalet* in them).

Fig. 1: The first paragraph

After the initial *baruch*, we have enlarged the word *Atah*, You, referring to the *Ein Sof*, who cannot be named but only thought of as the ultimate Other to whom we can relate. Immediately below we see its unfolding in the *olam ha'atzilut*, in which our different appreciations of the Divine are separated.

On the right, we have the ineffable name, *HaShem*, which signifies the quality of *chessed*, and on the left, *Elokeinu*, our G-d, which represents that of *din* (or *gevurah*). These are followed by *Elokei avoteinu*, G-d of our fathers, showing that the three patriarchs were the paradigm for the transmission of Divine beneficence to the next level of creation, the synthesis of *chessed*, and *gevurah* only being possible through their application in a human context (in our analogy, the actual writing). The next level of 'world' expands this synthesis in a new triad:

Here we see on the right, *Elokei Avraham*, the G-d of Avraham who represents *chessed*, and on the left, *Elokei Yitzhak*, G-d of Yitzhak who represents *gevurah*. These are synthesized as *Elokei Ya'akov*, the G-d of Ya'akov who represents *emet*, truth (cf. Mic. 7:20), the combination of the two opposing forces in a form that can survive at this lower level. In this context, one might note that it is only Ya'akov whose image appeared in Yechezkel's vision of the four faced beings (Ez. 1:10), as explained in the Midrash.

Thus, we have in the *olam haberiah* the actualization of this paradigm of Divine names as a blueprint in the three primal personalities on which creation rests, three of the four legs of the Divine throne, the fourth being that of David, representing the *Mashiach*, who will herald the completion of G-d's plan when His name, together with His throne, will be restored to their original completeness with the destruction of Amalek, the paradigm of evil (Ex. 17:14–16).

Unlike the *olam ha'atzilut*, where we find essentially only Divine names, in the *olam haberiah* each aspect consists of an intimate connection between the Divine and its actualization (in our analogy, the clear impression of the writing on the immediately underlying sheet). At this level, the Divine name is still attached to each of the patriarch's, whereas at the next level it is separated from the attributes that they represent, indicating the gradual detachment from the supernal world of Divine names to the material world of creation. At that stage, we have the Divine name *Kel*, which is one of those signifying *rachamim*, but on a lower level than *HaShem*. The next three words move on from these primal personalities in the *olam haberiyah* to the concepts they represent in the *olam hayetzirah*, each of which is combined with the Divine name *Kel*, though the connection is now only through the definite article (*Ha-*) appended to each, rather than a repetition of the Divine name with each individual attribute. *Hagadol* corresponds to Avraham, as is implied in the verse, "and I will make you (Avraham) into a great (*gadol*) nation" (Gen. 12:2). *Hagibor* corresponds to Yitzhak, through his willingness to be offered up as a sacrifice in response to the Almighty's command, representing the quality of *din*, taken in the Kabbalah as a synonym for *gevurah*. Finally, *Hanora* corresponds to Ya'akov, who appreciated this quality in his famous dream after which he exclaimed, "How awesome (*nora*) is this place, for it is the house of G-d, the gate of heaven" (Gen. 28:17) (in our analogy, the faint impression of the writing on the next sheet).

Having established the essential qualities of the patriarchs combined with the lesser Divine name of mercy in the *olam hayetzirah*, the text now enters the *olam ha'asiyah*, in which the Almighty wishes His will to be actualized. The name *Kel* now becomes exalted as *Kel elyon*, indicating that relative to this lower world the Divine *Kel* is now more exalted and thus distant from it. The descriptive adjectives *hagadol*, *hagibor*, and *hanora* now become yet more concretized as specific actions. *Gomel chassadim tovim* corresponds to *chessed* and *vekonei hakol* corresponds to *din/gevurah*, as expressed in the *piyut* "*vekonei avadav badin*," leading to the culmination of the Divine plan when, through remembering the kind deeds of the patriarchs (*chassdei avot*), He will bring a redeemer to their descendants (though this is primarily for His own sake, since that was His purpose from the beginning of creation). At this level, even the connection by the definite article has disappeared, leaving an apparent separation between the Divine and mundane or, more accurately, an indication of how G-d has "hidden" Himself in this world and is only manifested through His actions (in our analogy, the almost imperceptible impression of the writing on the lowest sheet).

It might be noted that as we descend from the highest to lowest "world," the Divine becomes progressively less closely connected to the attribute. In the *olam ha'atzilut*, we have only Divine names; in the *olam haberiah*, the Divine is still intimately connected with the names of the patriarchs; in the *olam hayetzirah*, it is linked through the shared definite article, whereas in the *olam ha'asiyah*, the link is merely implied. Also, the Divine becomes more exalted as we progress from the higher to the lower levels: *Elokei*, G-d of…, *Kel*, G-d, *Kel elyon*, Exalted G-d. Thus, as we descend, the Divine ascends, so to speak, implying a progressively more hidden connection between us and Him.

The blessing concludes with a sequence of four words describing the way the Almighty protects us, each corresponding to one of the worlds. The first, *Melech*, King, describes Him as being the complete controller of the world, yet so far above us that we cannot really appreciate how He is acting on our behalf; this corresponds to the world of *atzilut*, closeness to the Divine essence. The second, *Ozer*, Helper, corresponds to the world of *beriyah* where His actions are noticed even if He is, so to speak, in the background pulling the strings like a puppet master without actually being seen. The third, *Moshia*, Savior, is a position much closer to us, yet still sufficiently distant to be not completely appreciated, thus corresponding to the world of *yetzirah*. Finally, we come to the last term, *Magen*, Shield, with which His protection is close to us and thus completely tangible. In a sense, this sequence re-establishes the closeness of Divine and mundane whose divergence was hinted at in the main body of the *berachah*.

The blessing finally sums up the whole unfolding of the Divine scheme as praising Him as the "shield of *Avraham*," that is to say that the culmination of the Divine purpose is that He should protect us in the most manifest way, yet this protection should be through the medium of *chessed*, as exemplified by *Avraham*, and not *din*.

This last correspondence also explains one problem with this *berachah*; namely, that unlike the standard format of *berachot*, it does not contain a reference to *HaShem* as King without which a *berachah* is considered defective. Since the three *Avot* are three of the four legs of the Divine throne, on which, so to speak, the King sits, the phrase *Elokei avoteinu* can be seen as implying the missing word *Melech*, as if the latter were written in the text, thus removing the apparent problem.

Having set up the scheme of four sets of triplets corresponding to the four "worlds" through which the Divine beneficence "percolates" from the unknowable essence, *Ein Sof*, to our mundane world, the *olam ha'asiyah*, we are immediately confronted with an apparent contradiction to another kabbalistic teaching: that this chain of transmission proceeds through the ten *sefirot* (Fig. 2). We seem to have a set of twelve stages and not ten. The two teachings can, perhaps, be harmonized if we postulate that the *olam ha'atzilut*, world of closeness, is so far removed from our puny understanding, being essentially on the level of Divine names, that from our perspective it "collapses" into one *sefirah*, *keter*. There might be a hint to this in the text since there is no Divine name (*Kel* or *Kel elyon*) interposed between the first and second triplets. It is only when the Divine beneficence reaches the lower three worlds that we can even begin to talk of individual *sefirot*, but this whole concept is too highly esoteric and cannot be elaborated further here.

Fig. 2: The Sefirotic tree

However, it might be worth noting that the number twelve might be significant in the context of the ascent of the worshipper as a parallel to the various levels in the *Beit HaMikdash*, since it would be a hint to the ascent from the *ezrat kohanim* to the gate of the *ulam*, which consisted of twelve steps. This might be linked to the fifteen adjectival attributes in the morning *berachah* after *Kriat Shema* when the word *emet* is detached and appended instead to the *Shema*, thus commencing *veyatsiv*, which precedes the *Shemoneh Esrei*, which might hint at the fifteen steps from the *ezrat nashim* up to the gate of the *azarah* and the four sentences beginning with *emet* following them, corresponding to the four steps from the *ezrat Yisrael* to the *ezrat kohanim*, as we saw above.

The pattern described here can be thought of as setting up

the structure through which the Almighty allows His influence to flow down into our world. This might, perhaps, be the significance of the difference between the first paragraph of the *Shemoneh Esrei* and the remainder, in that it requires greater concentration. Strictly speaking, any lack of attention in it would oblige one to repeat it, whereas, for the remainder, this would not be obligatory. However, as the Rema points out, this is hardly likely to be effective since there is no guarantee that the second recital will be any better.

This concept of four "superimposed worlds" might help solve the apparent contradiction between the transcendence and immanence of G-d. In our world, *olam ha'asiyah*, we only see His actions, whereas He is far removed as *Kel elyon*, reflecting our perception of His transcendent majesty. As we have seen, however, our world is a mere imprint of the "real" one, *olam ha'atzilut*, which is completely suffused with the Divine. Thus, from this perspective, the paradox is a result of our inability to transcend our own limitations and, therefore, more apparent than real.

There seems to be a similar pattern in the second paragraph (Fig. 3), which might symbolize ascent to the *Ein Sof*, symbolized by the word *Atah* with which it commences. Furthermore, the third paragraph might be seen as having a similar but compressed triplet pattern (Fig. 4), showing the essential unity of the four worlds.

אתה

מחיה מתים אתה	גבור לעולם אדוני
מלך	
רב להושיע	

מחיה מתים	מכלכל חיים בחסד
ממית	
ברחמים רבים	

ורופא חולים	סומך נופלים
ומחיה	
ומתיר אסורים	

לישני עפר	ומקים אמונתו
ומצמיח ישועה	
מי כמוך בעל גבורות ומי דומה לך	

ונאמן אתה להחיות מתים

ברוך **אתה** יהוה **מחיה** המתים

Fig. 3: the second paragraph

Fig. 4: the third paragraph

Thus, the first three paragraphs might be thought of as forming a threefold unit in themselves, reflected by their invariant inclusion in all recitations of the *Shemoneh Esrei*: weekday, *Shabbat*, and festival. As is clear from many *kerovot* (*piyutim* inserted in the *Shemoneh Esrei*), especially those composed for the *Yamim Noraim*, these first three paragraphs themselves correspond to the three Patriarchs and therefore form a similar structure to the internal one described above (Fig. 5).

Once these structures have been assembled, we can turn to our personal requests or the sanctification of holier days, which we hope may reach the fountain of all blessings and flow down to us here in this world. Perhaps this discussion might add some depth to our appreciation of the profundity of *Chazal* in their arrangement of the *Shemoneh Esrei* and thereby enhance our ability to connect ourselves to *HaShem*, who both transcends the universe and is immanent in it in the most intimate way, if we could but realize it.

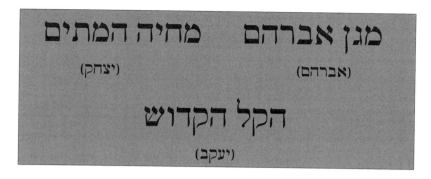

Fig. 5: the first three paragraphs

For further discussion of the inner meaning of the *Shemoneh Esrei* see Rabbi Mordechai Potash's *Making the Most of Prayer* (Mesorah Pub., 2008).

Ten Letters – Ten *Sefirot*

In the above, we suggested how some esoteric ideas like the "four worlds" and the "ten *sefirot*" may have been "coded" by *Chazal* into the *Shemoneh Esrei*. It is possible that they are even "hidden" in the *Torah shebichtav* itself, in the first *pasuk* of the *Shema*.

That the four-letter name alludes to the four worlds is well known from kabbalistic writings, but the choice of *Elokeinu* may be significant in that it contains six letters. It might have been more appropriate to have written *Elokim*, as used by the Torah itself in describing the creation, but it consists of only five letters, or even *Elo-ah* (not pronounced "eloha" as is sometimes heard). The latter might actually have been more appropriate since, like *HaShem*, it consists of four letters and might be seen as paralleling the latter in describing the descent through the "four worlds" through the path of *din*, whereas *HaShem* represents the descent through *rachamim*. We shall return to this idea below.

Thus, *HaShem Elokeinu* consists of ten letters which might allude to the ten *sefirot*. Furthermore the *milui*, "completion" (i.e., the result of replacing each letter by its name as spelled out [see *Through the Lens of Gematria* by R. Matityahu Glazerson,

pp. 159–163, 195]), of the word '*HaShem*' also consists of ten letters. Therefore the *pasuk* might be understood as meaning, "Hear
Yisrael, even though we connect to the Divine through the ten *sefirot*, nonetheless He is a perfect unity."

It might also be significant that the last paragraph of the
Shema ends with the apparently superfluous words, "*Ani HaShem
Elokeichem.*" *HaShem Elokeichem* also consists of ten letters, so
this might be intended to reinforce the same message that we can
connect to Him through the ten *sefirot*, to which we add the word
Emet, indicating that we acknowledge the truth of this concept.

Furthermore, these ten letters can be arranged in the *sefirotic*
tree as follows:

Fig. 6: The Divine names

The bracketed *vav* corresponds to the semi-*sefirah*, *daʾat*. It is omitted since this particular Divine name is always spelled *chaseir*, defective, in the present state of the world, but may be restored when
the world reaches its perfection in the days of *Mashiach*, when
all defects will be rectified as the *navi Yeshaya* predicts (35:7–10,
65:17–26).

The Significance of Four and Six

One might ask the question as to why the ten letters are split into two Divine names, one of four letters and one of six. This could be explained as indicating a division between the "higher" sefirot– keter, chochmah, binah (chabad) and the semi-sefirah, da'at, and six of the lower ones – chesed, gevurah, tiferet, netsach, hod, yesod (chagat nehiy), leaving the last sefirah, malchut, which is identified with the Shechinah, the Divine immanence, to be associated with the final Divine name of four letters itself, representing Divine mercy. As the Arizal explains, the purpose of mitzvot is the reunification of the Almighty with His Shechinah, and that lesson might be seen as implied in this form of wording HaShem (4) Elokeinu (6) HaShem echad (1).

The Four Letter Names – the Four Worlds

An alternative diagram shows the parallelism of the two four-letter Divine names with the four worlds:

א	olam ha'atsilut	י
ל	olam haberiah	ה
ו	olam hayetsirah	ו
ה	olam ha'asiyah	ה

Fig. 7: The four worlds

It might be noted that in the two lower worlds, both Divine names have the same letters, possibly alluding to our inability to distinguish between the middat hadin and the midat harachamim. Interestingly, at the highest level, both letters have the same mispar katan, 1, alluding to His complete unity from whichever side one approaches Him.

It is only at the second level that the letters are completely different, perhaps alluding to the fact that for creation to take place He had, so to speak, to first allow for differentiation. However, it should be noted that the numerical value of the lamed, 30, is six times that of the heh, 5, possibly alluding to the six days of creation, representing natural law i.e., din, followed by the single day of Shabbat, representing its supranatural purpose, i.e., rachamim, all of which consist of five levels parallel to the five parts of the soul (in ascending order): *nefesh, ruach, neshamah, chayah, yechidah*, which, as the *Ramchal* explains, are rooted in the *olam haberiah*. These five correspond to the five *sefirot* on the central spine of the *Eitz Chaim: malchut, yesod, tiferet, da'at, keter*, the lowest four of which can be seen as the synthesis, and thereby perfection, of the two *sefirot* above it in the complete *Eitz Chaim*, as we explained above.

There is one other lesson that might be learned from this comparison of the two four-letter Divine names. If the two final letters that they have in common are removed, we are left with two further ones: *Keil* and *Kah*. What is interesting is that *Keil*, which is formed from *Elo-ah*, a name associated with *din*, is itself associated with *rachamim*, whereas *Kah*, which is formed from *HaShem*, a name associated with *rachamim*, is itself associated with *din*. It might be argued that this is the secret of good and evil that is hidden from us by being rooted in such higher worlds that we cannot truly understand their distinction, but these matters are too recondite to allow elaboration here.

THE PARADOX OF PRAYER

Having set up the framework and conduits for the descent of Divine beneficence, we come next to the central section of the *Shemoneh Esrei*, the petitions to *HaShem* for our needs. Though at first sight these are quite a straightforward sequence of requests, as if one were a servant asking his master or a child his father, there are some deep theological problems with such a point of view. We will outline some of these first and then discuss some possible ways of answering them, none of which are entirely satisfactory.

One of the basic beliefs of Torah Judaism is that *HaShem* is absolutely perfect and, therefore, does not change. In consequence, our requests to Him must fall on "deaf ears" since they are, apparently, asking Him to "change His mind", so to speak.

Another basic belief is that He knows everything. Thus He knows what we are going to ask for and, therefore, it is not necessary for us to articulate our requests.

These problems would seem to indicate the futility of prayer, at least in the simple understanding outlined above. This problem has concerned the medieval Jewish philosophers and led them to propose an alternative understanding of the nature of petitionary prayer. In particular, Rabbi Yosef Albo, in his *Sefer HaIkarim* (Chapter 18), attempts to set up an alternative way of looking at it. Basically, his thesis is that prayer is not meant to change G-d's mind at all, but rather to change the person who is praying so that his requests now become consistent with the Divine will since he is now worthy of the Divine beneficence.

Though this approach is attractive, it is also not without problems, as Rabbi Seth Kadish shows in his book, *Kavana* (Chapter 5), in which he points out that this paradigm seems to be inconsistent with the actual wording of our prayers, in particular those included in the *Shemoneh Esrei*. Since we are exhorted not to make our prayers rote recitations, but rather heartfelt entreaties for grace and compassion to *HaShem* (*Berachot* 28b ff.), it is difficult to see how we can recite them with such thoughts in mind.

One might try to answer this objection by examining the wording of this section of the *Shemoneh Esrei* more carefully. It begins, perhaps surprisingly, not with a request but with a statement, "You grace man with knowledge and teach humanity understanding," and only then continues to ask for these, unlike the subsequent paragraphs that all commence directly with the petition. This would fit in very well with Rabbi Albo's approach, in that it can be seen as an acknowledgement of seeing them as, in some sense, an expression of our puny status in relation to Him.

Having humbled ourselves, our requests might be understood as merely an articulation of our problems before Him rather than a request that He actually respond to them. This approach might be seen as being reinforced by the nature of the conclusion to each request. For example, the eighth of the *berachot* in the *Shemoneh Esrei*, *Refa'einu*, "Heal us," concludes *Baruch Atah HaShem Rofei cholei amo Yisrael*, which is usually translated as "Blessed are You, *HaShem*, the healer of the sick of your people

Israel." According to Albo's understanding of the nature of prayer, however, it should rather be translated, "Blessed are You, *HaShem*, who is healing the sick of your people Israel," i.e., that *HaShem* is already in the process of providing the healing of those who merit it. Thus, the petitions can all be understood as taking the petitioner from a feeling of a need to ask *HaShem* for something to a realization that He is actually doing what is requested if He deems it to be justified, producing a sense of trust in Him to do that which is best from His perspective. Perhaps this is summed up in the last of the petitions that concludes "For You hear in mercy the prayer of Your people Israel (alternative version 'every mouth'). Blessed are You, *HaShem*, who is listening to prayer."

Chazal do specifically state that one may insert private petitions into the *Shemoneh Esrei*, with the proviso that this be done in such a way that the private request be included in that *berachah* that asks for the same thing in general terms, or in the last one, *shomeia tefillah*, which is itself a general request. (*Avodah Zarah* 8a). However, it would seem more appropriate to do so briefly and leave it to the Almighty, in His wisdom, to understand what has to be done. *Chazal* also tell us always to add something new to our prayers (*Berakhot* 29b), in order that they not degenerate into rote recitations, which might imply that our requests do have some independent validity. Just how one balances private and proscribed prayers is one of paradoxes of prayer.

In the last resort, we must conclude that we cannot really understand *HaShem's* essence and have to take it on trust that our prayers are something He wishes to hear for some unknowable reason. As *Chazal* put it: "Why did the Almighty make the Patriarchs and Matriarchs barren? Because He desires the prayers of the righteous" (*Yevamot* 64a).

A RESPONSE TO THE MISSIONARY MENACE

The recent full-page advertisement in the *London Times*, produced by Jews for Jesus, is a timely reminder of the strong missionizing emphasis still retained by elements within the Church of England.

The Jewish response is inevitably inhibited by the courtesy that has to be extended towards a host country, and therefore Jewish reaction has been somewhat muted.

The following article seeks a response within traditional Jewish sources. Since early within the Common Era, rabbinic leaders had to deal with the same problem, and the answers they provide are equally relevant today.

Though Christian missionary activity may appear to have taken a new turn with the appearance of such groups as the Jews for Jesus and the founding of so-called messianic synagogues, the approach taken differs only in presentation from that already encountered by *Chazal* (our Sages) when the early Christians, who were mostly of Jewish origin, tried to infiltrate the synagogue and persuade Jews that their ideas were already to be found in *Tanach*. They relied on the relatively low level of knowledge of the average Jew of those times to do so by quoting, or usually misquoting, verses from *Tanach* out of context.

The idea that we can combat the activities of the Jews for Jesus and similar Hebrew Christian evangelists by being able to counter their arguments is misplaced. The reason for this is that they see *Tanach* only as a source for proof-texts to support their theological position and are not interested in the true meaning of the passages quoted, as it is so well put in Psalms (82:5): "They do not know, nor do they understand; they walk in darkness."

Of course, all their arguments can be countered, and there are many books recording medieval disputations which do so, but these are in reality irrelevant to the true purpose of the missionaries. For the ordinary Jew, the best policy is to refuse to be drawn into any argument with the missionaries, however well versed he may feel himself to be. Perhaps the concluding words of the prophet Hosea are particularly apposite in this context: "Who is wise, let him understand; who is prudent, let him know that the ways of HaShem are right and that the righteous walk in them but willful sinners stumble in them."

Establishing Contact –
the First Stage in the Missionary Approach

The procedure adopted by the missionaries consists of several stages, the first being to insinuate themselves into the target group and establish a non-threatening relationship. Thus, in approaching Jews, they always emphasize their "deep love" and even "awe" of the Jewish People, or their support for the State of Israel. They often adopt externals of Jewish observance to try to give an appearance of Jewishness, and it is relatively easy for them even to appear more "frum" than the average Jew by these means.

This ploy can only be effective with those who see Judaism solely in terms of performing certain rituals. Unfortunately, too many Jews ascribe to this fallacy. In essence, it goes back to Mendelssohn's doctrine that Judaism consists of revealed legislation, but, unlike Christianity, does not have any fixed doctrines. That such a theory cannot form a firm basis for a living Judaism is clearly shown by the widespread apostasy among his followers and even his own descendants.

When conducting missions to other cultures, they do the same, using the literature of the people being evangelized in much the same way. The early Church virtually canonized the Roman poet Virgil on the strength of his fourth ecologue, which they chose to interpret as a prediction of their "savior."

The main aim of their approach is to establish contact with the potential convert and, by subtly reading their doctrines into his cultural heritage, make him feel that their message is not alien to his previous value system and therefore no threat to his identity.

Another basic technique is to adapt the externals of their target group but destroy its inner essence, much like some parasitic wasps that lay their eggs in a caterpillar to have them emerge as adults from the latter's empty shell. Thus, we see relics of pagan religious rites, most notably in their celebration of Christmas, which was adapted from the Roman Saturnalia, but also uses

Celtic symbols such as mistletoe and Germanic ones like holly or the now ubiquitous Christmas tree. This made the conversion of these peoples easier, since it preserved the popular outward forms of the heathen cults, allowing the Church several generations to wipe out their former significance. Many of the popular religious practices throughout the Christian world bear witness to this syncretic approach; that their pagan origins are no longer remembered bears witness to its success.

Our Sages understood quite well these conversion techniques used by the early Christians, which form the basis of those used by missionaries to this day. Their problem was how to provide the ordinary Jew, who only had a very sketchy Jewish education, with sufficient familiarity with Jewish doctrine to be immune to the missionaries' blandishments. The most direct method to educating them was through the *siddur*, which was probably the one Jewish book with which most Jews were familiar. Therefore, they included various passages in our daily prayers to help the ordinary Jew avoid being manipulated by the missionaries. Since the latter tried to influence Jews by using quotations from *Tanach*, they decided to include such a selection of verses that would present the true Jewish position on several crucial doctrines. There are three such major collections of verses inserted into *Shacharit*, as well as some shorter ones at various other points in the liturgy.

Guilt Generation – the Second Stage

Having established a rapport with their victims, the missionaries' next program is to work on their guilt feelings. Since, "there is no man in the world who is so righteous that he does good and never sins" (Ecclesiastes 7:20), everyone has some weakness that can be exploited.

Apart from the individual's personal problems, they develop their doctrine of "original sin" that they claim taints every person irrevocably from birth. They claim that, as a consequence of the sin of Adam Harishon, all mankind is liable to punishment and that this can only be avoided through belief in their religion, which will have some "saving" power. Of course we totally reject this doctrine and believe that the consequence of this "original sin" is that we have a *yetzer hara* that makes it possible for us to do wrong by making sin seem attractive, though we have the ability to resist it, especially through Torah study.

This assertion that *Mashiach* would come to redeem man from sin was first put by Paul, who wrote in his letter to the Romans (11:26–27): "and thus all Israel shall be saved as it is written: The redeemer will come from Zion, he will remove ungodliness from Jacob. And this is my covenant with them, when I take away their sins."

This is, of course, a complete distortion of the words of the prophet Yeshayah (59:20–21) and probably prompted our Sages to begin their composition of the *Kedushah Desidra* by quoting the original passage:

> And a redeemer shall come to those that turn from willful sin in Jacob, says HaShem; And as for Me, this is my covenant with them, says HaShem, my spirit that is upon you, and my words which I have put in your mouth, shall not depart from your mouth, nor from the mouth of your seed, nor from the mouth of your seed's seed, says HaShem, from now and forever.

A cursory glance at the original shows that it does not speak of a "redeemer from sin." On the contrary, it maintains that the Torah will never be abrogated, thus confuting yet another Christian doctrine that the "old covenant" has been superseded by a "new dispensation."

Thus they try to produce feelings of despair in their victim who is made to feel weighed down by sin and unable to relieve himself from this intolerable psychological burden. They then suggest to the person they are trying to convert that the Christian "savior" has sacrificed himself to atone for their sins, but only those accepting him will be forgiven. Thus they create an unbearable tension in the person and, at the same time, offer a way of release from it.

It is interesting to speculate on what motivates the missionaries to persist in their attempts to convert the world, and especially the Jewish People. Perhaps it lies in their own deep-seated doubts as to whether they have themselves been "saved" since, apart from their own subjective feelings, they have no guarantee. Thus they see every "unbeliever" as a threat to themselves, especially if that person is a Jew whom they recognize as having had, at least at one time, a special relationship with the Almighty, though they claim that it has been replaced by their own.

The continued existence of the Jewish People and its fidelity to the Torah must worry them since it raises the possibility that their whole religion may be based on false assumptions. The renewal of Jewish self-government in our days also undermines traditional Christian belief in the rejection of the Jewish People in favor of themselves as the "new Israel." This perhaps explains the desperate attempts being made specifically to convert Jews.

An example similar to the techniques of the present-day Jews for Jesus is the attempt by Ricci and his Jesuit successors in the seventeenth century to produce a "Chinese rite" adopting much Confucian teaching and permitting such religious rites as ancestor worship, as if they were merely civil or social ceremonies. This was eventually condemned by the Church in 1704 and we can expect a similar attitude to be taken to the so-called "Hebrew Christians" in due course. Their existence is only accepted at present on a temporary basis, as a halfway house to full estrangement from Jewish roots, by mainstream churches. The latter can expect this to happen within a couple of generations, from their experience with other ethnically based converts.

The Jewish Approach

Our Sages realized the consequence of sinking into despair through feelings of guilt and wished to emphasize the Jewish doctrine that repentance is effective and that HaShem will always forgive the true penitent. They realized that, for the average Jew who had little time for learning and was therefore at the greatest risk from missionary blandishments, the best vehicle was the *siddur* that he would use every day. To convey this message, they laid especial stress on the verse from Psalms: "He being merciful forgives iniquity and does not destroy; many a time He turns away his anger, not arousing all His wrath" (78:38). This verse is recited no less than four times on every weekday, and a fifth time, the long *Vehu Rachum*, introducing the addition to *Tachanun* on Mondays and Thursdays. Unfortunately, many recite the prayers by rote and do not learn the lessons that our Sages intended.

By examining the passages where this verse is quoted, we find it associated with others that together present the fundamental theological position of Judaism on sin and Divine mercy.

It forms the introduction to Ma'ariv, together with Psalm 20:10, "HaShem save! May the King answer us on the day we call," that is closely linked to it throughout the liturgy, forming a natural sequel as a request following the previous affirmation of HaShem's mercy.

In Shacharit we find it three times. The first forms an introduction to the collection of verses selected from *Tehillim* that follow *Hodu* (Chronicles I 16:8–36) at the beginning of *Pesukei deZimra*. These expand on the basic theme of HaShem's mercy and render the worshipper immune to the missionaries' attempts. The whole passage taken from Psalms is a panegyric on Divine mercy:

- He being merciful forgives iniquity and does not destroy; many a time He turns away his anger, not amusing all His wrath. (78:38)
- You HaShem – withhold not Your mercy from me; may Your kindness and Your truth always protect me. (40:12)
- Remember Your mercies, HaShem, and Your kindnesses, for they have been ever of old. (25:6)
- Salvation is HaShem's, Your blessing be upon Your people, *Selah!* (3:9)

- The Lord of Hosts is with us, the G-d of Jacob is our stronghold, *Selah!* (46:81)
- Lord of Hosts, happy is the person who trusts in You. (84:13)
- HaShem, save! May the King answer us on the day we call. (20:10)
- Save Your people and bless Your inheritance, feed them and earn them forever. (28:9)
- Our soul longs for HaShem – He is our help and our shield. For our Heart will rejoice in Him, because we have trusted in His Holy Name. May your kindness, HaShem, be upon us, as we have hoped for You. (33:20–22)
- Show us Your kindness, HaShem, and grant us your salvation. (85:8)
- Rise up to help us, and free us in Your kindness. (44:27)
- I am HaShem, your G-d, who brought you up from the land of Egypt, open wide your mouth and I will fill it. (81:11)
- Happy is the people for whom this is so. Happy is the people whose G-d is HaShem. (144:15)
- As for me, I have trusted in Your kindness; my heart will rejoice in Your salvation. I will sing to HaShem, because he has dealt kindly with me. (13:61)

Another technique used by the missionaries to undermine the Jew's inner faith is to assert that the covenant between G-d and the Jewish People has been abrogated with the coming of their founder. They like to justify this by claiming that the Temple was destroyed since, with this new dispensation, the old system of atonement for sin was no longer operative and had been replaced by "believing" in him, as in Paul's misquotation from Isaiah that we discussed above. In the next occurrence of our key verse at the conclusion of *Yehi Chevod*, our Sages have chosen a selection of verses to emphasize the inscrutability of the Divine purpose and the eternal covenant between the Jewish People and the Almighty:

- Many thoughts are in a man's heart, but the counsel of HaShem – only it will prevail. (Proverbs 19:21)
- The counsel of HaShem will endure for ever, the thoughts of His heart through all generations. (Psalms 33:11)
- For He spoke and it came to be; He commanded and it stood firm. (Psalms 33:9)
- For HaShem selected *Zion*. He desired it for His dwelling place. (Psalms 132:13)
- For G-d selected Ya'akov as His own, Yisroel as His treasure. (Psalms 135:4)
- For HaShem will not cast off His people, nor will He forsake His inheritance. (Psalms 94:1–1)
- He being merciful forgives iniquity and does not destroy; many a time He turns away His anger, not arousing all His wrath. (Psalms 78:38)
- HaShem, save! May the King answer on the day we call. (Psalms 20:10)

Our Sages' Message of Trust in G-d

The final passage in *Shacharit*, in which our key verse, the *Kedushah Desidra*, appears, can be understood as containing a comprehensive answer from *Tanach* to many Christian doctrines.

The *Kedushah Desidra* originally formed the final prayer in *Shacharit* and would have left the worshipper adequately prepared for the arguments of the early Christians, should he be exposed to them in his daily activities. Its omission on Shabbat and Yom Tov may have reflected the lesser likelihood of exposure to their propaganda on those days.

The daily recitation of *Aleinu* was only introduced in the thirteenth century, probably as a result of the profound impression created by its recital by the martyrs of Blois as they were consigned to the flames, the moving tune being noted even by the Christian bystanders. Previously, it had been recited only as part of *Musaf* on Rosh Hashanah. This daily recitation is first recorded by the

Rokeach (221) and the Meiri in his commentary on *Berahkot* (118), from which it is clearly not yet a fixed custom.

It commences, as mentioned above, with an answer to the doctrine of "original sin" and an assertion of the eternity of HaShem's covenant with the Jewish People.

It continues with the three verses together with the Targum, their Aramaic paraphrases, which give the whole passage its name *Kedushah Desidra*. It is intriguing to speculate as to why the latter were included, but one possibility lies in the use of the verse from Isaiah (6:3) by the early Christians to justify their doctrine of the trinity, based on the threefold repetition of the word "holy." To counter this, the Targum paraphrases the angelic praise as referring to the Almighty as being:

> Holy in the heights of heaven the abode of His Divine presence, holy in the world the work of His mighty power, holy for ever and to all eternity.

After the two verses of this *Kedushah*, together with their Targum and preceding our key verse, our Sages included the verse from King David's prayer of dedication of the materials for the construction of the Temple (Chronicles I 29:18): "HaShem, G-d of Abraham, Isaac, and Jacob, preserve this forever…and direct their hearts to You." The inclusion of this verse is somewhat strange, but might have been meant to remind us of the following verse in which he prays: "Give my son, Solomon, a whole heart so that he may keep Your commandments, testimonies, and statutes, to do everything to build the Temple for which I have made the preparations."

Together these verses stress once more the eternal validity of the Torah and its *mitzvot*, countering the Christian assertion that they have been abrogated and replaced by their new covenant of faith in their redeemer. This is further emphasized after our key verse by the next two verses:

- Your righteousness remains righteous forever, and Your Torah is truth. (Psalms 119:142)
- Grant truth to Jacob, kindness to Abraham, as You swore to our forefathers from days of yore. (Micah 7:20)

This is followed by the verses from Psalms (68:20, 46:8, 84:13, and 20:10) emphasizing trust in HaShem and followed by a short statement of the Jewish answer to the Christian attack on Torah:

> Blessed be He, our G-d, who created us for His glory, separated us from those who go astray, gave us the Torah of truth and implanted eternal life within us. May He open our heart through His Torah and put in our heart love and awe of Him that we may do His will and serve Him wholeheartedly so that we should not labor in vain nor bring forth confusion. May it be Your will, HaShem our G-d and the G-d of our forefathers, that we observe Your statutes in this world and merit that we live and see and inherit goodness and blessing in the messianic times and in the life of the world to come so that my soul might sing to you and not be silenced. (Psalms 9:11)

The closing words, perhaps, sum up the key concept of trust in Divine mercy, which forms the only real way to develop the inner strength to resist such brainwashing techniques should anyone, G-d forbid, find himself unable to escape the attentions of these groups. The last verse would seem to have been chosen, in particular, to counter the Christian claim that the multiplicity of laws in the Torah presents more situations for people to transgress and fall into sin, part of their conversion technique as we saw above, It emphasizes, as Rabbi Chananya ben Akashya explains (Mak 3:16) that, on the contrary, the Torah gives us more opportunities to perform mitzvot and thereby acquire merit in G-d's eyes, a fitting conclusion to the morning prayers, fortifying the ordinary Jew against their blandishments.

- Blessed is the man who trusts in HaShem, then HaShem will be his security. (Jeremiah 17:7)
- Trust in HaShem forever, for in G-d, HaShem, is an everlasting strength. (Isaiah 26:4)
- Those who know Your name will trust in You, and You have not forsaken those who seek You, HaShem. (Psalms 9:11)
- It pleased HaShem, for the sake if [Israel's] righteousness, to make the Torah great and glorious. (Isaiah 42:21)

ADDITIONAL STANZAS FOR MAOZ TZUR

Since my daughter Rivkah Leah was to be married on the third night of Chanukah, I decided to produce, as a souvenir of the occasion, an edition of some additional stanzas of *Maoz Tzur* that are little known.

The original was composed by an unknown medieval *paytan* whose name, Mordechai, is found as an acrostic in the initial letters of the first five stanzas, which describe the deliverances of the Jewish People up to the one commemorated on Chanukah. These are well known among Ashkenazim though unknown to the Sefardim, which suggests that the author must have lived in Germany in the late medieval period.

There is some dispute regarding the sixth stanza, of whose first three words, *chasof zeroa kodshecha*, the initial letters spelling *chazak*, often appended in *piyutim* to the author's name. According to Baer, this stanza is not found in any of the early editions and is therefore a later addition. However, it is possible that the omission was a case of internal censorship since it calls on the Almighty to wreak vengeance on the *malchut harsha'a*, a reference to Rome and, by extension, the Christian world that was persecuting the Jewish People at that time.

Like the sixth stanza, most of the additional ones dealt with the persecutions of the Jewish People in Christian Europe and were therefore never included in *siddurim* to avoid probable repercussions, though they were known, and sung, in many German Jewish homes until recent times.

The seventh stanza, *mei'olam*, is ascribed to Rabbi Moshe Isserles, who added his glosses to the *Shulchan Aruch* and whose name, Moshe, is to be found in the initial letters of the first three lines.

The eighth stanza, *yehi ratson milfanecha*, is by a Rabbi Yirmiyah of Wurtzburg, of whom little is known, whose name is formed by the initial letters of the words in the first line.

Stanzas nine and ten are by Rabbi Shmuel Halevi who was rabbi of the small community of Klein Steinach in Franconia and author of the work *Nachalat Shiva*. His name is found in the initial letters of the hemistiches of stanza nine, with *chazak* in the initial letters of the first three words of stanza ten.

These additional stanzas were printed for the first time in the second edition of the *Kitzur Shela* by Rabbi Yechiel Mechel Epstein, published in Fürth in 1693, and a further two were appended by the proofreader, Rabbi Shlomo Zalman London, their author. The *Kitzur Shela* was an extremely popular work and went through many editions during the eighteenth century. The text of these additional stanzas was unvocalized and, in many editions, full of typographical errors.

The first vocalized edition was published with a German translation and notes in Frankfurt am Main in 1922 by Rabbi Dr. M.L. Bamberger of Schönlanke as part of his *Zemirot Yisrael*. In this edition, he added a further stanza composed by his father, Rabbi Dr. Simchah Bamberger of Aschaffenburg.

A second vocalized edition with extensive notes was published in 1969 in Jerusalem in *Shanah Beshanah*, the yearbook of Heichal Shelomoh, by my late father-in-law, Rabbi Dr. A. Carlebach. A further version with English translation of four of the additional stanzas was included in the Artscroll Chanukah, published in New York in 1981.

In this edition I have included some additional stanzas that have never before been published. Stanza fourteen was written by Rabbi Seckel Bamberger of Kissingen, whose Hebrew name, Yitzhak, appears in the initial letters of the first four hemistiches,

and was included, in manuscript, in a copy of his brother's edition
of 1922 shown to me by Mr. S.B. Bamberger of Manchester, a son
of the editor. The remaining stanzas are of unknown origin but
the author of the fifteenth has included his name, Moshe *Chazak*,
in the initial letters of each hemistich.

In order to help the reader, I have included references, mainly
to *Tanach*, of the various phrases and unusual word forms in this
poem, and highlighted the acrostics. For translation and notes
I must refer the reader to the editions cited whose scholarship I
cannot match.

ראשי החרוזים מרדכי חזק

1

מָעוֹז צוּר¹ יְשׁוּעָתִי, לְךָ נָאֶה לְשַׁבֵּחַ.
תִּכּוֹן בֵּית תְּפִלָּתִי,² וְשָׁם תּוֹדָה נְזַבֵּחַ,³
לְעֵת תָּכִין מַטְבֵּחַ,⁴ מִצָּר הַמְנַבֵּחַ,⁵
אָז אֶגְמוֹר, בְּשִׁיר מִזְמוֹר, חֲנֻכַּת הַמִּזְבֵּחַ:⁶

¹Ps. 31.3; ²Is. 56.7; ³Ps. 116.17; ⁴Is. 14.21; ⁵Is. 56.10; ⁶Ps. 30.1

2

רָעוֹת שָׂבְעָה נַפְשִׁי,¹ בְּיָגוֹן כֹּחִי כָלָה.²
חַיַּי מֵרְרוּ בְקֹשִׁי,³ בְּשִׁעְבּוּד מַלְכוּת עֶגְלָה.⁴
וּבְיָדוֹ הַגְּדֹלָה, הוֹצִיא אֶת הַסְּגֻלָּה,⁵
חֵיל פַּרְעֹה, וְכָל זַרְעוֹ, יָרְדוּ כְאֶבֶן מְצוּלָה:⁶

¹Ps. 88.4; ²Ps. 31.11; ³Ex. 1.14; ⁴Jer. 46.20; ⁵Ex. 19.5; ⁶Ex. 15.5

3

דְּבִיר קָדְשׁוֹ¹ הֱבִיאַנִי, וְגַם שָׁם לֹא שָׁקַטְתִּי.²
וּבָא נֹגֵשׂ³ וְהִגְלַנִי, כִּי זָרִים עָבַדְתִּי.⁴
וְיֵין רַעַל⁵ מָסַכְתִּי,⁶ כִּמְעַט שֶׁעָבַרְתִּי,⁷
קֵץ בָּבֶל, זְרֻבָּבֶל,⁸ לְקֵץ שִׁבְעִים⁹ נוֹשַׁעְתִּי:

¹1 Kings 8.6; ²Job 3.26; ³Is. 14.4; ⁴Jer. 4.19; ⁵Ps. 60.5; ⁶Pr. 9.5; ⁷Cant. 3.4; ⁸Ezra
2.2 et al.; ⁹Jer. 25.12, II Ch. 36.21

4

כָּרֹת קוֹמַת בְּרוֹשׁ¹ בִּקֵּשׁ אֲגָגִי בֶּן הַמְּדָתָא.²
וְנִהְיָתָה לוֹ לְמוֹקֵשׁ, וְגַאֲוָתוֹ נִשְׁבָּתָה.
רֹאשׁ יְמִינִי³ נִשֵּׂאתָ, וְאוֹיֵב שְׁמוֹ מָחִיתָ,
רֹב בָּנָיו, וְקִנְיָנָיו, עַל הָעֵץ תָּלִיתָ:⁴

¹II Kings 19.23, Is. 37.24; ²Esther 3.1, 5.14 cf. Meg. 10b; ³Esther 2.5; ⁴Esther
9.13

5

יוֹנִים נִקְבְּצוּ עָלַי, אֲזַי בִּימֵי חַשְׁמַנִּים.

וּפָרְצוּ חוֹמוֹת מִגְדָּלַי,[1] וְטִמְּאוּ כָּל הַשְּׁמָנִים.

וּמִנּוֹתַר קַנְקַנִּים,[2] נַעֲשָׂה נֵס לַשּׁוֹשַׁנִּים,[3]

בְּנֵי בִינָה, יְמֵי שְׁמוֹנָה, קָבְעוּ שִׁיר וּרְנָנִים:[4]

[1]Mid. 2.3; [2]Shab. 21b; [3]Cant. 2.2 cf. Shab. 30b; [4]Shab. 21b

6

חֲשׂף זְרוֹעַ קָדְשֶׁךָ,[1] וְקָרֵב קֵץ הַיְשׁוּעָה,[2]

נְקֹם נִקְמַת דַּם עֲבָדֶיךָ,[3] מִיַּד מַלְכוּת הָרְשָׁעָה,[4]

כִּי אָרְכָה לָנוּ הַשָּׁעָה, וְאֵין קֵץ לִימֵי הָרָעָה,

דְּחֵה אַדְמוֹן,[5] בְּצֵל צַלְמוֹן,[6] וְהָקֵם לָנוּ רוֹעִים שִׁבְעָה:[7]

[1]Is. 52.10; [2]Dan. 8.19; [3]Deut. 32.43; [4]Ber. 61b et al.; [5]Gen. 25.25; [6]Ps. 68.15; [7]Mic. 5.4 cf. Suc. 52b

מהר"ר משה איסרלם (רמ"א)

7

מֵעוֹלָם הָיִיתָ יִשְׁעִי, כְּבוֹדִי וּמֵרִים רֹאשִׁי,[1]

שְׁמַע נָא לְקוֹל שַׁוְעִי, מַלְכִּי וֵאלֹהַי[2] קְדוֹשִׁי,

הַעֲבֵר חַטָּאתִי וּפִשְׁעִי,[3] גַּם בְּגָלוּת הַשְּׁלִישִׁי,

חֲזַק יִשְׂרָאֵל, הַכְנִיעַ יִשְׁמָעֵאל, מֵאֱדוֹם תִּפְדֶּה נַפְשִׁי:

[1]Ps. 3.4; [2]Ps. 5.3; [3]Ex. 34.6–7

מוהר"ר ירמיהו אב"ד וורצבורג

8

יְהִי רָצוֹן מִלְּפָנֶיךָ יָחִיד הוֹד וְהָדָר,[1]

גְּאַל שְׁאֵרִית צֹאנְךָ,[2] מֵאֱדוֹם יִשְׁמָעֵאל[3] וְקֵדָר,[4]

רַחוּם בַּקּוֹדֶשׁ נֶאְדָּר,[5] רֶוַח תָּשִׂים לָעֵדֶר,[6]

נַחֲלָתְךָ הוֹשִׁיעַ,[7] אֵל נְקָמוֹת הוֹפִיעַ,[8] בַּעֲמָלֵק מִדֹּר דֹּר:[9]

[1]Ps. 21.6 et al.; [2]Jer. 23.3; [3]Ps. 83.7; [4]Gen. 35.13; [5]Ex. 15.6; [6]Gen. 32.17; [7]Ps. 28.9; [8]Ps. 94.1; [9]Ex. 17.6

מוהר"ר שמואל בן מוהר"ר דוד הלוי בעל נחלת שבעה

9

שִׁמְךָ יְבֹרַךְ לְעוֹלָם,[1] מִתּוֹךְ קְהַל אֱמוּנִים,

וְכִסְאֲךָ יְהִי שָׁלֵם,[2] אִם תִּנְקֹם בְּזָדוֹנִים,

לְנַפְשׁוֹת נֶעֱנִים,[3] הַסְכֵּת[4] מִמְּעוֹנִים,

לְהוֹשִׁיעַ עַמְּךָ,[5] וּלְהַצִּיל שְׂרִידֶיךָ,

יְדִידֶיךָ כְּאָז בִּימֵי חַשְׁמַנִּים:

[1]Ps. 113.2; [2]Tan. Ki Teze 11 to Ex. 17.16; [3]Is. 58.10; [4]Deut. 27.9; [5]Ps. 28.9

מהר"ל

10

חַי זְקֹף קֶרֶן יְשׁוּעָה,¹ וְקָרֵב קֵץ הַגְּאֻלָּה,
וּמַלְכוּת זָדוֹן הָרְשָׁעָה,² תְּהִי מְעִי מַפֵּלָה,³
בִּנְפֹל בְּנֵי עַוְלָה,⁴ וּלְעַמְּךָ תַּעֲשֶׂה הַצָּלָה,
בְּצִדְקַת אֵיתָנִים,⁵ גְּאַל בָּנִים, וְתִבְנֶה הָעִיר עַל תִּלָּהּ:

¹II Sam. 22.3; ²Ber. 61b et al.; ³Is. 17.1; ⁴II Sam. 3.34; ⁵R.H. 11a; ⁶Jer. 30.18

מוהר"ר שלמה זלמן בן מתתיהו לונדון

11

שַׁדַּי לָמָּה כְּאַלְמָנָה,¹ תַּחַת יַד הָאַדְמוֹנִי,
רְאֵה כַּמָּה לַחַץ וּמוֹנָה,² עוֹד מְעַט וּסְקָלֻנִי,³
בְּנָקְמְךָ כְּבִימֵי מַתְּתִיָהוּ,⁴ רַבִּים יִרְאוּ וְיִתְמָהוּ,
שְׁלַח עֵזֶר,⁵ נְשֹׂא נֵזֶר,⁶ מָשִׁיחַ וְאֵלִיָּהוּ:⁷

¹Lam. 1.1; ²Ex. 22.20; ³Ex. 17.4; ⁴Hab. 1.5; ⁵Ps. 20.3; ⁶II Kings 11.12; ⁷Mal. 3.23

מהר"ל

12

חַזֵּק קִרְיַת מוֹעֲדֶיךָ,¹ וְקָרֵב יוֹם הַנֶּחָמָה,
קַבֵּץ צֹאן יְדִידֶיךָ,² וְיֵצְאוּ בְּיָד רָמָה,³
גָּרֵשׁ אֶת בֶּן הָאָמָה,⁴ וְהַר שֵׂעִיר תָּשִׂים שְׁמָמָה,⁵
הַכְרִיתֵם,⁶ וְהַצְמִיתֵם,⁷ וְיוֹדוּךָ כָּל מַלְכֵי אֲדָמָה:⁸

¹Is. 33.20; ²Ez. 36.38; ³Ex. 14.8; ⁴Gen. 21.10; ⁵Ez. 35.7; 15; ⁶Ps. 34.17; ⁷Ps. 94.23; ⁸Ps. 138.4

מוהר"ר שמחה בן מוהר"ר יצחק דוב הלוי באמבערגער

13

שַׂמֵּחַ לֵב בָּנֶיךָ, הַמְצַפִּים לִישׁוּעָתֶךָ,¹
שְׁלַח מְשִׁיחַ צִדְקֶךָ, וְהַחֲזִירֵם לִמְעוֹנֶךָ,²
זְכֹר בְּרִית אָבוֹת,³ אִם מְעַטִּים הַזְּכֻיּוֹת,
עֲשֵׂה לְמַעַן שְׁמֶךָ, עֲשֵׂה לְמַעַן שְׁמֶךָ,
לְמַעַנְךָ אִם לֹא לְמַעֲנֵנוּ:

¹Mic. 7.7; ²Ps. 26.8; ³Deut. 4.31

מוהר"ר יצחק (המכ' זעקל) בן מוהר"ר שמחה הלוי באמבערגער

14

יְהִי שָׁלוֹם בְּקִרְבֵּנוּ, צָהֳלָה וּבְרָכָה בְּמַחֲנֵנוּ,
חַי שְׁלַח מְשִׁיחֵנוּ, קְדוֹשׁ יִשְׂרָאֵל עִמָּנוּ,¹
קָרֵב יְמֵי שִׂמְחָתֵנוּ,² הַבָּאִים לִגְאוּלֵינוּ,³
עֲשֵׂה לְעֵינֵינוּ, עֲשֵׂה לְעֵינֵינוּ, עֲשֵׂה לְעֵת חַיֵּינוּ:

¹Ez. 39.7; ²Esther 9.22 cf. Neh. 12.27; ³Is. 63.4

116

מֹשֶׁה חֹזֵק

15 **מִ**גְדַּל עֹז שֵׁם אֲדֹנֵינוּ,[1] **שׁ**ֹמֵר הַכִּבְשָׂה בֵּין שִׁבְעִים זְאֵבִים[2]
הִשְׁקִיפָה[3] עַל לַחֲצֵנוּ,[4] **חֵ**יל שֵׂעִיר[5] וְחַתְנוּ[6] וְכָל הַגּוֹיִם[7]
זְרוֹעָם בְּפַחַד תִּפֹּל,[8] **קְ**רַע מֵעָלֵינוּ[9] אֶת הָעֹל,
הָעֵץ תֵּעָקֵר, הָאֶבֶן תִּשָּׁבֵר,[10] וְעָלוּ צִיּוֹן מוֹשִׁיעִים:[11]

[1]Pr. 18.10; [2]Esther R. 10 to Esther 9.2; [3]Deut. 26.15; [4]Is. 19.20; [5]Gen. 32.4; [6]Gen. 28.9; [7]Zech. 14.14; [8]Ex. 15.16; [9]I Kings 11.11; [10]Deut. 28.36; 64; [11]Ov. 21

16 חֲנֻכּוֹת שֶׁבַע בְּמִנְיָנָם,[1] כִּסְאוֹ וַהֲדֹם רַגְלָיו בַּתְּחִלָּה,[2]
הַשֵּׁנִית מְקוֹם מַתְּנַת דָּם,[3] וְאַחֲרָיו בֵּית יְדִידְיָה,[4]
מֵצֵל מֵאֵשׁ[5] וְהַתִּרְשָׁתָא,[6] וְשֶׁלָּנוּ[7] עַל יְדֵי הַחֲמִשָּׁה,[8]
מִקֵּץ הַגָּלוּת הַשְּׁלִישִׁי,[9] בִּבְשׂוֹרַת הַתִּשְׁבִּי,[10]
מְהֵרָה תָּבֹא הָאַחֲרוֹנָה:

[1]Pes. Rab. 2.2; [2]Gen. 2.1–3 cf. Is 66.1; [3]Num. 7 cf. Lev. 4.30 et al.; [4]I Kings 8 cf. II Sam. 12.25; [5]Ezra 6.13–18 cf. Zech. 3.2; [6]Neh. 12.27–42 cf. 8.9; 10.2; [7]Meg. Ta'an. 9, Shab. 21b; [8]Meg. Ant. 41.1, I Macc. 2.2–5; [9]Pes. Rab. 2.2 to Zeph. 1.12; [10]Mal. 3.23 cf. I Kings 17.1

17 עַל הַנִּסִּים וְעַל הַנִּפְלָאוֹת, שֶׁעָשִׂיתָ עַל יְדֵי כֹהֲנֶיךָ הַקְּדוֹשִׁים,
לֹא בְכֹחָם[1] עָשׂוּ גְבוּרוֹת, וְלֹא בְחֵילָם[1] נִצְּחוּ חֲלָשִׁים,
אֲשֶׁר בְּרוּחֲךָ[1] הַטְּהוֹרָה, פָּנוּ אֶת בֵּיתְךָ[2] הַנּוֹרָא
מֵטִיב הַיָּוֵן,[3] מְעֻוָּת לְתַקֵּן,[4] לְהָסִיר מִמֶּנָּה אֶת כָּל הַשִּׁקּוּצִים:[5]

[1]Zech. 4.6; [2]Gen. 24.31; [3]Ps. 40.3; [4]Ecc. 1.15, 7.13; [5]Ez. 11.18

CHAPTER THREE:

SHUL BEHAVIOR

As we enter the period of the *Yamim Noraim*, perhaps we should take stock of the situation in Anglo-Jewry. On the one hand, the *chareidi* sector is growing, being the only one that showed an increase in the number of marriages in the last year and with schools, *baruch HaShem*, bursting at the seams. However, the majority of the community still seems to be apathetic to Yiddishkeit and is assimilating rapidly. Although most Jews in the UK are affiliated with an Orthodox synagogue, their attachment to Judaism remains nominal. The growth of programs such as SEED shows a heartening increase in interest; this is only reaching a small proportion at present, though we all hope this will expand in the future.

On the other side of the community, the non-Orthodox movements are trying to expand. In reality, their membership differs little from the average "Orthodox by affiliation" Jew since, to such people, it matters little which shul they do not attend. They are achieving some success among those young Jewish couples who have settled in predominantly non-Jewish areas. By choosing to live far from Jewish centers, these people have effectively shown a lack of great interest in Jewish commitment, and only start to consider joining a shul when they start to have children and wish them to have some awareness of their Jewish origins. As might be expected, they have very little knowledge of Torah and cannot distinguish authentic Judaism from these other movements. The latters' claims to be more "up to date" and their lack of "inconvenient" obligations such as Shabbat is a powerful attraction to *tinokot shenishbu*. Those who harbor some nostalgia for tradition, even if it is only culinary, gravitate to Conservatism or Reform (in the UK equivalent to the "left wing" of the Conservatives in the USA) that preserve some "pleasant Jewish customs." Those with even weaker Jewish roots may join the Liberals (in the UK equivalent to Reform in the USA) who, despite their moral earnestness, resemble liberal Protestantism more than Torah Judaism. However, all these movements share the common feature that they deny fundamental concepts of the Torah such as its Divine origin and, in consequence, the obligatory nature of the *mitzvot*.

Though many join the breakaway groups as a result of intermarriage, since the latter are more ready to "convert" their non-Jewish spouse, it seems to me that this cannot be their be sole attraction; people will not admit to dishonorable motives such as a desire to be free from *mitzvot*. These movements have to present themselves in a positive manner in order to make themselves respectable. To do this they pick on some fault in the Torah community that they claim to rectify. This ploy has always been used in the past, even by those who in reality only wished to indulge in the most licentious behavior, like the Frankists 250 years ago.

As an example, we might consider the Karaites in the time of the Geonim, who arose originally from a dispute as to the succession to *Reish Galuta*. At that time, the study of *peshat* and *dikduk*, the literal meaning of *Tanach* and grammar, was somewhat neglected. The Karaites made great play of this neglect and, by their attention to these studies, gained a considerable following. They were only defeated when *gedolim*, in particular Rav Saadia Gaon, showed that this neglect had not been a matter of principle and exhibited a much greater skill in their study than the sectarians. This work was continued by such scholars as lbn Ezra and Redak and eventually the Karaites dwindled to insignificance as the fault on which they based their claims was rectified.

Perhaps this illustrates an underlying process whereby HaShem allows such movements to grow as a warning to us to mend our ways. They require some positive quality from which to draw their spiritual nourishment. This is necessary if people are to have a true freedom of choice since an obvious falsehood can only be rejected. They require some grain of truth to make it possible for the *yetzer hara* to seduce people to follow them.

Can we discern the fault in our community that gives them their strength? Perhaps if we examine their propaganda this will be possible. Since the various reforming movements wished to remodel Judaism to resemble the dominant religion, they concentrated their attention on the synagogue services. Here they found a careless attitude not in accordance with *halachah* among many Jews, who were very lax about talking during *davening*, despite the attempts of many *gedolim* to correct them. The reformers compared this to the great decorum to be found in the churches and claimed that their main program was to rectify this fault.

Unfortunately, we are still plagued with this problem and are therefore playing into the hands of the sectarians who can present themselves as devout in their public worship. This can attract serious-minded, but Jewishly ignorant, individuals and, in the end, gives them a respectability that allows them to infiltrate *goyim* into the community and, even worse, to spread *mamzerut*.

In his excellent work, *Kuntres Mikdash Me'at*, Rabbi Nosson Gestetner outlines the *halachah* on these matters and shows that there can be three basic prohibitions involved when one talks in shul:

First, it is forbidden to interrupt during certain *tefillot*. Of course nobody would dream of stopping to chat during *Shema* or *Shemoneh Esrei*, but when it comes to *chazarat haShatz* or *Kriat haTorah*, many are not aware of any restrictions on free speech.

Yet the *din* is that one must listen carefully to every word in both of the latter cases. While some *poskim* allow an individual to learn during *chazarat haShatz or bein gavra legavra* in *Kriat haTorah*, this is a concession to those who find it difficult to abstain from learning at all times. However, many of those who are found engrossed in a *sefer* during *davening* seem to be able to control this desire at other times, and seem to be victims of the *frum yetzer hara*. Their lack of attention to the *davening* creates a poor example to others who deduce that such a lack of concentration is not so serious, and proceed to indulge in idle chatter.

Secondly, the *Beit haKnesset* and *Beit haMidrash* have a degree of *kedushah* and one is forbidden to discuss everyday matters within their precincts, even when they are not in use. Thus, even at points during *davening* when one is permitted to make an interruption, the range of subjects allowed is severely limited to *divrei Torah* or matters of immediate concern. Clearly one may not discuss business affairs even on a weekday, let alone on *Shabbat*.

Thirdly, when one talks in shul at a permitted time and on a permitted topic, there is always the problem that this might distract one's fellow who is trying to concentrate on his *davening*. Thus, even then, one should be careful to avoid talking loudly, or near such a person. If one is not careful in this respect one is coming close to a kind of *gezel* that cannot be rectified, a *geneivat da'at* of sorts.

Unfortunately, in the eyes of many, talking in shul is seen as entirely innocuous or, at worst, as a minor fault, and those who abstain are considered eccentric or, at best, exceptionally pious. The resulting disorderly behavior opens the door to the accusations of the reformers.

This view is completely incorrect and many *gedolim* in all generations have spoken out against this fault, as can be found in *Kunires Mikdash Me'ai* or, with an English translation, in Cyril Domb's *The Dignity of the Synagogue*. For example the *Shulchan Aruch* (*o.c.* 124: 7) states with respect to talking during *Chazarat hashatz, gadol avono min'so*, "his sin is greater than he can bear." Many catastrophes that have befallen our people have been ascribed to carelessness in these matters. The *Tosafot Yom Tov* considered it to be the underlying reason for the terrible Chmielnitzky massacres in his days and was moved to compose a special *Mi Sheberach* for "those who control their mouths and tongues so as not to talk during the time of prayer." I have heard that one of the *gedolim* of the last generation was asked why the Jews of Eastern Europe suffered so severely from the Nazis, *yemach shemam*, whereas a large proportion of the German Jews escaped. He answered that the former were much more committed to Torah learning and observing the *mitzvot*, and the only fault he could find was that they were lax in the matter of talking in shul. Though he was loath to ascribe the *churban* to this cause, he suggested that it might have been their avoidance of this improper behavior that saved the Jews of Germany, despite the assimilation of so many of them, and also the Sefardim who were equally careful in this respect.

While I would not suggest that greater care in these matters will avoid all disasters, or cause the immediate disappearance of the sects that have broken away from Torah Judaism, it will certainly take away one of the accusations against us. In the words of the *payyetan* "*has kategor vekach sanegor mekomo* – let the accuser be silenced and an advocate take his place" so that we may reach a time when HaShem will "open the mouths of those who trust in Him" with the coming of *Mashiach bimhera veyamenu*.

A KING EXTOLLED WITH PRAISES

Imagine that you, as chairman of the building committee of your school, had with great effort managed to erect a new building. To crown your achievement, a business contact has managed to arrange for a very eminent person, the secretary of state or perhaps even a member of the royal family, to perform the official opening. You know that money must still be raised to pay for the work, but the prestige of being introduced to such a personality will surely impress potential donors and persuade them to be more generous than usual.

Of course you would prepare your speech of welcome carefully and practice it several times to ensure that your presentation was polished for such an important occasion. There would be no question of letting the slightest mispronunciation pass your lips, nor any phrase that verged on the colloquial with so much at stake.

Yet when we address *HaShem* in our *tefillot* we seem to be happy to ignore all this. How often do we think how the words should be enunciated or how they should be grouped into meaningful sentences? We assume that *HaShem* is an indulgent father who will overlook our childish mistakes. Though this may be true, is it right for us to play on His good nature when we are capable of doing better? Should we make the *tefillot* a meaningless gabble when with greater care we could present them correctly? It is an insult to *HaShem* for us to treat Him with less respect than the visiting dignitary who is coming to open our new building. The latter is, after all, only a human being and is not really doing anything apart from gracing us with his presence.

Not only are we careless in our diction, which can make our utterances meaningless, but in many cases our mispronunciations can completely alter the meaning. There are many ways that this can happen and only by studying *dikduk*, the rules of *Lashon ha-Kodesh*, can this be avoided. Unfortunately, many look askance at this study and consider it as almost verging on *apikorsut*, thus continuing to distort our holy texts. Perhaps this attitude had its roots in the time of the struggle with the *Haskalah*, since the study of *dikduk* was one of its main activities. However, it is surely a fallacy to condemn something just because it is pursued by *reshaim*; by that logic, *chareidishe Yidden* would not be allowed to live in *Eretz Yisrael* because the secular Zionists have set up their state in it.

A few examples will show how we can fall into serious error if we do not take sufficient care in these matters, sometimes almost making blasphemous utterances.

Milra and *Mil'el*

Normally Hebrew words are stressed on the last syllable (*milra*) though some words, especially the so-called *segholate* nouns, like *melech*, have the stress on the preceding one (*mil'el*). In the latter case, this is often indicated in pointed texts by a *meteg*, a short vertical line under the stressed syllable, though many texts omit it. Usually using the wrong stress on a word does not alter its meaning, but may be compared to the use of slang expressions in other languages, something that one would avoid in conversation with people of importance. As one *darshan* once told his congregation, "Your *emet* is *sheker* and your *sheker* is *emet*," by which he meant that they were pronouncing both with the stress on the first syllable. Thus they were correct with *sheker*, which is an ordinary *segholate* noun, but wrong with *emet*, which is not, having a *chataph seghol* under the *aleph*, which can never appear in a stressed syllable.

However, there are cases where the incorrect stress can change the meaning, for example, the word *ba'ah* with the stress on the last syllable means "she came," whereas when stressed on the first means "she is coming." Even more drastic is the word *banu*, which changes its meaning from "they built" to "in us."

Sheva Na' and *Sheva Nach*

As most people are aware there are two types of *sheva*, one sounded (*sheva na'*) and one that merely separates syllables and is not (*sheva nach*). The rules for distinguishing between them are quite involved and in certain cases in dispute. However, there are some rules that are universally accepted, in particular that a *sheva* under a letter containing a *dagesh* or following a syllable with a long vowel is always sounded. Yet how often do we hear *berachot* on *mitzvot* sound as though they are praising *HaShem* for "our *kitsch*," whatever that might be.

Sometimes this carelessness can completely change the meaning of the sentence, especially when the *sheva* follows a *kametz*, which is sometimes a long vowel and at other times a short one. This is found in words like *shamerah*, which, with a sounded *sheva*, is the third person feminine singular form of the perfect tense of a verb meaning "she has kept," whereas with an unsounded *sheva* is the jussive, meaning "please keep," which is completely different. In some texts there is a *meteg* after the *kametz* in the former case, but this is not always printed and one has to rely on the context to decide what the word means and thus how to pronounce it.

Sometimes the use of the wrong *sheva* can lead to very peculiar distortions. In *Mussaph Shabbat Rosh Chodesh* there occurs the phrase *charevah irenu*, with a sounded *sheva*, meaning "our city has been destroyed." When the *chazan* reads it with an unsounded *sheva*, I wonder what he had in mind since such an intransitive verb cannot have a jussive form. Surely he was not asking *HaShem* to destroy *Yerushalayim*!

The *Mappik Heh*

Sometimes the *heh* at the end of a word has a dot in it called a *mappik*, which means that the *heh* is to be pronounced. Usually it is a suffix indicating the third person feminine pronominal form; for example, *ishah* with a *mappik* means "her husband," as opposed to "a woman" without it (though the former contains an additional *yod*). Failure to pronounce the *heh* can completely alter the meaning in some cases; for example, in the *parshat nedarim* at the beginning of *Mattot*, it might make the casual listener think that a woman can annul her own vows, whereas this is the prerogative of her husband!

Correct Grouping of Words

If we really understood what we were saying we would put the words of our *tefillot* together in meaningful phrases, but one often hears *Ba'alei tefillah* make mincemeat of the text, especially when forcing it to fit a *nigun*. They can even run words into one another, in particular where words begin and end with weak letters such as an *aleph* or *heh*. Once I heard the *Shemoneh Esrei* begun as

Baruch...haKel hagadol, hagibor vehanorel, which seemed to as-sociate a hitherto unknown *malach* (*chas v'shalom*) with *HaShem* as the subject of the *tefillah*!

Sometimes the correct phrasing is not entirely clear, particu-larly in *piyutim*, and this can give rise to distortions that become widely accepted. An example of this is the *Melech Elyon piyutim* on *Rosh Hashanah*. The phrase *Melech Elyon* forms the introduc-tion to each stanza which then enumerates the attributes of the "exalted King," concluding with the phrase *le'adei 'ad yimloch*, "may He rule for ever." In the original versions, each *Melech Elyon* stanza was followed by a *Melech Evyon* stanza, contrasting the attributes of an earthly king, concluding with the plaint, *ad matai yimloch*, "how long will he rule," forming a complete *aleph-bet* acrostic. This is still to be found in the *Machzor Roma* of the Italian *Minhag*. The custom was to open the *aron* for the *Melech Elyon* and close it for the *Melech Evyon* stanzas; this must have been confusing and is the probable reason that most of the latter were omitted. *Ba'alei tefillah* who did not appreciate this consequently read the *piyut* as though each stanza concluded *le'ade 'ad yimloch Melech Elyon*, which admittedly makes sense, only is not the intention of the authors who were among the *Gedolei Rishonim*. Are we on such a *madreigah* that we can take such liberties with their compositions?

Most wrong groupings of words, however, render the text as gibberish and if we only listened to what we were saying, we would realize how ridiculous they were!

Many other errors are caused by rushing the *davening* and slurring the words. We sometimes read a vowel wrongly even in a *shem*, for example the first vowel in *Elokim* is a *seghol* yet is of-ten heard pronounced as a *tzere*. Other errors are the swallow-ing of the last letter of a word making, for example, *matar*, rain, into *matta*, below, or eliding similar sounding syllables making *lehachayot meitim*, to bring the dead back to life, into *lechayot meitim*, "for the dead living creatures (zombies?)"! The *Shulchan Aruch, Orach Chaim* (*siman* 61) brings many other examples of situations where care is required in pronunciation, primarily in regard to *Kriat Shema*, though equally applicable to all the *tefillot*. Although it rules *Kore ve'eino dikdek yatsa*, "one has done one's duty if one recites with slight inaccuracies," this is only *bediavad*, after the event; *lechatchilah*, in the first instance, one should try to say every word correctly. We would surely not be satisfied with a *bediavad* fulfillment of our personal desires!

All this applies to every Jew, but for those who wish to act as *sheliach tzibur* it is even more important. Only by greater knowledge and care can one address *HaShem* with *peh velibo shaveh*, "saying with one's mouth what one means in one's heart" and avoid mistakes that make us sound ridiculous. We should try to emulate the *melachim* who *kulam potechim et pihem…besafah verurah*, "all open their mouths with clear speech" to praise *HaShem* and so avoid the ultimate blasphemy of making Him *Melech mechulal baTishbachot*, "a King profaned with praises."

A TIME TO REQUEST

This article is going to be controversial; it is meant to be. Its purpose is to provoke a response from its readers and, hopefully, to make them think more deeply about the purpose of *tefillah* and, in particular, *Shemoneh Esrei*.

When it comes to *davening*, there are two types of person. The first finishes his *tefillot* as quickly as possible so that he can get on with the rest of his daily activities. This article is not meant for such a person; in fact, it could be positively deleterious to him. It is quite clear that one must be aware of the meaning of the words one is saying in order to fulfill one's obligation. Though someone might be so preoccupied with his problems and find it difficult to concentrate on a particular occasion, this cannot be seen as a blanket *heter* for rushing one's *davening* on a regular basis.

Rather, this article is aimed at those who appreciate the importance of *tefillah* and are prepared to extend their recitation of *Shemoneh Esrei*, concentrating carefully and at great length on each word. While the *Anshei Knesset Hagedolah* undoubtedly included deep mystical meaning in their composition, these are beyond the knowledge of most ordinary persons who have not been initiated into the *chochmat hanistar*. For them it might be presumptuous even to try to have such deep *kavanot*.

However, I doubt if many people aspire to such heights. On the contrary, they only wish to pour out their requests to the Almighty and do so at great length. While this is entirely understandable at times of personal crisis, I would like to challenge its desirability on a regular basis.

Perhaps it shows some lack of trust of *HaShem* to draw out one's requests to Him since He surely knows all our needs even better than we ourselves. The Prophet Isaiah (65.24), whom we quote in our *Shemoneh Esrei* every *ta'anit tzibur*, states, "Before they call, I will answer; while they are still speaking, I will hear." Extending our requests under normal circumstances might be seen as a form of "nagging" *HaShem*, like a child who keeps asking its mother over and over for a sweet. Perhaps what we think are our essential needs are not for our real benefit and it would be better to restrict ourselves to the formula composed by the *Anshei Knesset Hagedolah* and let *HaShem*, so to speak, fill in the details relevant to our personal situation.

The prophet's words are reflected in the actual wording of the *Shemoneh Esrei* itself, if we only pause to consider its structure. For example, let us consider just one of the requests, the prayer for forgiveness. In it, we commence with the plea, "Forgive us, our Father, for we have erred; pardon us, our King, for we have willfully sinned," which we follow with the reason, "because You are pardoning and forgiving. Blessed are You, *HaShem*, the gracious One Who pardons abundantly," which acknowledges that *HaShem* is already answering our request. Similar considerations would apply to the other requests.

Once this point has been appreciated, one might feel that it is somewhat presumptuous to extend one's personal requests unduly. Of course this is not to exclude those that *chazal* encourage us to include, such as to pray for specific sick people in *Refa'enu* or for one's personal *parnasah* in *Barech Aleinu*, only to be brief and leave it to the Almighty in His wisdom to understand what has to be done. As they tell us, we should not make our *tefillot* mere rote recitations and should consider the relevance of the words we recite to our personal situation.

There are some other problems that an over-long *Shemoneh Esrei* might cause to one's fellows. Firstly, one should remember that it is forbidden to sit in the proximity of someone *davening Shemoneh Esrei*. This could cause considerable distress to those in one's immediate vicinity, especially if they are feeling weak; this might be an even bigger problem on the *Yam'im Noraim*, yet one would wish to avoid disturbing others, especially at that season.

A second problem is that it is also not permitted to walk in front of someone *davening Shemoneh Esrei*. This might also cause problems especially if one is *davening* near the door.

Because these *dinim* are not widely known, people ignore them and the problems involved are relatively few but one should consider whether one is entitled to cause others to err through one's actions. Should one be extra *frum* at other people's expense? On the other hand, perhaps this is yet another case of *mutav sheyi-hyu shogegim*?

For those who come late there are *dinim* regarding what should be missed out in order to catch up with the *tzibur*. If they ignore them and blithely *daven* at their own leisurely pace so that they do not start their *Shemoneh Esrei* with the *tzibur*, but only with *chazarat hashatz*, it might be said *ki yosif al chatato pesha*! (Job 34:37).

They might care to remember the incident when Reb Yisrael Salanter was asked why he only used the minimal amount of water for washing his hands on a certain occasion despite his normal custom. He replied that he saw how the maid had to bring the water a long distance up a hill to provide for him and he did not want to cause her extra work. Similarly we might take into account the effects of our *avodat HaShem* on others.

Perhaps we should take Rabbi Akiva as a model. As the

Gemara (*Berachot* 31a) records, when in *shul*, he used to shorten his *davening* to avoid being *matriach* the *tzibur*. This point is particularly relevant to anyone acting as *sheliach tzibur* who should not keep the congregation waiting because of his wish to put extra concentration into his private *Shemoneh Esrei*.

From the above, it should be clear that overextending one's *Shemoneh Esrei* might not be an act of piety and one should consider whether one is justified in so doing. Perhaps one should restrict one's *kavanot* to concentrating on the meaning of the words we are reciting and their relevance to us and leave the rest to the Almighty, as we say at this season (*Tehillim* 27:14): "Hope in *HaShem,* be strong and let your heart be brave, hope in *HaShem*."

WHEN THE DAVENING FINISHED TOO LATE

In an article in the *Jewish Tribune*, "When the Davening Took Too Long" (Aug. 31, 1995), Rabbi Avrohom Katz, in his inimitable way, discussed two types of shul, comparing the davening to the two types of train that travel through the Swiss countryside. The first, the inter-continental express, races along in a blur of mechanized efficiency, whereas the second, meant for tourists, takes the most scenic route and travels at a leisurely pace to allow the passengers the opportunity to admire the breathtaking scenery and the soaring Alpine heights.

The comparison to the two types of *minyan* is clear and his obvious preference for the latter quite understandable. I most wholeheartedly agree with his judgment. It is most disturbing to feel that one has to daven ever faster in order to keep up with the *tzibur* and that every *meshullach* who comes makes one fall yet further behind. Such *minyanim* feel like being on a treadmill where one is afraid to sneeze lest one fall two pages behind, and are hardly conducive to *tefillah* in the true meaning of the word. This is particularly true where the texts are unfamiliar, such as the *selichot*, which are full of obscure references requiring a slower pace, yet are often recited, if anything, even faster than the regular *tefillot*.

However, there is one aspect of the problem that he failed to tackle. For those gentlemen who do not have to be at work at a fixed time, the leisurely *davening* is ideal. They may even have time to learn a bit after the end of *shacharit* before returning home for a leisurely breakfast. Unfortunately, there are still many who have a tight schedule in the mornings, perhaps having to drop children off at school before going to open their businesses. While this might not be a problem in a small town like Gateshead, travelling times can be considerable in larger cities.

A yeshiva or kollel can arrange its *tefillot* as part of its daily *seder* and no *baalabos* can complain if it finishes too late for him. If he doesn't like it, he can go elsewhere. However, a shul has to accommodate the not-unreasonable requirements of its members. The problem, then, is how to allow sufficient time for the davening and still finish early enough for those who have to seek a *parnassah*. Unfortunately, I have not yet found a *minyan* that has solved the problem. Despite what seems to be a widespread opinion, work is not a four-letter word of Anglo-Saxon origin not used in polite company!

With great trepidation I present a few thoughts about how these objectives could possibly be reconciled. First, the *minyan* must decide how long each part of *shacharit* should take. This will necessitate some compromise, since what is leisurely for one is impossibly fast for another. However, it should be possible to satisfy most of the latter provided that the former are assured that they will be able to leave for work in time. On the other hand, these times should not allow for latecomers to catch up; there are *dinim* that they should know, for deciding which sections should be missed out in such circumstances. Once this timetable is established, at least everyone knows what to expect. A friend told me that when he was an *avel* he once davened before the *amud* in Zurich and the *gabbai* pointed out to him such a list of times that was on the *amud* next to a watch and how this made him feel that he knew what the *tzibur* expected and could avoid causing them any problems.

Having established this framework, it is simple to calculate back from the desired finishing time to establish when *shacharit* must begin. Unfortunately, it will become almost immediately apparent that this will be rather earlier than most members are used to, but there is no alternative that will satisfy both requirements.

Of course, it will be essential that davening start on time, but that is the responsibility of the *gabbai*, who should make sure that someone is ready. If the person designated to say *berachot* does not wish to continue, the *gabbai* must make sure that the replacement is ready to take over without delay. If no one else is willing, he should do so himself; of course this will necessitate his being ready, with his *tallit* and *tefillin* on, well before the official time of commencement. Where there is an *avel r"l*, or someone with *yahrzeit*, who wishes to have the *amud*, the *gabbai* should ensure that someone else is ready to start, should the latter be late in arriving. To be *sheliach tzibur* is a privilege and not a right.

On the other hand, should there not be a *minyan* in time for the *kaddeishim* before *Pesukei deZimra*, the *avel* should carry on and be satisfied with saying only those at the end of *davening*. To delay at that stage means either speeding through the remainder or finishing late, which is an unfair imposition on those who may have to leave for work.

Another source of *tircha detzibura* arises where somebody has taken on saying *kaddish* for someone for whom he is not a *chiyuv* and he insists on saying one at every possible opportunity, even in the absence of those with a genuine *chiyuv*, instead of restricting himself to the one after *alenu*. Such multiplication of *kaddeishim* is no honor to the *niftar* since it might be thought to imply that every effort has to be made to drag him out of Gehinnom!

Similarly, should a *bachur* who does not wear a *tallit* be given an aliyah, the *gabbai* should make sure one is available so that no *tircha detzibura* is caused while the *oleh* searches for one. Another cause of *tircha detzibura* is when a visitor is given a *petichah* but is not told how to open the *parochet* or which *sefer* to take out. Every shul seems to have a slightly different system, yet this *mitzvah* is most frequently given to a visitor, which also embarrasses him as he searches for the possibly non-existent cord, which is, of course, even worse.

It will also be necessary to have fairly strict controls on who can act as *sheliach tzibur*, and ban anyone who fancies himself as a chazan, especially on days when the *davening* is longer than usual. While a melodious rendition of *hallel* may be very pleasant, it should be strictly reserved for Yom Tov. Similarly, since nowadays we are not *yotzei* with *chazarat hashatz*, there is no reason for saying it with excessively great deliberation, so long as every word is enunciated clearly. Conversely, those who have difficulty in *davening* aloud fluently should have the decency to decline the *amud* even when they are *aveilim*. It is a greater honor to the departed in such cases *not* to insist on one's "rights."

The custom in most shuls is to wait for the *rov* of the shul to finish *Shema* and *Shemonei Esrei* before continuing the *davening*. In some places this is extended to visiting *rabbonim* and *roshei yeshiva*. Since the latter are usually not aware of the honor shown them, they *daven* at their customary speed, which, though appropriate in their usual *makom tefillah*, causes delays in the shul in which they find themselves. On the other hand, the local *rav* knows his congregation and would hopefully not impose on them in this way. If he wanted to spend longer over his *tefillah* than he realizes they can allow, he would waive this honor, as for example did the late Manchester Rosh Yeshiva, *ztz"l*.

Though the various suggestions above may individually save only a minute or so each, the cumulative effect could be considerable.

In order to meet the objectives of reasonable pace and a sufficiently early finish without starting too early, the *davening* will inevitably be too fast for a few individuals. For them I can only suggest that they start before the *tzibur* and arrange their timing so that they reach some crucial point, such as *Barechu* or the beginning of *Shemoneh Esrei*, at the same time as it. This is clearly not ideal but it would, hopefully, avoid the unseemly spectacle of people rushing out before the end of *davening*, or what is much worse, that some members feel constrained not to come to shul at all and *daven* at home instead. After all, it is hardly correct to be frum at other people's expense, a thought that we should perhaps take to heart at all times.

KADDISH YATOM – THE ORPHAN'S KADDISH

However far a Jew may have strayed from his Jewish roots, there is one observance that still exerts a hold on him. Even if he never enters a synagogue at any other time, when a *Yahrzeit*, the anniversary of the passing of a parent, comes again, he feels the irresistible urge to recite *Kaddish* in memory of the departed. Many who rarely grace its portals become, during the year of *avelut*, mourning, regular worshippers in the synagogue for this purpose. For some this is the beginning of an on-going religious commitment, but, alas, for many, the end of the eleven months signals a return to their previous way of life. Yet many who are punctilious in their recital of the *Kaddish* have but a faint idea of its true purpose, or even the meaning of its Aramaic wording, so that it becomes a meaningless rendition performed at breakneck speed.

Originally, *Kaddish* had no connection with remembering the dead and, apart from the extended version recited at the graveside, has no reference to death whatsoever. It is, on the contrary, a doxology praising of the Almighty centered on the communal response, *Yehei shemeih rabba mevorach le'alam ule'almei almaya,* "May His great Name be blessed for ever and ever."

Its main purpose is to separate distinct units in the liturgy and then consists of the so-called *chatzi* (half) *Kaddish*. Though called half *Kaddish*, it is the essential part and in no way a shortened version. All other versions contain it with some additions appropriate to their nature. As such a "punctuation mark," it is extended after *Shemoneh Esrei* by adding three extra stiches to form the *Kaddish Shalem* (at *shacharit* on ordinary weekdays this is said after *Kedushah deSidra*, which is considered to be connected to it). This *Kaddish* is also said after *Selichot*.

Another type of *Kaddish* is the *Kaddish deRabbanan*, which was instituted as a prayer for the welfare of Torah scholars to be recited after a homiletic discourse. This may be said by anyone, though nowadays it is usually recited by mourners, many of whom stumble over its unfamiliar extra paragraph. Finally, there is the *Kaddish Yatom*, the orphan's *Kaddish*, which is recited after *Alenu* or a chapter of *Tehillim*. The former is an integral part of the service and should be said by somebody even when there are no mourners present, whereas the latter is optional.

How this *Kaddish* became associated with memorializing the dead is an interesting problem. It seems that the source is a *midrash* found in the Tanchumo, Noach, and, in a slightly different form, in Massechet Kallah.

There we are told that Rabbi Akiva once met a strange-looking man with a coal-black face running along with an enormous load of wood balanced on his head. Rabbi Akiva was puzzled and so stopped him to ask what he was doing. He replied that he had died and was being punished in this way for his wicked life. He had been a tax collector and had treated the poor very harshly while being lenient with the rich.

Every day he had to chop a large amount of wood with which he would subsequently be burned. Rabbi Akiva asked if there was any way in which he could be released from this, and the apparition replied that if he had left a son who could cause the congregation to respond, *Yehei shemeih rabba*, his torment would cease. Unfortunately, he had died childless though his wife had been pregnant at the time. He said that he came from Laodicea, so Rabbi Akiva went there to find the family. On his arrival in the town he asked about the tax collector, but, on hearing his name, everyone responded, "May his bones rot," in a tone of utter disgust. When he inquired after the wife, who seems to have shared her husband's lifestyle and had also died, they replied, "May her memory be blotted out," in revulsion. Finally, he asked if they had left a child and was told that there was a boy, but, like his parents, he was completely estranged from Judaism and had not even been circumcised. Rabbi Akiva eventually found the boy, had him circumcised, and taught him Torah. He then brought him to the synagogue and had him recite the *Kaddish* to which the congregation responded, *Yehei shemeih rabba…* That night the tax collector appeared to Rabbi Akiva in a dream, thanking him for securing his release from Gehinnom, and prayed that he be rewarded for his great kindness with a place in Gan Eden.

Whatever the true meaning of this midrash, we see that the essence of *Kaddish* is to evoke the response of the congregation, not the recital of the words as such. Thus, the usual situation in many shuls today, where several mourners race each other and, as a result, none can be heard, is clearly incorrect since it precludes this response.

Perhaps this situation came about as follows. There were originally two modes of recitation of *Kaddish*. Among Ashkenazim, it would be said by one mourner only, who would go to the front of the shul to do so. When several mourners were present, the various *Kaddeishim* would be shared, each mourner saying one. Among Sefardim, on the other hand, the mourners would recite it together in unison so that each word was audible to everyone. Problems would arise among Ashkenazim when the number of mourners exceeded the number of available *Kaddeishim*. As a consequence, rules of precedence were established (*Kitzur Shulchan Aruch* 26). As they are quite complicated, there was a tendency for disputes to arise and some later authorities, for example R. Ya'akov Emden, *ztz"l* (1697–1776), in his commentary on the *siddur*, recommended the adoption of the Sefardi mode. The *Kitzur Shulchan Aruch* (*loc. cit.*) points out that leading a life of Torah and *mitzvot* is a greater honor to the departed than the recital of *Kaddish* and such disputes are, on the contrary, a source of disgrace. Thus, apart from a few congregations of Jews originating from Germany, most Ashkenazim eventually adopted the Sefardi mode of recitation.

Unfortunately, there is one difference between the two communities. Among Sefardim, it is customary for all prayers to be said aloud in unison, whereas among Ashkenazim, each individual would pray at his own speed, oblivious of all around. While this might be helpful to the individual in his private concentration, the resulting situation was one of noise and disorder to an outside observer. In most sections of the *tefillot*, this may have not been too bad, but with *Kaddish*, where the essence is the congregational response, it was disastrous.

This seems to be the origin for the situation found today, which is clearly unsatisfactory. We should try to remedy it so that the Orphan's *Kaddish* should once more be a praise of the Almighty recited by an orphan, and not itself be an orphan whose call nobody can answer.

CHAPTER FOUR:

THE KIDDUSH WIDOW

I<small>T IS PAST</small> one o'clock on an overcast *Shabbat*. Outside, the rain has reduced to a steady drizzle, and Miriam is sitting alone waiting for her husband to come back from *shul*. Well, she is not really alone; she has the three youngest children for company: Yanky, who is four, Yossy, who is almost three, and the baby, Channy, who will soon be three months. Of course, thinks Miriam, the baby is no trouble. She only wakes up for her feeds and is so contented, but she does seem more restless than usual today. Perhaps she is teething or coming down with a cold. The other children would, of course, be company if they did not keep fighting over the tricycle – in between pestering her for a *nosh* – but then they must be tired and hungry, since it is long past their regular lunch time.

Miriam's nerves are frayed as she wonders yet again where her Chaim has gone. It is at least an hour since *shul* would have finished and, as far as she was aware, there were no simchas this week to drag out the *davening*. Chaim must have heard of some *kiddushim* and gone to them with the older boys. Of course, one should be happy about other people's simchas, but she does wish he would come home first and at least tell her; how would he feel being cooped up with squabbling children, not knowing when dinner would be? She had gone to so much trouble to make an especially tasty *Shabbat* dinner and now they would probably come home unable to eat it.

Life seemed so dismal; her *oneg Shabbat* ruined. The trouble is Chaim is such a *chevraman*, he cannot resist going along with all the others at the *minyan*. He just does not realize the problems he causes; perhaps if she speaks to him he will see how unhappy it makes her.

She remembers how things used to be when they were first married. In those days Chaim used to go to the *hashkamah minyan* and come back right away to make *kiddush*. He had always then been careful to wash and make *hamotzi* straight away. She had so enjoyed those *Shabbat* breakfasts together while the children played; it had somehow made her day. Afterwards, Chaim's *chavruta*, Moshe, would come and they would learn for an hour or so. Sometimes Moshe's wife, Hadassah, would come as well and Miriam would have a good *schmuss* with her. She had been at seminary with Hadassah and they had both married the same summer. Miriam always felt sorry for her as she had not yet had any children, but it had the advantage that Hadassah could get out on Shabbat. Then Moshe and Hadassah had gone to live in *Eretz Yisrael* and, *Baruch HaShem*, they had twins the next year.

That was when she was expecting Yanky, and Chaim had decided that it was time for him to take their oldest boy, Dovidle, to *shul* with him. Of course the *hashkamah minyan* was too early and anyway, no other father came with such small boys. So they reorganized their *Shabbat* schedule and gave up the breakfasts together.

Chaim soon found a *minyan* where he felt at home and before long he was one of the crowd. The only thing Miriam did not like about it was that they seemed to go to every *kiddush* in the neighborhood after *davening*; it seemed as though they made a point of not missing any. At first Chaim tried to slip away, but as he became more involved with the group, he went to more *kiddushim.* It would not be so bad if she could at least take the children to *shul* to meet him, but there was never a time when there was not one at home who could not walk, at least not that far. It must be wonderful for Hadassah, in Bnei Brak with an *eruv*, to be able to get out on *Shabbat*! Here in Manchester, it seems that there is no hope for one. When the idea was raised once, it came to nothing because of the opposition of the secularist Jews on the town council.

A thought crosses Miriam's mind: next *Shabbat* she will give Chaim a quarter of an hour to come back from *shul* and, if he has not returned, she will make *kiddush* for herself and the children and have the *Shabbat seudah*. Chaim can eat on his own when he gets back and, if the *cholent* has gone cold, so be it. Immediately she feels ashamed of such feelings of *nekamah* and regrets that they should even have entered her mind. However, it would not be wrong, she thinks, to go over her old seminary notes on the *dinim* of *kiddush*, just in case. Just then her thoughts are interrupted by a knock on the door – Chaim and the boys are back, at last!

*   *   *

It is now half past nine on a Monday morning and the house is quiet. The boys have all gone to school; even Yossy has started kindergarten and can hardly wait to get out of the house in the morning. Miriam has cleared up the breakfast dishes and put a load in the washing machine, so she has at least half an hour to daven until Channy wakes up for her feeding. It often strikes her that it is strange that she can always find time to *daven* during the week, but on *Shabbat* she is always too busy keeping an eye on the children.

On her way to the living room, she notices the mail on the doormat and picks it up. There are a few bills as usual, but the large envelope catches her eye. When she opens it, she sees it as an invitation to the *bar mitzvah* of the Cohens' youngest son. It is so kind of a *gevir* like Shmuel Cohen to think of them; they cannot approach his lifestyle, but he always makes them welcome.

She remembers the *bar mitzvah* of his oldest boy when she was expecting Dovidle; that had been a sumptuous *kiddush*. People had talked about it for months afterwards. Of course, by today's standards, it would not have been so remarkable. That seems to be the trouble, she thinks. Everyone wants their *simchah* to be more outstanding than anyone else's. At one, they had five types of *kugel* as well as *cholent*, and at another, they even made *fleischigs*!

This really makes it hard for those who cannot afford it, Miriam thinks on. She remembers how embarrassed she felt when Channy was born and they made a modest affair. Somehow she sensed that people thought they were being stingy; after all, it was their first girl after five boys, but they really could not afford to waste money just then after having had the house rewired. Miriam is dreading Dovidle's *bar mitzvah*, but at least they know when it will be and can put aside a little money every week towards it.

As she puts the card on the sideboard, Miriam remembers that she had decided to go over the *dinim* of *kiddush* again and takes the old folder with her seminary notes from the top of the bookcase and blows off the dust. When she has finished *davening*, she will look over them until Channy wakes up and she will have to get on with the housework.

Miriam opens the folder and thumbs through the pages until she gets to the notes on *kiddush* for *Shabbat* morning (adapted from *The Radiance of Shabbat*, by Rabbi S.B. Cohen, in the *Artscroll Mesorah* Series).

"It is a *mitzvah derabanan* to recite *kiddush* on Shabbat morning. The *mitzvah* is incumbent upon all adult men and women, and children old enough to be trained in *mitzvot*."

She reads on and comes to the section on eating before *kiddush*:

"Adults are forbidden to eat or drink anything, even water, before fulfilling their *kiddush* obligation. Minors (boys under thirteen and girls under twelve) are permitted to eat before *kiddush*.

"The *kiddush* obligation of *Shabbat* morning does not take effect until after one has davened *shacharit*.

"Since before *davening* one is not yet obligated to make *kiddush*, one is permitted to drink water. Tea and coffee are also permitted."

As she goes on through the *dinim* of the *kiddush* cup and the amount to be consumed, she remembers the *shiurim* at seminary. Reb Avraham used to be able to make them so interesting and he always kept their attention with his humorous comments. She comes next to the section on *kiddush* with *chamar medinah*, which she never really understood properly. It is a good thing that women do not go in for strong drink, she thinks as she remembers the time she picked up a glass of vodka by mistake at a *kiddush*, thinking it was a liqueur. She reads on…

"If both wine and *chamar medinah* are available, it is preferable to use wine for *kiddush*. However, one who prefers beer or whisky may substitute it, being careful to use a cup that contains at least a *reviit*, of which he must consume a *melo lugmav* [the greater part ot a *reviit*]. Some authorities rule that when whisky is the *chamar medinah*, it is permissible to use a whisky glass from which he need only drink a small amount."

The thought of somebody drinking a *melo lugmav* of whisky makes Miriam shudder. She now turns to the section on *kiddush bemakom seudah*:

"The obligation to make *kiddush* in the place where one eats applies to the *kiddush* of *Shabbat* morning just as it does on Friday night."

Miriam turns back to the notes on *kiddush* on Friday night, where she reads:

"*Kiddush* is valid only when it is followed by a meal. This involves the following conditions:

"The *kiddush* is recited where the meal is to be eaten and the meal must be eaten immediately after *kiddush*.

"If either one of these requirements is lacking, the *kiddush* is not valid."

Miriam remembers that there is some dispute about what constitutes a meal and thumbs through her notes to that part:

"For the *kiddush* to be valid, it is necessary that both the person who recites *kiddush* and the one who listens to it consume at least a *kezayit* of bread, cake or other food made from one of the five species of grain. This *kezayit* must be consumed within a *kedei-achilat-pras* and before sampling other foods."

Miriam notices that she has made a note that some authorities require bread *davka* and recalls how Chaim used to say that that way one was *yotzei* according to every opinion. He had then said that if one made *kiddush* and only ate cake, one might have to make *kiddush* again at the proper *Shabbat seudah*. Then she remembers how Reb Avraham had warned them that to be *koveia seudah* one had to eat sitting down and that they should be careful about this at *kiddushim*, particularly for the first *kezayit* of cake. He must have said it during a different *shiur* because it does not seem to be in her notes on *kiddush*. It is strange, Miriam thinks, that people are not *makpid* on this and there are usually very few chairs around at any *kiddush* she had been to. If so, she muses, perhaps they are not *yotzei kiddush* at all and are eating after *shacharit* and before *kiddush* which is against *halachah*. Miriam finds this all very confusing and decides to ask Chaim to learn these *dinim* with her. It cannot be that most people act wrongly; perhaps he will be able to be *melamed zechut* on them. It would also give her a marvelous opportunity to make him aware of her problems in a tactful way.

She now turns back to her *Shabbat* morning *kiddush* notes and reads the last paragraph:

"If one eats cake after *kiddush*, he must try not to become satiated so that he will retain an appetite for the meal."

When she reads this, Miriam sighs as she remembers how the boys could not manage to eat any dinner last *Shabbat*. Of course if one eats that much *mezonot*, one has to wash first and *bensch* afterwards, but Miriam cannot recall ever seeing anyone do so. It would be so much better if people made an "At Home" instead, which would avoid all *halachic* problems. In the summer, when *Shabbat* goes out late, they could have it after *shalosh seudot*, and in the winter it would be a nice way to spend the long *Motzoei Shabbat* evenings. They could even have one on Sunday, which would mean that friends who lived too far or had small children would be able to come.

The thought of small children jolts Miriam out of her reverie. She looks at the clock; it is half past ten! She has been so engrossed in her thoughts that she had completely lost track of time and forgotten about Channy. The poor child must be starving. She rushes upstairs and as she opens the door, Channy wakes up, rolls over and gives her a big smile.

CHAPTER FIVE:

DEAR CHAIM LETTERS

[*The following fictional exchange of letters provided an interesting opportunity to air several issues that come up in many shuls around the world.*]

BERA MEZAKEH ABBA

Dear Chaim,

I was very sorry to hear of the *petirah* of your father, *a"h*. As I also went through the same experience just over a year ago, I know exactly how you must feel. That his last few weeks were spent in the hospital must have been particularly distressing for you, as the geriatric wards are at the best of times depressing places. I am sure that he really appreciated your being with him every day and your *kibud av* was an example to us all.

Now that you have gotten up from *shiva*, you will be *davening* before the *amud* and I thought I might pass on to you some of the thoughts I have had from my own experience last year. Perhaps you have wondered why an *avel* is considered to have this particular *chiyuv*. Perhaps the clue lies in one of the qualifications required of a *sheliach tzibur*, that he be acceptable to the whole *tzibur*. When one thinks how easy it is for people to become irritated with one another, can there be any greater *zechut* for the *niftar* than for his son to be so popular that no one has any *ta'anot* on him?

Of course this puts a great responsibility on one to live up to such a high standard but, as the *Kitzur* writes, this is what is most important, rather than having the *amud* or saying many *Kaddeishim*. He also writes that one should rather give up one's "rights" to these than come to *machloket* over them, or *chas ve-shalom* hurt someone else's feelings. Unfortunately, there are too many people who consider that their "right" to the *amud* is absolutely sacred and are not willing to give way to others, even if they have a higher priority *al pi halachah*. If someone like that should come to your *minyan*, let him have his way and do not worry that you may have missed an opportunity for *kibud av*. Even if as a result you lose the chance to say a *Kaddish,* do not be upset. The Chasam Sofer writes that when someone takes a *Kaddish* away from someone else, it goes to the merit of the one for whom it should have been said. So you will not have lost anything; in reality, he has only acted as your *shaliach* in saying it.

Another situation that sometimes arises is where the other person does not exactly drive you away from the *amud* but suggests, rather, that one of you take part of the *minyan* out in the corridor so that you can both act as *sheliach tzibur*. This is also not a good solution, since often the place where the *"austritt minyan"* goes may not be a suitable place to *daven*. It also goes against the principle of *b'rov am hadrat Melech*. By letting the other person have the *amud*, and not insisting on your rights, you bring more *zechut* to your late father than a hundred *Kaddeishim*.

While on this subject, might I suggest that saying extra *Kaddeishim*, ostensibly in his honor, might, in reality, have the exact opposite effect? In *sefarim* it says that each *Kaddish* raises the *niftar* a bit further out of Gehinnom. Only the completely wicked stay there the full twelve months and that is why a son only says *Kaddish* for eleven, so as not to imply that his parent comes into that category, *r"l*. By trying to say more *Kaddeishim* than absolutely necessary, you might be thought to be making that same implication, *r"l*. This is quite apart from any *tircha d'tzibura* involved, especially on weekday mornings when most people have to hurry to work after *davening*.

Another aspect of *tircha d'tzibura* that you may find difficult to avoid is getting to *shul* on time in the mornings. I know your wife has not been well recently and that you cannot leave the toddlers crying in their cribs, which inevitably makes you occasionally late. Perhaps it would be better for you to tell the *gabbai* about your problem and ask him to find someone else to say *birchot hashachar* if you are not in *shul* by five minutes before the official start of *davening*. After all, the main *chiyuv* is to *daven* from *Barechu* and it is a *genai* for your late father that people should mistakenly think that his son can't get out of bed in time in the morning, even if you have a very good reason for your lateness.

When Shmuli Levy was an *avel* a couple of years ago, people were forever complaining that he always rushed in at the last minute, or even a few minutes late; nobody knew whether he would turn up or not until he appeared. When the *gabbai* suggested that someone else should say *birchot hashachar*, he was indignant and said that the *tzibur* should not be so bothered since he had the right to the *amud*. As someone pointed out, he would not have turned up late to catch a train, but some people just do not realize the problems their attitudes can cause others.

To add insult to injury, Shmuli would then rush the *davening* to try to finish on time. At least we can rely on you not to do that. I remember when we were in *yeshiva* how careful you always were to *daven* with proper *kavanah* and, since you started working, you have always tried to keep up this *hanhagah*. Unfortunately, you will find it difficult to continue to do so when acting as *sheliach tzibur*.

Remember when old Mr. Cohen had *yahrzeit* a few months ago and finished a quarter of an hour late? Of course, he has been retired for many years and has no need to hurry, but the result was that he hardly had a *minyan* left by the time he got to *Aleinu*. A question that you might wish to consider is whether *davening* before the *amud* will interfere with your own *avodat HaShem* and, therefore, be counterproductive. It would be a much greater *zechut* for your late father for people to be impressed by your private *davening* than to have them complain about having to rush out of *shul* before the end of *shacharit*. In the circumstances, you might feel happier only taking the *amud* from *Ashrei*.

Shlomo Hamelech says, *Tovah tochachah megulah mei'ahavah mesutaret*, "Better open rebuke than hidden love" (Prov. 2:5), so I hope that you will understand my remarks in that spirit and not take them as a personal criticism. They are only meant to help you through what will certainly be a very difficult year. Before making any decisions, you should discuss them with the *rav*.

Your Torah learning and *tefillot* will certainly be a great *zechut* for your father, and I hope that you will see only simchas in the future together with your family until the time when *bila' hamavet lanetsach umachah HaShem Elokim dimah mei'al kol panim*.

Your friend,
Moshe

SOME TIPS ON BEING SHELIACH TZIBUR

Dear Chaim,

Many thanks for your letter. From it, I can see that you have already tasted some of the "pleasures" of being *sheliach tzibur*. Don't be too upset if some people complain that you *daven* too fast and others that you are too slow. If you get roughly the same number of each, you have probably gotten your speed just about right. It is impossible to please everybody in this matter. So long as you are consistent in your "timetable," everyone will know what to expect. Those who are a bit slower can always start a bit earlier and let you "catch up" with them at *Barechu* or *Shemoneh Esrei*. Those who have to leave earlier will also be able to arrange their *tefillot* appropriately; for example, they can say the *Shir Shel Yom* while waiting for you to start *chazarat hashatz*.

Of course there are some people who find it impossible to get up in the mornings. *Ya'alzu chassidim bechavod, yerannenu al mishkevotam* (Ps. 149:5)! Do you remember Yanky Gross, who was my *chavruta* in *yeshiva* during our first *zeman* and was notorious for always coming late? At the end of *zeman*, he had to catch an early plane to go home and I heard that Reb Shloime *davened* that he should oversleep and miss it so that there should be no *kitrug* against him in *shamayim* for always being late for *shiur*. It seems that his *tefillot* were answered! Interestingly, from then on, Yanky was much more punctual, so perhaps he learned his lesson.

I really felt for you yesterday when Mordechai Greenberg made such a disgraceful scene. He always turns up ten minutes late, whatever time the *davening* starts, and so it was pure *chutzpah* to complain that you did not give him time to catch up. I remember the time when he had *yahrzeit* and came rushing in late, just in time for one of the *kaddeishim* at the beginning of *shacharit*, but he did not know whether it was the *kaddish yatom or kaddish derabbanan*. One would have thought he would have been embarrassed by the incident, and learned his lesson, but at *minchah* he was also late and even had the *chutzpah* to snatch the *tallit* off the *sheliach tzibur* in the middle of *Ashrei*, because, in his eyes, he had the right to be *shatz*!

Of course some people never can get anywhere on time and even miss their plane, but Mordechai is not like that. I once had to see him on a business matter and we arranged to meet at two o'clock. It was the day of the bomb scare and the traffic in town was completely snarled up. Because of that, I left my car and walked to his office. I knew it would only take twenty minutes because I had to walk that way to the hospital on *Shabbat* when our Yitzy was born. So I allowed myself half an hour to get there but, despite that, I was about five minutes late for the appointment. You should have heard the way he went on about how I would have been on time if I had really wanted the contract! If I remember correctly, his words were, "When something really matters, one always meets a deadline."

Though that time it was a pure *ones*, I have noticed how people generally do leave things to the last moment. The way some people drive home from the *mikveh* on *erev Shabbat*, it is a *nes* that there are not more accidents. If they went five minutes earlier, they would not be in such a mad rush. They seem to be more afraid of not getting out of their cars before *bein hashem-ashot* than knocking someone down, *chas veshalom*. It is all part of the tendency to think only of oneself and not consider what one's actions will do to others.

Having just made it home in time, these gentlemen usually rush into shul late and start *davening* right by the door, blocking the way for anyone else. This almost seems to have become their *makom kavua* as they are almost always *davening* there. When there, their piety is on such a high level that they spend well over ten minutes on *Shemoneh Esrei*. Their lack of consideration is hardly *midat chassidut*, but, rather, they form a *"bur" birshut harabbim*!

Of course there will always be occasions when someone is late for a genuine reason and I suppose one should try to be *melamed zechut* on everyone, but it seems as though it is always the same people who come precisely ten minutes late, whether it is *shacharit*, *minchah*, or *ma'ariv*, weekdays, *Shabbat* or *Yom Tov*, which makes this very difficult.

Generally speaking, I have noticed that those who *daven* a very long *Shemoneh Esrei* do not appreciate the problems they can cause their neighbors, especially if the latter know the *halachot* concerning sitting within their *daled amot*. We all know Yossi Weiss is absolutely genuine in his *davening* and can't help taking so long, but the *gabbai* should move him further away from old Mr. Levy, who finds it very hard to stand so long. I am sure if someone told Yossi about the *tza'ar* he is causing, he would be shocked, but he is so immersed in his *davening* that he just does not know what is going on around him. When I asked our *rav*, he said that starting one's own quiet *Shemoneh Esrei* with *chazarat hashatz* is definitely not preferable to missing out parts of *Pesukei deZimra* in order to start it with the *tzibur*, quite apart from disturbing everyone else by loudly *davening* earlier parts of the *tefillah*, which one could have skipped to do so.

If everyone took this to heart and did not leave things to the last moment then they would find life so much less stressful. Rushing around all the time is counterproductive in the long run, and it is doubtful whether anything very useful is achieved in the minutes that are "saved." Unfortunately, I suppose that this trait is just human nature and it would require a lot of self-discipline to overcome it.

Of course all these considerations do not make life for you as *sheliach tzibur* any easier, but perhaps these trials are all part of the process of coming to terms with one's *aveilut* and help in the long run.

Your friend,
Moshe

SHUL ETIQUETTE

Dear Chaim,

We were all so happy to welcome you back from what we had thought was a business trip and discover that your Yossi had become a *chatan*. My cousin tells me that the *kallah* taught two of his daughters and they thought the world of her. Considering the way children sometimes talk of their teachers, Rivkah must be an exceptional girl; your Yossi is a very fortunate young man. It all goes to show that it is possible to achieve such a high *madreigah* despite having grown up in a small provincial community and having had to go away from home to school at such an early age.

Your new *mechutan* is also a remarkable person in building up his *kehillah* despite being far away from the centers of Yiddishkeit. I have often been there on business and seen the level of Yiddishkeit rising over the years, and I am sure it is entirely due to his influence. It is easy for us to live a life of Torah and *mitzvot* when everyone else seems to be doing so; it is quite a different matter where such a lifestyle is not taken for granted among the people with whom one mixes. That he should have been *zocheh* to have all his children grow up with such *yirat shamayim* and *midot tovot* would be a credit even to someone living in a 100% frum environment. If only there were more young *rabbanim* like him with a charismatic personality who are able to be *mekarev* people, the situation in Anglo-Jewry would be transformed.

Still it must have come as quite a culture shock for you to *daven* in a shul where almost everyone is there to say *Kaddish*. Of course, the time they finish *shacharit* is really too late for any-one who has to get to work, so it is not entirely surprising that the only other people present were retired gentlemen. It makes a change from having to search for someone who is prepared to be *sheliach tzibur*! It must have been quite a novel experience to hear how each one rattled off the *Kaddeishim* with no regard for the others, so that it was impossible for anyone to hear and an-swer *Amein, yehei shemeih rabba* to any of them – a real case of *trei kalei lo mishtamei*.

You were lucky that there were so few of them who could act as *sheliach tzibur* so that you had a chance to have the *amud* a few times while you were there. Still it must have been quite difficult for you to *daven* at their speed after what you are used to here. As your *mechutan* said, he is still working on getting them to take a little longer, at least for *Shema* and *Shemoneh Esrei*, but it is very difficult in such a community. I suppose that is why he does not expect them to wait for him before starting *chazarat hashatz* in the mornings. It was fortunate that you were not offered the *amud* at the first *shacharit* so you had a chance to find out their "time-table." Your *mechutan* once confided to me that he always dreaded when he had *yahrzeit* and had to *daven* at their speed, but he felt he had no choice. It is this sort of sensitivity to his congregation that has been largely responsible for his success so far. Perhaps in a few years time they will also want to *daven* at his pace.

What you say about the gentleman who had yahrzeit stay-ing for the shiur after *minchah* to say the *kaddish derabanan* and then walking out before *maariv*, joking that he would be "back again next year," was really disgraceful and just shows the warped sense of values of some people, as though Torah and *mitzvot* are restricted to *maftir* and *niftar*! Still if it gives them some vestigial connection with Yiddishkeit, one should be grateful; who knows that without it they might even have married out.

They seem to have some minhagim that we could very well copy. The idea of saying *Tehillim*, starting five minutes before *davening*, is an excellent idea. I have always found our *minhag* of saying them at the end not to be very good, as people tend to be in a hurry. As a result, they walk out in the middle, which looks as if they do not care to *daven* for the *cholim* that, even if not true, is unfortunate. It has the added bonus that they do have a minyan in shul for *berachot*, which they probably would not have had otherwise. I have read that saying *Tehillim* before *davening* improves one's *kavanah*, which is an added bonus for those who manage to come early enough.

Unfortunately, I can see our *ba'alei batim* objecting to such a change in the *minhag* they are used to. On the other hand, calling out the names of the people for whom the *Tehillim* are being said and why they need our *tefillot* seems an excellent practice. It is so much easier to *daven* for someone if one has a name and *matzav* in mind, even if one does not know him or her personally. Perhaps you could suggest that we introduce it. Nobody can object that that would be a change in our *minhag hamokom*.

At least now that you are back, you can *daven* at your usual pace once again. You must have been really upset about the disappearance of your *siddur* while you were away. After all, it had belonged to your grandfather, *a"h*, and he had given it to you, just before his final illness. Whoever took it out of your desk did a big *avlah*, as *chazal* say, *hashoel shelo mida 'at harei hu gazlan*, "someone who borrows an object without permission is a thief." At the very least he should have put it back afterwards, *veheishiv et hagezeilah asher gazal*, "and he shall return that which he has stolen," as the Torah commands us.

It is not as though we do not have enough *siddurim* in shul! The way they are left around makes the shul sometimes look as though it had been hit by a hurricane. I often wonder if those responsible would put up with such a terrible mess in their own homes. Someone once said that the first thing one should learn from a *mussar sefer* is to put it back when one has finished with it. Then at least one's *chaver* will be able to find it easily. At least this time your lost *siddur* was soon found.

Aveilut is in itself a stressful time and little irritations like the loss of a *siddur* can get magnified out of all proportion in one's mind. I only hope that Yossi's engagement will be an end to all *tza'ar* for you and you should go *miyagon lesimchah, me'eivel leyom tov.* May we all be *zocheh* to the ultimate *simchah* of *biat goel tzedek bimheirah veyamenu.*

Your friend,
Moshe

HOW TO RUN A *MINYAN*

Dear Chaim,

Congratulations on your election as our *gabbai* for the next year. Obviously our members must have confidence in you. They must have noticed how, during your year of *aveilut,* you were always in *shul* early and ready to start *davening* on time, even the time your wife was in the hospital. At the time everyone said that it would have been understandable if you had been late; after all, you have quite a few small children at home, *kein ayin hara.*

We have not really had a capable *gabbai* since Reb Nachman was *niftar* over ten years ago. Somehow Reb Nachman seemed to have the knack of keeping everyone happy. I hope you will be as successful. Reb Nachman was always there, with his *tallit* and *tefillin* on, at least ten minutes before the official starting time so that he could start if nobody else wanted to. In his time everything ran like clockwork.

At least while you were an *avel,* Yankel Klotz could rely on you to be on time, but that did not really entitle him to take advantage of you and turn up ten minutes late practically every morning. Unlike you, he does not have any small children at home.

When you were away for a few days when your Yossi got

engaged there was chaos. I don't think that Yankel was on time once. Finding someone to start *berachot* held us up for several minutes each morning and more often than not whoever was pressed to do so would not *daven* any further. On Monday morning we had the same performance at *Yishtabach* as well; the gentleman just walked off, leaving the *siddur* open on the *amud*; did he believe *"mei'eilav yikarei"*? Then Moishe Klein took over, but he had to leave early to take his children to school.

To make matters worse, Yankel gave a visitor *petichah* but did not have the sense to go up with him to show him how to open our a*ron*, so he had to fumble around to find the cord. Yankel had also not thought to tell him which *sefer* to take out. Of course, he took the one we had found was *pasul* the previous Shabbat, but which had not yet been corrected, so Yankel had to run up to tell him to take a different one. By then, the poor fellow was terribly embarrassed. In the end, we were running more than a quarter of an hour late, and by the time we finished there was hardly a *minyan* left in *shul*. Admittedly, it was not quite as bad on the other days.

It is these pointless delays that are so irritating for those who have to be at work on time. A little forethought can easily avoid them. I don't know why our *ba'alei batim* are so loath to *daven* before the *amud*. It is almost as if they are looking forward to someone becoming an *avel, rachmana litzlan*, so that they can "relax."

You must also have noticed that, since we lost Reb Nachman, attendance in the mornings has dropped, as those who have to get to work on time have stopped coming. I hope you will be able to attract them back by setting a more reliable timetable. It is not so much the speed of *davening* that matters so long as it is consistent. If one knows that, for example, we will get to *Barechu* after twenty minutes he can pace himself as he wishes. Unfortunately, you will find that when everything runs smoothly no one will thank you, but should anything go wrong, you will hear about it right away. Some people are very easily offended, so you can expect plenty of *tzores* from your job, almost all of which will be completely unde-served. That is probably why we have had such a rapid turnover of *gabbaim* over the years.

When you feel a bit fed up, you might remember Reb Nachman's favorite story of the fellow who was given *revi'i* and said to the *gabbai, Bei uns gibt man revi'i zu a pferd.* ("Where I come from we give *revi'i* to a horse."). To which the *gabbai* answered, *Bei uns gibt man es zu a eisel!* ("Here we give it to an ass."). I don't think he ever actually said it to anyone but I am sure he must have felt like doing so more than once. Now that he is no longer with us, everyone looks back to the good old days of Reb Nachman and they have long forgotten any disagreements they may have had with him. So you see that so long as no one has any worse complaints than getting *revi'i*, you will be doing a marvelous job.

Wishing you every success in your endeavors to improve the running of our *shul,*

Your friend,

Moshe

Dear Chaim,

Now that you have completed your first month as *gabbai*, you must be getting into the swing of running the *shul*. Things are certainly improving; it makes all the difference that you are always on time to see that we get started though it looks as if you will end up being the *chazan kavua*, at least on weekdays.

I wish I could help you out more often, but, as you know, my business takes me away very frequently. Even when I am in town, I cannot always stay until we finish *davening*, especially when one of our less time-constrained members has the *amud*. Perhaps now that you have put a card on the *amud* with a timetable for *shacharit*, they may not drag things out so much and more people will be able to stay to the end.

Unfortunately, there will always be two factions in every

minyan: those who have to leave by a certain time and those who don't and can therefore spend as long as they like on putting extra *kavanah* into their *tefillot*. The times you allowed for each segment of the *davening* seem to me quite generous, but I am sure you will still get complaints from those who want to put in extra *kavanah*.

Your idea of getting the youngsters to *daven* before the *amud* might mean that at least in the next generation that won't happen. As *chazal* say: *Im ein gediyim ein tayashim*, if there were no kids there would be no goats. Have you noticed how they are coming earlier now in the hope of being asked? They may make a few mistakes at first, but people are more likely to tolerate that in children and, when they are pointed out, they soon learn.

Do you remember when I was in Yerushalayim a few years ago over the *Yamim Noraim* and *Succot*? I *davened* in a small *Yekkishe shul* where, of course, everything ran like clockwork. There is a lot to be said for such quiet efficiency and we could learn from it.

One thing I noticed was that there the *tzibur* did not drown out the *sheliach tzibur*'s *davening*. For example, the *gemara* tells us that in *Hallel* we have a *zecher* of all the forms of *shirah* that were used in the *Beit Hamikdash*. One of these was that one group of *Leviim* would sing a *pasuk* and the second would respond with a set refrain. In *Hallel* this was preserved in the section *Hodu laShem…*, where each *pasuk* was to be said by the *sheliach tzibur*, who was *motzi* the *tzibur*, who responded *Hodu…*each time, as is printed in some older *siddurim*. They still keep that *minhag*, unlike many places where the *tzibur* drowns him out when he says his *pasuk* and has to say it themselves.

You are certainly removing many problems in the running of our *shul*. May we all be *zocheh* to the time when all the *batei kenessiyot* and *batei midrashim* will be transported to Eretz Yisrael with the coming of *Mashiach zidkeinu, bimherah veyameinu*.

Your friend,
Moshe

Dear Chaim,

You have certainly been busy improving the running of our *shul* while I was away. I really like your idea of making little cards to give out to those to whom you want to give matzos. I remember seeing something similar in Yerushalayim when I *davened* in that *Yekkishe shul* a few years ago. They told me that the *minhag* in Germany used to be to give out little silver plates engraved with the various *kibbudim*, which were distributed before *Kriat haTorah*. Apparently it was not uncommon for two people in a *shul* to have the same name and this avoided any confusion when someone was called up. I never was very happy about the way the *gabbai* would go round on *Shabbat* during *chazarat hashatz* to tell people to take *petichah*, or during *Kriat haTorah* to give out *hagbahah* and *gelilah*. Once one starts talking at those times, albeit *beheter*, it is difficult to stop others doing so *be'issur*. It is well known that the *Mechaber* writes that talking during *chazarat hashatz* is *gadol avono min'so*, and many *gedolim* attributed disasters that befell our people due to this particular *aveira*. Unfortunately, *beavonoteinu harabim* it is still all too common.

I must say I like the way you have managed to limit the number of names allowed in *misheberachs*. Some people seem to go overboard and want to mention everyone in *shul*. If one tries to mention all one's friends and misses one, that person is likely to feel offended, so cutting the number of names allowed should, if anything, increase harmony.

If someone wishes to honor specific people with a *misheberach* they could be allowed to do so in a second one provided they offer the *shul* a suitably high donation for each name mentioned. If the charge were high enough it would discourage most people from doing so and, when someone occasionally does insist, the *tzibur* will be *mochel* since the *shul* funds will be benefiting noticeably. In any case, these long lists of names result in people losing interest in what is going on and starting to chat among themselves, which, strictly speaking, is *assur* even *bein gavra legavra*. I have always thought that ending these lists with the phrase *vechol hamitpallelim kan* might imply that one suspected the named persons of not *davening* properly so that they had to be named separately in order to include them. Perhaps it would be preferable to change it to *vechol she'ar hamitpallelim kan*!

Your friend,

Moshe

MAKING YOUR SIMCHAH A SIMCHAH FOR EVERYONE

Dear Chaim,

Your twins' *bar mitzvah* really showed how one can run a *simchah* without inconveniencing the regular *mitpallelim*. Our shul just does not have the space for too many visitors, so asking friends who live locally not to come was a great *chessed*. When some people make a *simchah*, they seem to ask the whole town to come and the place becomes unbearably crowded. I am sure if the fire officer were to turn up on such an occasion, he would close the shul down on safety grounds. It is all right for those who daven in the big shuls that are empty most of the year to invite all their friends, but in smaller *battei midrash* like ours it is not really very clever.

It was a *mechaye* that you managed not to make any *hosafot* even if that meant you did not get an *aliyah* yourself. It was particularly difficult that week with so many other *chiyuvim,* so your self-sacrifice was even more appreciated. If only other people would also consider the rest of the *tzibur*! Why should they make their *simchah* at the expense of everyone else's *tsa'ar*? At the reception, your *shver* told me that he had insisted on not having an *aliyah* for the same reason; at least your efforts on our behalf did not cause any friction in your family.

Making your reception after *minchah* in your house was a brilliant idea. I always felt that *kiddushim* on Shabbat morning raise too many problems. Do you remember the Shabbat before last when there were three bar mitzvahs and four *aufrufs*? Some men did not get home until almost two o'clock. It was not fair on their poor wives who were cooped up with toddlers all that time.

161

By the time they came home they had eaten so much that they could not manage to eat their Shabbat seudah. What that does for *shalom bayit* I hate to think! Of course everyone is hungry after *davening*, but the way some men gorge themselves they probably are *mechuyav* to bensch, though I have not seen anyone do so. On the other hand, my wife tells me that most women hardly eat anything at a *kiddush*, so they may not be *yotzei kiddush* because they have not eaten a *kezayit mezonot* to make it *bemakom se'udah*. At this time of year when Shabbat goes out so late, I think people really enjoy the chance to have such a social gathering later in the day. Similarly, in the winter, one could make a reception on *motza'ei Shabbat*, which also avoids these problems. It also means that if one invites people who may not be *shomer Shabbat* one does not have to worry that one might be putting a *michshol lifnei iver*.

Everyone commented that your "at home" was really enjoyable. It goes to show that one does not have to make an overly elaborate affair. The way some people go overboard with a *simchah* is incredible; it is as if they want to be that much more impressive than anyone else and are willing to go to any expense to do so, even if they can't really afford it.

Your *simchah* showed that it was possible for everyone to share your happy event without being forced to take out a second mortgage. Sometimes I wish that the *rabbanim* would put a limit on what is allowed; that has been tried in the past when they had greater control than nowadays, but it never worked because the wealthy ignored their restrictions. The only sanction would be for them to refuse to attend a function that was overly lavish, but it would be difficult to risk offending their most prominent *ba'alei battim*.

The biggest expense is the *seudah*, and I think that you were quite right to limit that to your immediate family. I only hope that you may set a new trend and break the escalating size and cost. Once this has been controlled, it will be possible to put on a slightly more elaborate reception and, like you did, invite the whole *kehillah* to participate. The extra cost will be comparatively small and, as we saw at your twins' *bar mitzvah*, is enjoyed by everyone. Also in a less formal context, one can mix more freely whereas, at a formal *seudah*, one is "stuck" at a table with people with whom one may have little in common.

Some people make their sons' *bar mitzvah* celebrations seem like a wedding and when their daughter gets married, it might as well be a coronation banquet. Of course, everyone is entitled to do what they like with their own money, but the amount of food that simply gets thrown away is pure *bal tashchit*. That makes it very difficult for those who cannot really afford such ostentation yet do not want to seem cheap by comparison with what has become the norm in their social circle.

May you be *zocheh* to make many more such simchas together with your family in the future, until the ultimate *simchah* of the coming of *Mashiach bimherah veyameinu.*

Your friend,
Moshe

FOR EVERYTHING THERE IS A TIME

Dear Chaim,

Many thanks for your letter, which arrived two weeks ago. I must apologize for the delay in my reply, but I have been out of town on business and only came back just before *Shabbat.*

At this time of the year we all try to accumulate extra *mitzvot* and give extra *tzedakah*, but I think you were quite right to be upset over that incident with the *meshullach*. Unfortunately, it was not so atypical. After all, he should have seen that you had just put on your *tefillin shel yad* and were about to put on your *shel rosh*. A donation for his *yeshivah* could have waited an extra minute. A similar thing happened to me once when I was about to say *Shema* with my hand over my eyes and someone shouted, "*hachnassos kallah*," down my ear. It completely destroyed my *kavanah*. Admittedly, he would have had to wait a bit longer than in your case, but that hardly excuses such behavior.

We all realize the time constraints *meshullachim* work under, but that does not justify soliciting funds at such inappropriate times. I consulted our *rav* about this some years ago and he assured me that there is no obligation to interrupt one's *tefillah* for them. We might say in our *yamim noraim tefillot*: *uteshuvah utefillah utzedakah ma'avirin et ro'a hagezerah*, "repentance, prayer and charity annul the evil decree," but, to paraphrase *chazal, zeman tefillah lechud uzeman tzedakah lechud*, "there is a time for prayer and a time for charity." I suppose that we must be grateful that not all *meshullachim* show so little sensitivity in these matters.

Of course, if it were a case of *pikuach nefesh* it would be different, but I have never seen anyone who was about to collapse from starvation collecting in shul. In such a situation a monetary donation would probably be too late, and a gift of some food would be more appropriate. I wonder what would happen if one offered a particularly obstreperous *meshullach* a sweet to help him survive until the end of *davening*!

I once saw a gentleman who had a little card on his desk during *davening*, which he pointed out to anyone who tried to talk to him. I think it read something like:

בס"ד

"העוסק במצווה פטור מן המצווה"

Unfortunately I cannot attend to you at
present so unless it is a case of

פקוח נפש ממש

please come back

after

חזרת הש"ץ

והקדיש שלאחרי'

"זמן תפילה לחוד וזמן צדקה לחוד"

I have always wondered how this problem has come about. Perhaps it all goes back to when they were children and were encouraged to go round with a *pushke* during *chazarat hashatz*. Thank G-d we don't have that *minhag* in our shul, but it is quite common, despite the fact that the *Pri Megadim* writes so strongly against it. He should have understood the bad effect it would have on children, since he always described himself as a *makrei dardekei*, an elementary-school teacher. I have quite often seen that people ask for change or even crack a joke with the child. Obviously, children learn from this practice that *chazarat hashatz* is not so terribly important and one can talk then. They do not realize the severity of the prohibition, which the *Shulchan Aruch* describes as *gadol avono minso*, "his sin is greater than he can bear." I suppose for people who chat anyway, a charitable donation may be a palliative, a sort of *pidyon* for their *aveirah*, but it can only be a second best to giving undivided attention to the *sheliach tzibur*. However, the children should be told in no uncertain terms not to rattle the *pushke*, since this can be very distracting to those who are trying to concentrate.

On the other hand, where this custom is firmly established, it would be difficult to abolish. If everyone knows about it, they can have a coin ready in advance and avoid any distraction, but the same cannot be said of the many *meshullachim* who turn up. It would be best if a notice barring them at such times was put outside the shul door and the *gabbaim* ensured that they did not disturb the *mitpallelim* at such inappropriate times.

There is another custom of collecting after *kriat haTorah*, which is in my opinion infinitely preferable. One *shul* I went to on one of my business trips had this custom, and it worked well for many years. Then they decided that they could raise more money by collecting every day. In order to avoid *chazarat hashatz*, they sent a child round during *Ashrei* on other days despite the *Pri Megadim*'s reservations. It did not take long before the children forgot the original custom and collected then also on Mondays and Thursdays. I am sure the extra amount collected did not justify the disturbance caused. People do not realize the importance of *Ashrei*, whose recitation three times a day, *Chazal* tell us, assures us of a place in the world to come.

One incident I witnessed struck me quite forcefully as to how this *minhag* taught the children not to appreciate the importance of *tefillah*. It happened one Sunday morning that one of them noticed that the *pushke* was not in its usual place, having been put away in the cupboard under the *amud* over *Shabbat*, and tried to extract it during *chazarat hashatz*, seeming not even to be aware that he might be disturbing the *sheliach tzibur* in the middle of his *davening*.

Of course this observation does not apply to *meshullachim* who, in any case, do not come to *daven*. After all, they need some time in which to collect, and talking during *Ashrei* and *Uva leTzion* is a less serious matter than during *chazarat hashatz*. Similarly, one can hardly object to their collecting during *Pesukei deZimra* especially since there is a custom, according to the *Arizal*, to give *tzedakah* when one reaches *Vayevarech David*. They should, however, realize that one cannot talk during *Pesukei deZimra*, and always have change ready should someone not have available the precise amount he wishes to donate. I have not infrequently had problems with *meshullachim* who did not do so and could not understand why I had to gesture to them to that effect, demanding that I tell them verbally what I wanted even when I pointed into my *siddur* to show him why I was silent. However, from *Barechu* until after *chazarat hashatz*, when one should have even greater concentration, it would be more appropriate if they desisted from disturbing the *tzibur*. Whether they should approach the *sheliach tzibur* at all is another matter; after all, the latter is the agent of the congregation and should not interrupt his duties for any reason, any more than an employee may undertake personal affairs during work time.

Perhaps the *teshuvah*, answer, to those who put giving money to charity above all else by saying *tsedakah tatsil mimavet*, "charity saves from death," is that through *tefillah* one becomes a true *ben olam haba*, one who really merits eternal life.

Your friend,
Moshe

A MAN DOES NOT EVEN KNOW HIS TIME

Dear Chaim,

Many thanks for your letter. I can appreciate how busy you must be, so don't feel bad about the delay in replying to me. What you write about the developments in our *kehillah* always makes me feel part of it even when I am away on these long jobs, but that is the disadvantage of my profession. Still, I will be back for Yom Tov.

What you write about your guests on that Friday evening coming so late really upset me. Even if they did not want to *daven* with you they should at least have gone somewhere that did not finish any later. To keep you waiting for almost two hours was disgraceful. Even if the shul they went to had decided at the last moment to arrange a *derashah* after *ma'ariv*, I am sure the speaker would have understood if some people might have to leave, especially as their families would not have been aware of the change of program. After all, some people have small children at home who can't be blamed for getting restless when their dinner is delayed for so long. I suppose there must be people who have never heard that *derech eretz kadmah laTorah*. We have had similar experiences in the past on several occasions. I remember when my Yitzy was a baby we invited some youngsters for a Friday night dinner. We made a point of telling them that our shul brought in Shabbat early with *plag haminchah* in the summer and told them when we would be *davening*. After about an hour's wait we decided they must have made a mistake with the week and started without them. They showed up just as we were serving the soup which was, of course, only lukewarm by then.

On another occasion when a guest did not turn up for Shabbat lunch, we found that she had been taken ill overnight and had no way of letting us know. So you see that it is not always their fault. However, since that occasion I have made a point of telling guests about it and saying that if they have not turned up within quarter of an hour of the time we have told them we plan to eat, we will assume that they will not be coming after all. The Gemara writes

(Niddah 16a) that there is a *chazakah* of *oreach bizmano ba*, "a guest comes on time," but I suppose that this is yet another case of *nishtaneh hativim*, a change in the nature of things.

While on the subject of time-keeping, I must say how much we enjoyed your Yossi's wedding. It was marvellous that the *chupah* was not late and that, at the dinner, people were washing within a quarter of an hour of the time on the invitation. It must have given some of our "*heimishe chevra*" a bit of a shock when they came in and found the *chatan* and *kallah* had already arrived and everyone was enjoying the main course.

The same happened when our Leah got married because so many of the *chatan*'s side had come from out of town and had nothing to hold them up. Afterwards, my *mechutan* told me how grateful their friends were that we finished at a reasonable hour and that they did not have to drive home as dawn was breaking. Still, I can't understand why so many people bother to give a time when they don't expect anyone to even turn up until at least an hour later. I must admit that I was tempted to put 7.28 PM instead of 7.30 on our Leah's wedding invitation so that people would realize we meant the time, but my wife was afraid that it would not help and, in any case, people would simply laugh at it. I hope that when it comes to our Rachel's wedding they will remember what happened at Leah's and not be so late, but I suppose that would be a case of *hilchata demeshicha*.

Of course, there are always going to be some people who cannot come at the set time. For example, Rabbi Kahan gives the *daf hayomi shiur* every evening until half-past nine. He gets invited to so many weddings that it would be impossible for him to get someone to stand in for him every time. Also, sometimes people have problems getting small children settled or are let down by the babysitter coming late, but that can't apply to the vast majority. I think that people just assume that nothing will happen on time and act accordingly.

On one occasion, I was also late for an out-of-town wedding but that was because the people who kindly offered me a lift did not seem to value punctuality at all. I must say that I was terribly embarrassed and I can only hope that our hosts assumed that we were delayed by an accident on the highway or something similar. In reality, we were late because my driver chose to visit some friends instead of proceeding directly to the hall. When I tried tactfully to suggest that this was not the most perfect example of *derech eretz*, since I knew that the *ba'al simchah* was rather a *yekkishe* person, I was rather shocked by the driver's reply that, "we must show these people that they should not be so particular." Even if our hosts had been obsessive about being punctual, it is not for a guest to upset them and spoil their *simchah*.

I am glad you followed the advice of the Sassover Rebbe z"l and restricted the dancing to when the *chatan* and *kallah* came in, and after *sheva berachot*. I am sure the caterer's staff appreciated not having to go home after midnight for once. I remember once when we went to a *chatunah* out of town and the *chatan*'s family arranged a bus for their friends. Because of the late start, and prolonged dancing between courses, the whole proceedings dragged on and, eventually the bus driver told us he was leaving in five minutes, so we were forced to leave in the middle of the main course. I know that *al pi din* one must stay until the end of *sheva berachot*, but under the circumstances, we really had no alternative.

Unfortunately, time-keeping is generally perceived to be restricted to a few eccentrics, so I doubt if we will see any great improvement in the near future. Still, you have made the effort and it is just possible that the so-called "Jewish Mean Time" will eventually approximate more closely the times on invitations. In the *zechut* of greater punctuality, may we merit the coming of *Mashiach bimherah veyamenu*, which *HaShem* has promised *be'itah achishenah*.

Your friend,
Moshe

GIVE HONOR TO THE TORAH!

Dear Chaim,

Many thanks for your letter. The incidents you mention unfortunately show how we allow ourselves to feel too at home in shul and do not always give it proper respect. When one reads what the *Shulchan Aruch* writes *lehalachah* about *kavod Beit HaKnesset* (*o.c.* 151:1), one cannot but understand the truth of the words of the *Semak*, which the *Magen Avraham* quotes: "Because of this sin, synagogues were converted to houses of idol worship," *r"l*.

This is quite apart from the terrible sin of talking during *davening*, which the *Mechaber* describes as *gadol avono minso*, "his sin is greater than he can bear" (*o.c.* 124:7 *cf.* Gen.4:13). Our *Gedolim* have said that many of the disasters that have befallen our people could possibly be traced back to this, so much so that the *Tosefot Yom Tov* went so far as to compose a special *Mi sheberach* for those who "guard their mouth and tongue from talking during the time of *davening*."

It is unfortunately all too common in smaller *batei midrash* to see the *bimah* used as a dumping place for *siddurim*, etc., and many people even leave their *tallit* bags on it. People seem not to realize that it is the place from which the *sefer* Torah is read and has, therefore, the status of *tashmishei kedushah*. It is even doubtful if the *gabbai* is allowed to lean on it during *Kriat haTorah*. In the big *shuls*, where the *bimah* is raised and enclosed, this happens less often because it is less easily accessible, but this only puts a greater responsibility on those who *daven* in the *shtieblach* to be more careful.

The *Sefer Chassidim* (262) even writes, "Where it says that one should not always point out people's wrongdoings because it is better that *Yisrael* should sin unintentionally rather than intentionally, this does not apply to behavior in *shul*."

There are several old *minhagim* associated with *Kriat haTorah* that are intended to impress on us the honor we should always give a *sefer* Torah as containing the words of *HaShem*. For example, when one is given an *aliyah*, one should always go up quickly, and by the shortest route, to show one's eagerness to read its words. On the other hand, on returning to one's seat, one should go slowly, and by the longest route, to show one's regret at leaving its company. Some people even run on their way up, but even those who do not go quite so far in this *hiddur*, should go up promptly on being called. It is certainly not right to delay to talk to one's friends on the way.

Similarly, what you say you saw during *Kriat haTorah* was certainly incorrect and the *gabbai* had no right to complain that you were being overly *frum* when you drew his attention to it. There is a *minhag* that someone should hold on to the *eitz chaim*, the spindle on which the *sefer* Torah is rolled, when it is lying on the *bimah*, at least when it is not covered by a *mappah*. This is based on the *pasuk: Eitz chaim hi lemachazikim bah vetomecheha meushar*, "It is a tree of life to those who take hold of and happy are those who support it" (Ps. 3:18), which we say when we return it to the *aron*.

It is also proper that the *mappah* cover it when it is not being read (*o.c.* 139:5), because of *kavod haTorah* as the *Mishnah Berurah*, writes (*s.k.* 22). Though he rules that this applies only when there is a long interval, such as for a *Mi sheberach* (*s.k.* 21), this does not mean that one should *not* cover it at other times; he only wanted to be *melamed zechut* on those who did not cover it for shorter intervals because of *tircha detzibura*. So, when the *gabbai* told his son not to put the *mappah* over the *sefer* Torah while the person who had *shelishi* said his *berachah*, and wait until the *shatz* said *kaddish*, he was certainly wrong, even according to the *Mishnah Berurah*.

There is also a *minhag* that those who had *hagbahah* and *gelilah* should accompany the *sefer* Torah when it is taken back to the *aron hakodesh*, and wait in front of it until it is closed, to show honor to the Torah. I have noticed that many people do not bother to do so, especially on a *Shabbat* or *Yom Tov* when more than one *sefer* is used. Perhaps one might be *melamed zechut* on them if there were not enough room on the *bimah* for so many people to wait, but this hardly applies on days when only one *sefer* is used. By not following this *minhag*, they are implicitly showing disrespect to the Torah, *r"l*.

A few weeks ago, when I was on business in New York and had to stay over *Shabbat*, I *davened* in a shul where they made a detour with the *sefer* Torah to take it to their *rav*. I have seen it done in several other *shuls* in the course of my travels, and always thought it showed a lack of respect. When I returned, I discussed it with our *rav*, and he told me it was definitely an incorrect custom and showed me a *Tzitz Eliezer* (12:40) to that effect. He said that such a detour could only possibly be justified for a handicapped person, but even that situation was not ideal.

Chazal tell us that the second *Beit HaMikdash* was destroyed because the people did not give sufficient honor to the Torah and that it will be restored when we rectify this fault. Through *kavod haTorah vehaTefillah* may we soon be worthy to see its restoration and the end of this long *golus*. Then the words of the *navi* will be fulfilled: "Behold the days are coming, says *HaShem*, when it will no longer be said '*HaShem* lives Who has brought the Children of Israel out of the land of Egypt' but '*HaShem* lives Who has brought the Children of Israel out of the land of the north and from all the lands where He has driven them,' and I will bring them again into their land which I gave their fathers" (Jer. 16:14–15) *beviat goel tzedek bimhera beyameinu*.

Your friend,
Moshe

DON'T BE OVERLY PIOUS –
AT OTHER PEOPLE'S EXPENSE!

Dear Chaim,

Many thanks for your letter. It was really not fair of Aryeh Ze'ev to hold up the *davening* the way you describe, especially on *Rosh Chodesh* when it would finish late anyway; I can understand how irritated everyone must have felt. You say that at least fifteen people had finished *Shemoneh Esrei* before he did and you had told him so. Why could he not have taken your word for it? After all, one does not have to be a professor of mathematics to count to ten.

Under the circumstances, he should have started *chazarat hashatz* and not insisted on counting for himself and then claim he could only see eight. When he delays starting *chazarat hashatz* so long, some people get fed up waiting and go out to read the notice boards and then, of course, they are not there for him to count when he finishes.

As you say, he could not see Mr. Katz, who was already sitting down at the back of the *shul*, but that would only reduce the number to fourteen, which would have been more than enough for him to start. I suspect he did not want to count the boys who were recently *bar mitzvah*. I suppose he was worried in case they had not yet brought *shtei se'arot*! Perhaps he also did not want to count old Mr. Levy who has a hearing aid, in case he only heard the *berachot* through it and not directly. The trouble with him is that since he came into that large *yerushah*, he has forgotten that most people do have to get to work on time and just are not free to spend as long on their *davening* as they might like.

I remember that something similar happened a few years ago when he also had *yahrzeit* and he would not start *chazarat hashatz* when the *rav* finished his *Shemoneh Esrei* and waited until he was satisfied that he had nine people to answer him, even though almost everyone had already finished. You know how long our *rav* takes! At least that time it was on a Sunday morning at the end of *Nissan* when there was no *tachanun*, so we were not in quite such a hurry. At the time I thought that it was not very respectful to the *rav*, but he is such an *anav* that he had not realized how slowly he had *davened*. Aryeh Ze'ev said to me at the time that he did not really like to start *chazarat hashatz* until there were over twenty people to answer because, in his opinion, at least half the *tzibur* do not seem to pay enough attention to be counted. Unfortunately, if one thinks along such lines, one might as well abolish *chazarat hashatz* completely.

Of course, he is right that the *mechaber* (*Orach Chaim* 124:4) writes that unless nine people answer *amen* to the *sheliach tzibur*, his *berachot* are almost *levatalah* and he wanted to avoid that at all costs, but that it is really more a duty for the *tzibur* to pay attention than an *aveirah* for the *ba'al tefillah*. I have always wondered how this can be reconciled with the long-established practice in many communities to start *chazarat hashatz* when only *rov minyan* have finished their *Shemoneh Esrei*. I suppose that the fact that six have completely finished indicates that at least four more will be saying *Elokai netzor* and so be able to answer *amen* by the time the *sheliach tzibur* gets to *Magen Avraham*. The same must be the case when one starts when the *rav* steps back without counting how many others are also ready, unless he is considered like Eliezer for these purposes (Rashi on Gen.14:14). Otherwise it might be a case of *Vesalachata la'avoni ki "rav" hu*! However, I saw somewhere a suggestion that the *sheliach tzibur* should make a *tenai* before starting his *Shemoneh Esrei* that it be a *tefillat nedavah* if he thinks that less than nine people would answer his *berachot*.

At least he did not tell you that he wanted to wait for *rov minyan* and that less than half the *tzibur* had finished their quiet *Shemoneh Esrei*. You would be surprised how many people make this mistake and think that the word *minyan* means the same as *tzibur*, making *rov minyan* a *chumrah* instead of a *kullah*.

To be fair to Aryeh Ze'ev, one must remember that he is very particular about all *mitzvot* and tries to avoid the possibility of anything less than the optimum way of performing them, something for which he also wants to give others the opportunity. He once said that he tried to give people who came late a chance to catch up in time for *kedushah*; he seemed to be unaware that they should miss out parts of *Pesukei deZimra* and, if they chose not to, then their loss was their own fault.

Furthermore, I suspect he adds into his *Shemoneh Esrei* his own private *techinot*, which also makes it take much longer. I once asked the *rav* about this and he told me that this was certainly not allowed because of *tircha detzibura*. In fact he confided that when he *davened* before the *amud* on a *yahrzeit*, he even missed out *Elokai netzor* so as not to keep the *tzibur* waiting. Unfortunately, there seems to have been a problem of reconciling Aryeh Ze'ev's scrupulous attitude with the needs of the *tzibur*. Perhaps he should have remembered that the *sheliach tzibur* is the messenger of the congregation and has to act in accordance with their wishes even if he holds a more stringent view on the matter; after all, we have the principle *chazakah sheliach oseh shelichuto*!

This is something we need to take to heart particularly at this time of year, as we approach the *Yamim Noraim*; after all, *Yom Kippur* only atones for sins committed against the Almighty, not for any wrongs done to our fellow man. Of what use are our *tefillot* if taking on extra *chumrot* leads to other people's suffering?

So being extra-punctilious in our *davening* may be counter-productive if it causes distress to others. As Reb Yisroel Salanter put it: "One should not be overly pious at other people's expense."

Your friend,
Moshe

VE'AL TITOSH TORAT IMECHA

Dear Chaim,

What you write about the events in shul is really worrying and it upsets me that I have been forced to be away on business for such a long time at this crucial juncture and, therefore, unable to take an active role. It would appear that it is being taken over by some "Young Turks" who are determined to change its nature. It was founded by refugees from Germany to preserve their distinctive traditions, yet this seems to mean very little to them.

The Jews in the smaller Jewish communities in Germany before the war were simple, if not particularly learned people of great piety whose loyalty to Jewish tradition was very deep-rooted.

It expressed itself in the meticulous preservation of its minhagim, especially the traditional niggunim for the different seasons of the year, which added so much color to the davening. Such familiar tunes evoked a deep echo in the souls of these simple folk – something not appreciated by those unfamiliar with their traditions.

It is not surprising that the Rema (Hil. Yom HaKippurim, O.H. 619:1) writes that it is forbidden to change such local customs, *even the niggunim*! The Rema recognized how important niggunim were to keep the unlearned close to Yiddishkeit. This ruling is based on the *Sefer Maharil* (Machon Yerushalayim edition, pp. 339–340), which recorded how once, when the Maharil made some, to him justifiable, minor change in the custom of Regensburg, he was punished, as he himself recognized, by the death of his daughter.

What I find quite difficult to understand is why the "modernizers" are so opposed to the traditional *niggunim*. I would have thought that, though they might have had no significance to them, they would have been prepared to leave them alone. If one comes to a strange shul and hears a *niggun* with which one is unfamiliar, the normal reaction is to note the difference, not treat it as some sort of existential threat to oneself. Since the *niggunim* are important to the original membership, any reasonable person would not wish to upset them over what, to him, is a relatively unimportant matter.

Unfortunately, it has been fashionable in certain circles to look down on the so-called *Yekkes* and their distinctive minhagim, so much so that many of their descendants have become alienated from that ancient tradition.

This is a terrible shame. It makes no sense to squabble over which tradition has a superior status, let alone to despise those of others. People are different and being different doesn't have to be better or worse. Different is just that – different. It is these small differences that add color to life. Imagine an artist's palette with a variety of paints through the judicious use of which he can produce a work of great beauty, yet, if they are all mixed together, they indeed produce a uniform color, but it is a muddy brown completely useless for the purpose.

However, changes will inevitably occur – this is typical of all human activities. One has only to look at the way languages develop over the centuries to realize this; after all, Anglo-Saxon is unintelligible to most modern English speakers. Yet these changes have been taking place over 1,000 years and the number occurring in any one generation has always been small. Since some changes are inevitable, perhaps one should consider what criteria should apply. Obviously, the primary one is that they are halachically permitted; there can be no question of allowing, for example, mixed seating or playing an organ, but I very much doubt if the "reformers" have anything like that in mind.

You mention that one of their first innovations was to cut out the *selichot* on Yom Kippur, ostensibly because the day was rather short that year. I took the opportunity of meeting Dayan Scwartz from Yerushalaim at a simchah the other day and took the liberty to ask him about it. He was appalled, and said every effort should be made to have them reinstated. He said that the *Minchat Yitzchak* (vol. 8, no. 1) held that important minhagim could simply not be altered, especially if there were any objectors. The reason that most congregations hailing from Eastern Europe do not say them is really quite revealing. It was entirely the fault of the printers who found the large variety of customs as to which ones to say too much trouble and merely inserted at the appropriate point in their editions of the machzor, "Here one says *selichot*." The editions produced in Germany by Sachs and Heidenheim, on the other hand, did print all of them, suitably numbered, so that each congregation could say those to which it was accustomed. That was also our custom and each year a sheet would be distributed giving the numbers of those to be said, more when the day was longer and fewer when it was shorter, so that the davening would continue all day without a break.

Later I decided to ask about the criteria for changing minhagim and was given the following interesting psak: where a minhag is based on an opinion in the Shulchan Aruch, it cannot be changed even if most *kehillot* follow alternative ones. A typical example was a shul where only the *Shatz* says *Nekadesh* at the beginning of Kedushah, it could not change to the more common practice of the *tzibur* saying it either before or with him. However, where the minhag seemed not to have any source in the halachic literature, there was more flexibility.

All this must depend on the change being acceptable to the overwhelming majority of active members, not merely those who pay a membership subscription, but hardly ever attend, and those wishing to make the changes should make every effort to persuade objectors of their desirability. The Magen Avrohom (O.H. 619, s.k. 7) points out how changes tend to confuse the congregation and can only lead to discord in such circumstances. They should certainly not be forced through over their heads by packing the meeting with those occasional attenders with no real interest, who have been asked to come to counter the opposition of "troublemakers," as seems to have been the case in our shul.

It is up to those who wish to make changes to justify them since there is a general principle of *shev ve'al taaseh adif*. In particular, they must show that they should be overwhelmingly beneficial and will not cause any problems, or at least the latter would be insignificant, relative to the benefits.

The one reason I find unacceptable is the wish to obliterate any distinctive traditions in order to be like "everyone else." In my opinion, diversity is valuable and even if a certain "style" is currently less popular, it should not be abandoned since fashions change and what may now be unfashionable might become fashionable again at a later date. If it is destroyed now, then it will be virtually impossible for later generations to revive.

There was *din* Torah in Johannesburg some years ago over precisely this sort of attempt to make the shul more similar to "everyone else" and the *psak* was that so long as they remained in their original building, they could not make any changes. In a teshuvah (*Igrot Moshe, Orach Chaim* second series, siman 21), Rav Moshe Feinstein discusses a shul where most of the original (Ashkenazi) members had moved out of the area and there had been an influx of new members who davened *nusach* Sefard and wanted to change the shul accordingly. He ruled that this was not permitted so long as even one of the original members objected. So you see that there is some considerable halachic objection to what the "reformers" are doing.

That old Mr. Salzberger should have been driven out for voicing his opposition verges on the criminal. If I am not much mistaken, his late father was a founder of the shul and he was the first child born into the kehillah. The way it was done was absolutely disgraceful – dumping all the contents of his shul desk on his doorstep with a note that he was no longer welcome. The last straw was putting guards at the door to prevent him entering. That is something that has not been done since Yeravam ben Nevat posted guards to prevent his subjects being *oleh regel* because he was afraid they would see he had to stand in the Beit Hamikdash while his rival Rechavam was allowed to sit. It is so sad that people act so childishly when they think that they are not given enough honor. The whole episode suggests a whole new meaning to the words of David Hamelekh (Ps. 19,14) "*Gam mizeidim chasoch avdecha, al yimshlu bi az eitam venikeiti mipesha rav.*"

Mr. Salzberger was absolutely right to take the shul to a *Din Torah* and I am so happy that he won. It is disturbing that those running the shul are refusing to accept the psak of the Beit Din and, even more so, that they should have sent the dayan such a *chutzpadig* reply. Unfortunately, this is a case of *Im ein shotrim, ein shoftim* and, as a consequence, we have the law of the jungle, *kol de'alim gevar.* Let us only hope that they will see sense before the Beit Din gives him a *hetter arkaot* and he takes the case before the civil courts. Still, under the circumstances, he has little alternative even though their stubbornness will result in a terrible *chillul HaShem.* The only good that can come of it is that it will serve as a warning to those running other shuls not to abuse their positions of authority.

But he was right when he compared the different *edot*, with their different traditions, to the *arbat haminim.* Just as the latter are all very different, when they are bound together they can be used for the mitzvah yet, if one of them is missing, the whole bundle is useless. In the same way, if one of the ancient traditions of our people is lost, there is a spiritual incompleteness in the Klal Yisrael which can only act to delay, *rachmana litzlan*, the coming of *Mashiach tzidkeinu bimhera b'yameinu*.

Your friend,
Moshe

CHAPTER SIX:

BOOK REVIEWS OR *PURIM TORAH*

THEY HAVE REASON TO DECEIVE

by Rabbi Dr. Jacob Lewis, Nicholas De Lyra University Press, New London, Ohio, 2003 (xvi + 640 pp, $150).

Reviewed by Rabbi Dr. Leon Bake, lecturer in Bible studies, Jewish Institute of Theology, New Heaven, Con.

This volume, by one of the most influential thinkers in the Jewish world, is the culmination of a lifetime's work in trying to convince any remaining doubters of the dangers of fundamentalism for the survival of Judaism or, for that matter, any text-based religion. It takes the form of a history of the modern approach to Bible studies, starting with the insights of Spinoza and Astruc through Wellhausen's brilliant reconstruction of Biblical history up to contemporary scholarly studies. This is followed by some of his own observations, which demolish the latter's criticism of Wellhausen. To give an example of his approach, I can do no better than quote one passage (pp. 263–4), which shows the depth of his scholarship, which destroys the possibility that any unprejudiced person could ever take seriously the pre-modern fundamentalist approach to the Pentateuch.

"In the Book of Numbers (ch. 26), there is a passage, the

record of the census taken just before the Israelites crossed the Jordan to conquer the Promised Land, which most modern readers skip over as of little relevance. In it, however, there are minor variations in the way by which the various tribes are denominated, which betray its late date of composition, forever destroying the fundamentalist belief that the whole Pentateuch could be of Mosaic origin.

"We find some tribes referred to adjectivally: *'Reubenites'* (v.7), *'Simeonites'* (v.14), *'Zebulunites'* (v.27). Others are referred to by their tribal name: *'Judah'* (v.22), *'Issachar'* (v.25), *'Manasseh'* (v.34), *'Dan'* (v.42), *'Naphtali'* (v.50). The remainder are all called 'children of...', or 'sons of...', the same word being used in the original Hebrew (though this variation may be an indication that the King James Authorized Version was compiled by more than one person), as in *'children of Gad'* (v.18), *'sons of Ephraim'* (v.37), *'sons of Benjamin'* (v.41), *'sons of Asher'* (v.47).

"On the basis of this variation in nomenclature, it is clear that this passage is a composite of three documents, one from an author from the tribe of Ephraim (E), another from the tribe of Judah (J), and a third from the tribe of Reuben (R). While the precise tribal affiliation of the author of each is not entirely certain, I have assigned it to the leading tribe in each group for obvious reasons. From the groupings we can ascertain the historical period in which this census took place.

"Such groupings make no sense in the context of the legendary invasion under Joshua, as implied in the Book of Numbers. However, their inclusion there would suggest that the redactor hoped for a reunification of all twelve tribes, probably just after the fall of Babylon prior to Cyrus' permission for their return, rumors of the pending announcement of which must have been circulating at the time.

"The problem, however, of the date of the original documents remains. Obviously, it cannot be at the time of the United Kingdom, since one would not expect such terminological differentiation in a unitary state. Similarly, they cannot have been composed once the two states of Israel and Judah were definitively separated since the tribal groupings do not correspond to their final crystallization. Thus, we must place it during the turbulent period following the death of Solomon before the two states had established their separate identities.

"At that time, the rebellious tribe of Ephraim, led by Jeroboam, had not yet garnered much support, only having attracted Gad and Asher and, surprisingly, Benjamin, which later reverted to the Davidic kingdom. The latter probably reflected its lingering loyalty to the house of Saul and resentment at its displacement by the Davidic dynasty.

"Most other tribes still remained loyal to Rehoboam except for Reuben, Simeon and Zebulun. The first two, traditionally descended from Jacob's two oldest sons, probably resented the dominance of Judah, his fourth, let alone the upstart Ephraim, whom they no doubt viewed as usurpers claimed by Ephraimic propagandists to have been favored by their mythical ancestor, Jacob, as later interpolated by them into the text of Genesis (48:5). As regards Zebulun, its maritime commercial interests probably made it wary of joining a state based on either hill tribe, whose economy was based on agriculture.

"So we see how a close look at the Pentateuchal text shows that the idea of a unitary origin of the text in the Mosaic period cannot be upheld by any right-thinking person."

No one could put the case against fundamentalism more convincingly, and anyone who could believe a word of it must have the word "gullible" missing from his or her vocabulary!

SHORSHEI KEREM ROSH NEVALIM[1]

by Mordekhai ibn Shakhran, edited with introduction and notes by Rabbi Alter Brandwein[2] (Mesirah Publications, Beit haKerem, 5767), 240 + xii pages, $50.

Reviewed by Shimmy Benkish, Emeritus Professor of Palaeooinology[3], University of Weinberg.[4]

As has been reported widely in the press, the *sefer Shorshei*

Kerem Rosh Nevalim by the 10th century Spanish Jewish exegete, *Ibn Shakhran*, was found recently in the wine cellars of the Vatican, where its folios had been used as stoppers in some ancient amphorae. We are truly indebted to Rabbi Brandwein for his effort in making this important work available to the Torah world.

The author obviously chose this name for his *sefer* as an acrostic of his own name [שכרן]. It is also a reference to his hometown, Gibraltar, which had been known before the Arab conquest as *Nebelberg*, from the Visigothic word meaning "foggy mountain," because of the clouds that often envelope its summit. There is a further reference to his birthplace, which had been uninhabited prior to the Arab invasion, hence its selection as the landing point from which they rapidly overran the whole Iberian peninsula. It had been known previously to the local Spanish speakers merely as *el Peñon*, the Rock, as the local population still calls it, or, in medieval Jewish works, *HaTzur*. The Arabs renamed it *Jebal Tariq*, the Mountain of Tariq, after their commander; it was later corrupted to Gibraltar. So, as an act of defiance, the indigenous Christian population called it among themselves "*el Peñon del Cabecilla,*" literally "the Rock of the Head of the Gang of Scoundrels," *Rosh Nevalim* in Hebrew.

Until now, this early Spanish Jewish grammarian and commentator was only known from quotations of his comments in the works of the *Rishonim,* but now we can appreciate his deep understanding of the Holy Scriptures in all its brilliance.

It seems that his support of the idea that Hebrew words were derived from four-letter roots from which one letter was removed to give different nuances of meaning, drew the ire of his contemporary, *Dunash Ibn Labrat,*[5] who wrote of him "*Ben Kaf keVen Kof,*"[6] presumably implying that, with such opinions, his name should have been שקרן[7] rather than שכרן[8]. This may also be the first reference to the introduction of the colony of Barbary apes[9] that still live in his hometown. *Ibn Ezra*[10] was moved to defend our author against this calumny in what is perhaps the best-known of his comments on *Tehillim* (81:17), *Umitzur devash asbi'eka – kemo hamefaresh hagadol Ibn Shakhran me'ir Tzur shemidevarav anu sevei'im devash.*[11]

This comment may itself be an allusion to *Ibn Shakhran's* introduction to the *Megillah*, "Why is *Shushan* always referred to as '*HaBirah*' – because it was the center of beer production in *Achashverosh*' empire," when one remembers that in Biblical usage *devash* invariably refers to date honey rather than that from bees, and this was the raw material from which beer was manufactured throughout *Bavel*, barley beer being peculiar to the land of *Madai* (*Beer Production in the Bible and Talmud*, by Professor Yehoiyada Flix, Beer Shekhar[12] University Press, 5715[13]).

Unfortunately, most of *Ibn Shakhran's* comments had been lost, but we can now peruse what must be some of his most original insights. To give the readers some idea of his approach, we quote a few on the *Megillah*, which I am sure will whet their appetite for more.

Noach and the *Megillah*

Ibn Shakhran notes in this seminal work that throughout the *Torah* the name of *Noach* is spelled *chaser*, i.e., without a *vav*. Even the *navi Yeshaya* (54:9) uses this form, yet in the *Megillah*, we find it spelled *malei* in three places.

He notes (Esther 9:17) that this must be a reference to the *beraita* brought in the *Avot deRabbi Natlan* (Schlechter edition[14], 1:1–3, Van De'stijl[15] Brothers' Press, Weinheim[16], Baden, 5526[17]):

> *HaBakbuk kibel haYayin meKerem umesarah leNoach, ve-Noach liVnot Lot, uVenot Lot leOved Edom haGitti, veOved Edom haGitti leNaval haKarmeli* (there seems to be a chronological inaccuracy here since *Naval* was earlier than *Oved Edom*, but perhaps this is a case of *ein me'uchar umukdam be-shikhrut* – when drunk one has no perception of chronological order – S.B.), *veNaval haKarmeli leBelshatzar, uvBelshatzar leAchashverosh, veAchashverosh asah mishteh lekhol sarav*

ve'avadav...Noach hayah omer 'Al sheloshah devarim haOlam omed, al haYayyin ve'al haShekhar ve'al haSaraf'...Hu hayah omer 'Im ein kerem ein yayin ve'im ein yayin ein shikrut.'[18] Since there is a *mitzvah* of *livesumei bePurya ad delo yada*[19] (Meg. 7b), he opines that this is an indication that one should be as *malei yayin*[20] as *Noach.*[21]

He continues to note that this form is repeated (Esther 9:18) and forms a scriptural support for the saying of Rav Yeina Saba[22] in *Massekhet Shikurim*[23] (Falsher[24] edition 7,12, Tokayer[25] Press, Martha's Vineyard, Mass., 5716[26]) that the *mitzvah* must apply to both days of Purim *meshum sefeika deyoma machmirin bazeh.*[27]

In his comment on *ya'asu eits gevoah chamishim amah*[28] (Esth. 5:14), *Ibn Shakhran* explains that this shows that *Haman* must have been a *ben Noach*[29] since he must have obtained this piece of timber from *Noach* who had used it as one of the cross beams of the ark.[30] It is interesting to note that he must have had access to many *midrashim* which are no longer extant since he quotes as a proof the *Midrash Shekhar Tov*[31] on this verse:

> How is it that *Noach* was drawn into the *Megillah*? Our Sages teach that when *Zeresh* told *Haman* to hang *Mordechai* on a gallows fifty *amot* high, he asked her where such an enormous piece of timber might be found. To this she replied 'Did not your ancestor *Noach* build his ark with such mighty beams? Go to him and ask for one!' This advice greatly pleased *Haman* and he did so. When he came to *Noach* with his request *Noach* refused, so *Haman* grabbed one end and tried to make off with it. At this, *Noach* became enraged and grabbed the other end to prevent its loss but, being an extremely elderly man, could not stop *Haman* who thereby dragged him with the beam into the *Megillah*.

As Rabbi Brandwein points out, there is an alternative version of its provenance found in *Midrash Abba Gorion ad.loc.*, which seems not to have been available to *Ibn Shakhran*, but, as he so wisely notes, *ein shoalin al hadrush*.[32]

Since it says (Esth. 9:16) *veNoach mei'oyeveihem*, which he translates as "and *Noach* from among their enemies," *Ibn Shakhran* points out that *Haman's* hatred of Jews must also have come from *Noach*, as an inheritance together with the rest of his junk.[33]

The Mothers-in-law of *Achashverosh*

In a later part of his work, *Ibn Shakhran* brings the famous *machkloket*[34] as to whether *Achashverosh* had three or four mothers-in-law.

It seems that the techniques of surrogate motherhood were still known in his days, only being lost later, since he comments on the verse, "*Gam Vashti haMalkah asetah mishteh nashim*"[35] (Esth. 1:9), *HaKetiv 'mishteh' im hei, vekakri 'mishtei' im yad, vezeh sod gadol – achat lezera veachat le'ibbur*."[36] Later he notes that both ladies are named in the *Megillah*, one was called *Bo'arah* (1:12) and the other *Keshokh* (2:1). The former was obviously the biological mother as he explains, "*venikreit al shem zeh mipnei shehe'erah bah ba'alah*[37]," so the latter must have been the surrogate. He notes that it is clear that these two must be the mothers of *Vashti*, since they are brought in connection with her downfall.

In his note to the words *kam bechamato*[38] (Esth. 7:7), he writes, "*al tikri 'kam bechamato' ela 'beKam chamato' vezeh shemah shel imah shel Esther*."[39] He notes that she was also known as "*Shokhakhah*" (7:10) and these two names must refer to Esther's mother since they appear in connection with the affair of Haman being settled by Esther. Furthermore, he notes in his comment to the latter, "*ve'ein zeh hakhchashah ledivrei hapasuk 'ein lah av va'em' (2:7), sheshemah hayetah nishkakhat. Yesh mefarshim sheyesh leEsther gam shtei imahot kemo Vashti aval zeh ta'ut gadol, shemah 'Kam' kemo shekatavti le'eil, veshem 'shokhakhah' rak kinui bealma*."[40]

There are many further insights brought by *Ibn Shakhran* but limited space precludes their inclusion here. The reader is recommended to obtain a copy and intoxicate himself with its wisdom, *"halo hem ketuvim al sefer."*[41] We hope that Rabbi Brandwein will merit publishing more works of this great scholar to fulfill the comment of *Ibn Janakh* on *Tehillim* (104:13), *Mashkeh harim me'aliyotav mipri ma'asecha tisba' ha'aretz – eleh divrei Hamashkeh, HaGaon Ibn Shakhran min haTzur, shemeihem kol yoshvei ha'aretz nisba'im beshekhar.*[42]

ENDNOTES

1. Roots of the Vineyard of the Head of the Scoundrels (Heb.)
2. old brandy (Ger.)
3. the study of ancient wine (Gr. *palaios* – ancient, *oinos* – wine, *logos* – study)
4. wine mountain (Ger.)
5. 10th century Spanish Jewish philologist and poet
6. cf. Rashi to Gen. 23:1
7. (son of) a liar (Heb./Ar.)
8. (son of) a drunkard (Heb./Ar.)
9. *kof* – ape (Heb.)
10. Spanish Jewish exegete, c.1092 – 1167
11. "and from the rock I shall satiate you with honey – just like the commentator Ibn Shakhran from the city of *Tzur* (Gibraltar) from whose honeyed words we are satiated." *Devash* is also often used to mean mead, a fermented drink made from honey, in which case the last phrase might be rendered "from whose words we are intoxicated with mead."
12. well of strong drink (Heb.)
13. ה'שטו"ת – the nonsense
14. *schlechter* – worse (Ger.) cf. *Avot deRabbi Natan*, Schechter ed., *natlan* – a taker from root *natal* – he took, *natan* – he gave (Heb.).
15. from the distillery (Dut.)
16. home of wine (Heb.)
17. ה'שכו"ר – the inebriated
18. *HaBakbuk* (name of Sage literally meaning "the bottle") received the wine from *Kerem* (name of Sage literally meaning "vineyard") and passed it on to Noah (who became drunk, cf. Gen. 9:20–21), and Noah to the daughters of Lot (who plied their father with wine until he became completely inebriated, cf. Gen. 19:31–36), and the daughters of Lot to *Oved Edom haGitti* (*gitti* = my winepress, cf. 2 Sam. 6:10), and *Oved Edom haGitti* to *Naval haKarmeli* (who made a drinking party at which he became very drunk, cf. 1 Sam. 25:36, any hint to a modern Israeli wine manufacturer is coincidental), and *Naval haKarmeli* to *Belshatzar* (who made a drunken orgy at which he was killed, cf. Dan. 5), and *Belshatzar* to *Achashverosh* and *Achashverosh* made a drinking party for all his ministers and servants (Esth. 1:3)…Noah used to

say, "On three things the world depends – Wine, beer, and brandy" (cf. Avot 1:2) – He also used to say, "If there were no vineyards, there would be no wine, and if there was no wine, there would be no drunkenness." (cf. Avot 3:21)

19. to become so intoxicated on Purim that one cannot distinguish [between "Cursed be Haman" and "Blessed be Mordechai"],

20. intoxicated by (literally filled with) wine

21. cf. Gen. 9:21

22. Rabbi Ancient Wine (Aram.)

23. Tractate Drunkards (Heb.)

24. false one (Ger.)

25. a well known Hungarian wine

26. ה'שתו"י – the intoxicated one

27. because of calendrical uncertainty we should be strict in this matter (Aram.)

28. they made a gallows fifty cubits high

29. literally "son of Noah" (Heb.), a term for any human, in particular a non-Jew

30. Gen. 6:15

31. Midrash, "Good strong alcoholic beverage," cf. *Midrash Shocher Tov* on *Tehillim*

32. we are not allowed to raise questions based on the conflicting homiletic teachings

33. colloquial "rubbish," but also the name of a Chinese trading ship

34. dispute

35. and Queen Vashti also made a drinking party for the women

36. the word *mishteh* is written with a *hei* (meaning drinking party) but should be read as if it were written with a *yad* (meaning two); this is a great secret – one for conception and another for pregnancy

37. and she was called by this name because her husband had commenced to have conjugal relations with her (but not completed them)

38. he arose in his anger

39. do not read "he arose (*Kam*) in his anger" but "with *Kam* his mother-in-law" and this is a hint to the name of Esther's mother

40. and this is no contradiction to the verse "she had no father or mother" because her name had been forgotten. Some explain that Esther also had two mothers like Vashti but this is a terrible mistake since her mother's name was *Kam*, as I have explained above, and *Shokhakhah* was only a nickname

41. behold they are written in a book (cf. Esth.10:2)

42. He waters the hills from above, the world is satisfied with the fruit of Your works – these are the comments of the one who provides strong drink, the Sage, Ibn Shakhran from Gibraltar, from which all the dwellers on earth become intoxicated

CHAPTER SEVEN:

MATHEMATICAL CURIOSITIES

A REMARKABLE APPROXIMATION TO PI

In the first Book of Kings, we find a description of the Temple built by King Solomon in which the measurements of the various parts are given. In Chapter 7, v. 23, the "molten sea," a large basin containing water used by the priests to wash their hands and feet before performing the rites, is described. The verse states (in the A.V.):

> And he (Solomon) made a molten sea, ten cubits from one brim to the other; it was round all about, and its height was five cubits; and a *line* of thirty cubits did encompass it round about.

From this verse, it appears that **pi** is taken to be 3, which is clearly inaccurate. Various explanations have been advanced by commentators; for example, that the Bible is not interested in giving exact constructional details and so rounds to the nearest integer, or that the verse has taken into account the thickness of the material, i.e., the ten cubits is an external diameter, whereas the 30 cubits is the internal circumference. In this note, I will take a different approach, based on the Masoretic text and certain peculiarities that one finds in the original Hebrew of this verse.

Before discussing our problem, it is necessary to note two points. Firstly, in the Masoretic text there are certain peculiarities of spelling found occasionally (*ketiv*) that are read differently (*qeri*). Both of these are found in Hebrew Bibles, the former in the text and the latter in the margin or at the foot of the page. In our verse there is one of these; the word translated *line* is written (in transliteration) *kvh* but read *kv*. (Vowels are not considered as proper letters in Hebrew and so have not been included; the word is in fact read *kav*.) Incidentally, the same verse appears in the parallel passage in 2 Chronicles, Chapter 4, verse 2, with no such unusual spelling.

The second point concerns the numerical notation of the ancients. Both the ancient Greeks and Jews used letters to denote numbers, the first nine letters representing the units 1 to 9, the next nine 10 to 90, and the following letters 100, 200, etc. Numbers were represented by a combination of letters in no particular order, and so every word had a numerical equivalent. This is the basis of numerological interpretations of Scripture that seem very forced to those of us who do not use letters to represent numbers. However, to the ancients, a word was a number, and so equating words of the same numerical value seemed quite natural.

If it is assumed that Scripture is Holy Writ, i.e., that it contains no meaningless items, the problem of the discrepancy between *qeri* (*kv*) and *ketiv* (*kvh*) is apparent. Why does our verse have an extra *h*? The following numerical calculation may prove interesting to the reader.

In Hebrew, the letters *k*, *v*, and *h* have numerical values 100, 6, and 5 respectively. Thus, the word translated *line* in its written form has numerical value 111, whereas as read (and written in Chronicles) the value is 106. If we take the ratio of these numbers as a "correcting factor" for the apparent value of **pi** and calculate $3 \times (^{111}/_{106})$, we obtain 3.141509 to 7 significant figures. This differs from the true value of **pi** by less than 10^{-4}, which is remarkable. In view of this, it might be suggested that this peculiar spelling is of more significance than a cursory reading might have suggested.

CALCULATIONS BEFORE CALCULATORS

With the advent of calculators, much of the tedium has been taken out of elementary mathematics, and pupils do not appreciate the difficulties faced in the past. Teachers who have had experience in the use of logarithms and other tables can convey some feeling for the problems they faced in their younger years. However, have these teachers ever considered the problems faced by earlier generations, when even such tables did not exist? If they think back to medieval times, when not only could such aids not be called upon, but even the notation used to represent numbers was much inferior to our decimal system, they will be able to give their pupils an appreciation of why mathematics developed as it did and in particular why geometry dominated its study.

The ancient Greeks and Jews represented numbers by letters. In this system the first 9 letters represent 1–9, the next 9 letters represent the numbers 10 to 90, etc., and each number is represented by a "word." To do anything more advanced than adding numbers in this notation is a considerable feat and it is remarkable that the ancient Greeks discovered the irrationality of $\sqrt{2}$. For them it was a terrible shock to find that the length of the diagonal of a unit square could not be expressed as a fraction since that meant that the number could not be written down at all, a truly irrational, i.e., unreasonable, situation.

The use of Roman numerals was an improvement on the older notation, but as anyone who has tried to multiply with them will have found out, they are not nearly as easy to handle as our notation. A problem that faces anyone who tries to do calculations in these ancient systems is that we automatically translate them into decimal number notation.

In order to bring home the complications involved in calculations, the discussion given below of the problem of showing $\sqrt{5000} > 70\,\tfrac{2}{3}$ may be useful. This problem arises from a dispute between Rabbi Judah and Rabbi Akiba, two Second-Century scholars, concerning the size of a square equal in area to the area of the biblical Tabernacle courtyard. Since the latter was 100 cubits by 50 cubits, this is in effect a dispute concerning $\sqrt{5000}$. The discussion is found in the Babylonian Talmud, Tractate Eruvin, folio 23b. The text is extremely elliptic and can only be understood with difficulty and then only by experienced scholars. The salient points of the underlying argument depend on the literal interpretation of the Hebrew text of Exodus 27:18, which reads: "The length of the court shall be 100 cubits and the breadth 50 by 50."

The last words "by 50" are peculiar and Rabbi Judah makes a cryptic comment: "Take away fifty and surround fifty," from which he goes on to deduce that a square of side 70 ⅔ cubits is certainly smaller in area than 5000 square cubits.

The following explanation from Rashi (1040–1105) in his commentary shows considerable ingenuity in demonstrating the underlying argument, considering the lack of suitable notation. In order to make his argument clearer, I have added some words in square brackets and diagrams. The latter will make the text much clearer although it was not available to medieval students. If this is taken into account, the problems of our ancestors in doing calculations will be appreciated by our pupils.

Rashi comments on the phrase, "Take away fifty and surround fifty," as follows:

> The length exceeds the width, so surround the excess 50 [around the first 50] giving 70 cubits and four fistbreadths square [i.e., 70 ⅔ cubits since 6 fistbreadths = 1 cubit]. How is this done: make of them [i.e., the excess area of 50 × 50] five strips each one cubit wide and 50 cubits long.

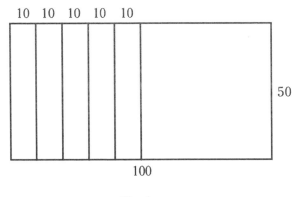

Fig. 1

Place one strip on the east and one on the west [of the base area 50 × 50] giving [an area] 70 cubits wide and 50 cubits long. Next, place a strip on the north side and another on the south side, giving a square 70 by 70 cubits, except that the corners are missing, each one 10 × 10 cubits because of the strips we have added.

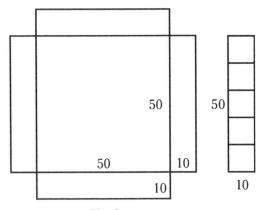

Fig. 2

Take from the 50 [cubit length of the remaining strip not yet used, which was 10 cubits wide] four pieces 10 × 10 cubits and place them in the four corners – thus completing [the 70 × 70 cubit square]. There now remains one piece 10 cubits by 10 cubits, which is 60 fistbreadths by 60 fistbreadths [since 6 fistbreadths = 1 cubit].

Make them into thirty strips, each two fistbreaths wide and ten cubits long, which [if placed in a line would be] 300 cubits long. Take 70 [cubits of this strip and place it] on each side [of our 70×70 cubit square]. This gives us a square of 70 cubits and 4 fistbreadths by 70 cubits and 4 fistbreadths, except that the corners are missing a square two fistbreadths by two fistbreadths.

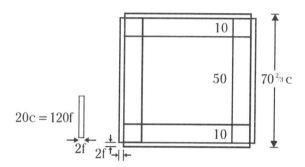

However, we have left [from our 300 cubit long strip of two fistbreadths width] 20 cubits [since we have only used 4×70 = 280 cubits]. Take from these 8 fistbreadths and place it in these corners and fill them. This leaves over 18 cubits and four fistbreadths length strip two fistbreadths wide – this is the small amount [referred to by Rabbi Judah]. For if you were to split it up and surround [the square] it would not be sufficient to increase its dimensions by ⅔ of a fingerbreadth [which is negligible relative to the size of the square] since we would have to split it up into a strip of length 282 cubits and 4 fistbreadths in order to go round all four sides [of the square].

SOME PROBLEMS WITH CALCULATING
THE TIME OF SUNRISE
Bird of prey...or prayer?

Problems of the environment seem to be one of the major current topics of concern in general society, with the preservation of endangered species threatened by industrial pollution attracting considerable attention. Such effects tend to be more pronounced

196

the higher up the food chain one goes, since chemicals become more concentrated in the bodies of predators who feed on other animals. For example, DDT, once a commonly used insecticide, has been found in very high concentrations in the bodies of many birds of prey. One result of this has been that the eggs of these birds have been found to be sterile, thus endangering these species. This phenomenon was already noticed over thirty years ago and was the subject of Rachel Carson's *Silent Spring*, a work that first made environmental problems a matter of concern to the general public.

In view of the old saying, "*Wie es christelt so juedelt es sich,*" it did not come therefore as a great surprise when I saw notices in the synagogues of Broughton Park, the Orthodox Jewish quarter of Manchester, that appeared at first glance to give daily reports of the numbers of hawks sighted, and that the numbers seemed to be increasing. This impression was gained from a cursory glance at the heading *nets minyan*. On closer examination, of course, it was obvious that the notice had nothing to do with nature conservation, but was a call for those who wished to recite *shacharit* in the manner of the *vatikin*, starting *Shemoneh Esrei* at the precise time of sunrise (Berachot 9b).

However, the authors of the notice had made a very common error in that they referred to sunrise as *nets hachammah*, whereas the correct term is *hanets hachammah*. The work *hanets* is the infinitive of the *hiphil* of the root *natsats*, as should be obvious since the *heh* is vocalized with a *kamatz*; this initial *heh* is characteristic of this particular *binyan* of the verb. It is definitely not the definite article, which would be vocalized with a *patach* and could, in any case, not be appended to a noun in the construct form.

The use of the term *nets hachammah* raises problems of which most people are unaware. Literally, this phrase means "hawk of the sun," which might seem innocuous until one realizes that the hawk was the symbol of the ancient Egyptian sun-god. Thus, using this phrase smacks of *avodah zarah*, or at least of transgressing *kema'aseh eretz Mitzraim*…Though this may seem fanciful, one might note that *chazal* may have had a similar motivation when they composed the first *brachah* before *Kriat Shema* in the morning, *yotzer or uvore choshech oseh shalom uvore et hakol*. This is adapted from a verse in Isaiah (45:7) where the prophet wrote "*ra*" in place of "*et hakol*." Although in Hebrew 'ra' means evil, it happens to be the name of the Egyptian sun-god whose symbol was the hawk. If they had not made this change, the text of the blessing could have been read *uvore ra, hameir la'aretz...*, as though this *avodah zarah* had some reality.

Many are the Calculations in the Heart of Man But...

The notices advertising the sunrise *minyan* gave the times of sunrise correct to the nearest minute, which seemed somewhat ambitious to me. However, when I heard that moves were afoot to calculate them to the nearest five seconds, I felt that this could not possibly be done since it seemed unlikely that the data used would be sufficiently accurate.

What seemed to be happening was that somebody had obtained a calculator that gave eight or ten digits and assumed that the results obtained were, in fact, that accurate. This is a fairly common mistake made by those who do not appreciate the limits imposed by one's data.

I therefore examined the way sunrise was being determined and analyzed the reliability of this data and the effect each item had on the accuracy of the final result.

In order to compute the time for any position of the sun we need five pieces of information:

    a. the latitude of the observer
    b. the longtitude of the observer
    c. the altitude of the sun
    d. the declination of the sun
    e. the equation of time

The longtitude and latitude can be obtained from a large-scale ordinance survey map and could be assumed to be accurate to the nearest second (of angle).

The altitude of the sun is the angle above (or below) the horizon of a line from the observer to the center of the sun's disc, an angle of 0° being when the sun's equator is on the horizon, i.e., half the sun's disc is visible. Since we define sunrise as the time when the sun first appears above the horizon we must have an altitude somewhat less than this.

A further complication is caused by refraction, i.e., bending of light in the atmosphere, which means that we see the sun when it is in reality below the horizon. For average conditions, these two effects mean that visual sunrise corresponds to an altitude of 50 minutes below the horizon (Fig. 1).

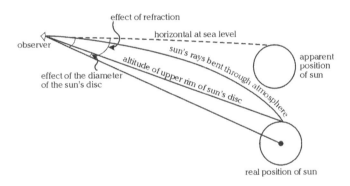

Fig. 1 – Effect of refraction on altitude

A further complication arises when the observer is above sea level, since he can then see further, so that visual sunrise corresponds to an even larger altitude (Fig. 2). The height above sea level can be estimated using the contour lines on the ordinance survey map, but this is clearly much less accurate than the longitude or latitude, and could be in error by up to five feet. If the observer were surrounded by hills, the sun may only become visible when it is well above the horizontal; unlike Yerushalayim, this was not the case in Broughton Park.

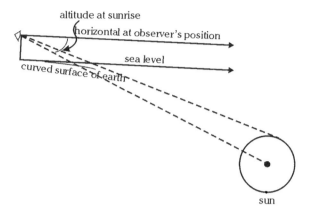

Fig. 2 – Effect of height above sea level on altitude

The declination is the angle between the line joining the centers of the earth and sun and the earth's equatorial plane (Fig. 3). The equation of time is a correction necessitated by the fact that the earth's orbit is an ellipse and not a circle. Both vary throughout the year, but do not depend on the position of the observer; their values can be found in *Whitaker's Almanac*. Unfortunately, their values are only given at midnight for each day of the year and can vary by as much as 30 seconds in 24 hours. In order to obtain their values at sunrise, we must interpolate, but, in order to do so, we must know the time of sunrise. In consequence, the calculation must be done iteratively, i.e., we estimate the time of sunrise, perhaps at 6 AM, and calculate these quantities and then use these to recalculate the time of sunrise. We then repeat these calculations until the calculated time of sunrise changes by less than, for example, one second. In *Whitaker's Almanac*, the equation of time is given to the nearest second and so should not be in error by more than half a second. However, the declination is only given to the nearest minute (of angle). If this is insufficiently accurate, then the *Nautical Almanac*, which gives it to the nearest tenth of a minute for each hour of each day, would have to be used.

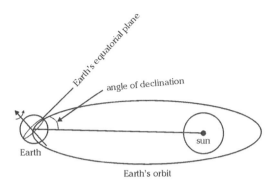

Fig. 3

Because of the way the time of sunrise, or for that matter any other position of the sun, is calculated, each error is subject to a magnifying factor, i.e., it must be multiplied by a factor to determine how much it contributes to the total error in the computed time. A full mathematical analysis entitled "Sunrise, Sunset – A Modelling Exercise in Iteration" may be found in my paper published in the *Journal of Teaching Mathematics and its Applications*, Vol. 9, no. 4 (1991), pp. 159–164.

For the latitude and longtitude, the maximum error can be shown to be at most a tenth of a second, while for the equation of time it is not more than half a second. As regards the declination which *Whitaker's Almanac* gives correct to the nearest minute (of angle), an error of up to four seconds might be introduced; if the *Nautical Almanac* tables are used, this can be reduced to less than half a second.

For the altitude, there are two sources of error. The first is caused by inaccuracies in the elevation, which in our case at about 195 feet above sea level could contribute up to almost 2 seconds to the total error. The second source of error in the altitude is due to variations in refraction caused by changes in atmospheric pressure and temperature. From the *Nautical Almanac* tables it can be calculated that this error could be almost 40 seconds! This is clearly the major source of error in our problem and we see that sunrise can only be calculated to the desired accuracy if it is taken into account. Since atmospheric conditions cannot be known in advance, this makes publication of such times problematic. When all the errors are taken into account, the times calculated could be in error by as much as 45 seconds to either side of the calculated time.

From all this we can see that unless the atmospheric pressure and temperature are measured, we cannot predict the time of sunrise even to the nearest minute. In consequence, it is futile to publish such accurate times in advance, but the calculation has to be done each day shortly before the required time. This would not prove impossible if a program for the calculation were available on a programmable calculator.

If we rely on the *poskim* who rule that we can use an average refraction in the atmosphere, and not take temperature and pressure into account, the maximum accuracy that we can expect from our calculations is to within about 6 seconds, though I doubt if any *sheliach tzibur* can time himself so well!

The Sun Knows the Time of its Coming

Perhaps the lesson to be learned from all this is *al tehi tzaddik harbeh*, that one should not be overly clever. As the Psalmist says, "the sun knows the time of its coming" (14:18), but we cannot. Unfortunately, "man must go out to his work" (ibid. 23), which means that most have to make an earlier start, at least in the winter months.

However, we all look forward to the time when "a new light will shine on Zion" and that "we should soon be worthy to benefit from its light," so that we might be able to fulfill the *retzon HaShem* in the best possible way, rising with the sun to praise Him.

IT'S A LONG, LONG TIME FROM JUNE TO SEPTEMBER

Though the young man in the Sixties ballad may have been protesting his undying love, the problem of writing a computer program to calculate the number of days between two given dates is by no means trivial. It or its inverse, the date a given number of days after a given date, can give rise to some interesting exercises for our students, especially if the dates are not necessarily on the usual Gregorian calendar. A further problem related to these is the determination of the day of the week on which a particular date falls, for which Conway, Berklekamp and Guy give an interesting algorithm for the Gregorian and Julian calendars.[1] These problems arose in some work that I was doing on a problem in rabbinic law concerning the detection of patterns in tables of dates of the onset of menstruation where these dates were recorded on the Jewish calendar.[2] There are some interesting complications in the Jewish calendar that might raise the exercise from the relatively trivial to a more worthwhile piece of work.

Types of calendar

In this paper I propose to discuss three calendars at present in use: the Gregorian (and Julian), the Moslem, and the Jewish. Of these, the first is purely solar, i.e, the year is fixed by the time of one circuit of the earth around the sun, and months are arbitrary divisions of it. The ancient Iranian calendar is similar.

The second is purely lunar, *i.e.*, the months are fixed by the time of one circuit of the moon around the earth and the year is defined as a period of 12 such lunar months. Since the lunar month consists of 29 days, 12 hours and 44 minutes (to the nearest minute), this means that months are taken to be of alternately 29 and 30 days. To allow for the extra 44 minutes, the twelfth Moslem month, which normally has 29 days, has an extra day added 11 times in each cycle of 30 years.

A solar year consists of 365 days, 5 hours, 48 minutes and 46 seconds (to the nearest second), and since the lunar month consists of 29 days, 12 hours and 44 minutes (to the nearest minute), there is a discrepancy of about 11 days between the length of the solar and lunar years. Thus, the months of the Moslem year shift back relative to the seasons which are fixed in the solar (Gregorian) year; this is the reason why, for example, Ramadan sometimes falls in the summer and sometimes in the winter. Determining the corresponding dates on the Moslem and Gregorian or Iranian calendars makes an interesting and non-trivial exercise[3].

The Jewish calendar has lunar months, like the Moslem, and fits them to the solar year by intercalating an extra month seven times in 19 years, a system attributed to the Alexandrian mathematician and astronomer Meton. The problem of correlating the Jewish and Gregorian calendars was used as a student group modeling exercise, designed to improve the students' transferable personal skills.[4]

The Gregorian Calendar

This is the calendar generally used, having been introduced to replace the Julian calendar by Pope Gregory XIII in March 1582. The latter, which had been instituted 1,627 years previously by Julius Caesar in order to correct the chaotic state of the calendar in republican Rome,[5] took the year to consist of 365 & ¼ days. This was arranged by having 12 months of alternately 30 and 31 days, except for the last month, February, which had only 29 days instead of 30. To get the extra ¼ day this was extended to 30 days every fourth year. Not long afterwards this was changed to its present arrangement by Augustus Caesar, so that the month named after him should also consist of 31 days like that named after his predecessor. This lengthened the summer by one day and by consequence February was made to consist of 28 days, or 29 in a leap year.[5] That months were originally counted from March is clear from some of their names, e.g., September is the seventh month from March.

The Gregorian reform reduced the number of leap years by making the century years non-leap except for every fourth one. This made the mean length of the Gregorian year 365 days, 5 hours, 49 minutes and 12 seconds, an error of 26 seconds in 400 years.

Because it was introduced by the Pope, this calendar was resisted in Protestant countries, but because of its greater accuracy, it was eventually accepted. Restoring the months to the correct seasons required deleting 11 days when it was introduced in England in 1752 and led to riots. Until the introduction of the Gregorian calendar the year was deemed to start on March 25th, the vernal equinox, when Julius Caesar introduced his calendar. This became April 5th on the new calendar, explaining the strange way the Inland Revenue fixes the commencement of the tax year. With the introduction of the Gregorian calendar, January 1st became New Year's Day.

Russia continued to use the Julian calendar until 1917, hence the anniversary of the "October Revolution" falls in November!

In order to calculate the number of days between two Gregorian dates we require two functions, one to calculate the length of a month, and the other that of a year. These are easily written in PASCAL using CASE statements, the only problem arising with leap years. A simple loop can then be set up to count the total number of days between the two given dates. The date of a given number of days after a given date can be found through the use of a similar program.

The Moslem Calendar

In the Moslem calendar, the months are alternately 30 and 29 days long, commencing with the first month, Muharram, except that the twelfth month is 30 days in an intercalary year (Ramadan is the ninth month and consists of 30 days).

To determine whether a particular Moslem year I is intercalary, we calculate $R = (11I + 14) \mod 30$ (the remainder when $11I + 14$ is divided by 30), in which case year I is intercalary if $R < 11$[5] Given this result, it is even easier to write the appropriate functions for the length of months and years on the Moslem than the Gregorian calendar.

The Jewish Calendar

The Jewish calendar is considerably more complicated than either of the others considered and would present a real challenge to students. The complications are consequent on it, using both lunar months of alternately 30 and 29 days and fitting these to a solar year with which it is not commensurate. As mentioned above, this is done by adding an extra month of 30 days in the Jewish year, J, 7 times in 19 years. This month is inserted after the eleventh month, this thirteenth month in a leap year being of 29 days. A criterion for determining whether year J is a leap year is to calculate $R = (7J + 1) \bmod 19$, in which case year J is a leap year when $R < 7$ p. 1000[5].

Although the Jewish year begins in the autumn, the New Year day is the first day of the seventh month[6] consequent on the Biblical instruction to count months from the spring month in which the Passover festival falls.[7] There are, however, some further complications in that the eighth month can have an extra day, making it 30 days long, and the ninth month can lose a day, making it 29 days long. (Both cannot occur in the same year.) Thus, there are three possible types of ordinary year, of 353, 354 or 355 days, and three types of leap year, of 383, 384, or 385 days. In order to determine to which of these year types J belongs, it is necessary to do some complex astronomical calculations to determine the expected sightings of the new moon at the beginning and end of the year, *i.e.*, the length of the year is a "boundary value problem." Normally the day on which it is sighted is *Rosh haShanah*, the New Year day, but it is sometimes postponed by one day or, exceptionally, two days.[8]

With these corrections, the average length of the Jewish year is 365 days, 5 hours, 55 minutes, 25 & $^{25}/_{57}$ seconds, an error of less than 7 minutes. This leads to an advance of one day in the solar year every 216 years. Various suggestions to avoid this problem have been advanced.[9]

Finding the Length of a Jewish Year

An algorithm for calculating the Gregorian date of the Jewish New Year is given by Conway *et al.*[1] which fixes it in the solar year. If the Gregorian date of the following New Year is determined, the length of year *J* is easily found, since the Gregorian year is 365 days long, or 366 in a Gregorian leap year.

We will write [*x*] to mean the largest integer less than *x*. In order to determine the date of *Rosh haShanah* as September *N*, we calculate *(i)* the Gregorian year number, $Y = J - 3761$; *(ii)* the Gregorian leap year number, $L = Y$ mod 4; *(iii)* the Gregorian century correction, $C = [Y/100] - [Y/400] - 2$ {for Julian years C = 0}; *(iv)* the Golden number $G = Y$ mod 19 + 1; *(v)* the Metonic correction $M = 12G$ mod 19.

Next evaluate:

x= C + L/4 + 765433M/492480 -(313Y+ 89091)/98496

Now $N = $[x] except when this makes *Rosh haShanah* fall on:

i.   a Sunday, Wednesday, or Friday,
     in which case $N = $[x] + 1
ii. a Tuesday when x – [x] ≥ 1367/2160 *and M > 6*,
     in which case $N = $[x] + 2
iii. a Monday when x – [x] ≥ 23 269/25 920 *and M > 11*,
     in which case $N = $[x] + 1

To find the day of the week on which September [x] falls, note that September 1st falls on a Saturday in 1990 and advances one day in the week each ordinary year and two days each Gregorian leap year. A Gregorian leap year is one for which $L = 0$ except when *Y* is divisible by 100 but not by 400.

Calculating the Length of a Jewish Month

The Jewish year commences with the month numbered seven, as explained above. The months of the year, with their number as counted from the spring month, *Nisan*, and lengths, are:

7. *Tishrei*	30 days
8. *Marcheshvan*	29 days, except when the year has 355, or 385 days when the month has 30 days
9. *Kislev*	30 days, except when the year has 353, or 383 days when the month has 29 days
10. *Tevet*	29 days
11. *Shevat*	30 days
12. *Adar*	29 days, except in a leap year when the month is called *Adar Rishon* and has 30 days
13. *Adar Sheni*	29 days (but only in a leap year)
1. *Nisan*	30 days
2. *Iyar*	29 days
3. *Sivan*	30 days
4. *Tammuz*	29 days
5. *Av*	30 days
6. *Elul*	29 days

Conclusion

Thus, the subroutines for calculating the lengths of Jewish months and years and the organization of the loop to count the number of days between two given dates is considerably more complicated than for the other calendars discussed and makes a slightly unusual programming exercise. It has been used as part of several student projects at both HND[10] and B.Sc.[11] levels.

ENDNOTES

1. Berklekamp, E.R., Conway, J.H., and Guy, R.K., "The Doomsday Rule" in *Winning Ways*, Academic Press, London. 1982, pp. 795–797, 800.
2. Stern, M.D., "Menstrual Cycle Analysis: a Problem in Pattern Recognition" *International Journal of Mathematical Education in Science and Technology*, vol. 21, no. 3 pp. 469–481 (July1990).
3. Stern, M.D., *Mathematics Review*, vol. 1, no. 1 (Nov.1990).

4. Stern, M.D, *Theta*, vol, 3 No. 1, 35–42 (Feb. 1989).

5. "Calendar" in *Encyclopedia Brittanica*, 11th edition, 1911, vol. 4, pp. 989, 990, 1000, 1001.

6. Mishnah, Rosh haShanah 1.1 cf. Leviticus 23:24.

7. Exodus 12:2.

8. Feldman, W.M., *Rabbinical Mathematics and Astronomy*, M.L. Cailingold, London, 1931, pp. 185–210.

9. Fax, D. H., *Intercom*, 1978, **17**, No. 1, 8–14.

10. Robson, C.H., "Menstrual Cycle Analysis – A Problem in Pattern Recognition," project dissertation for the HND in Mathematics, Statistics & Computing, Manchester Polytechnic, 1989.

11. Goldwater, S.H., "Calendar Problems," project dissertation for the B.Sc. in Combined Studies, Manchester Polytechnic, 1989.

CHAPTER EIGHT:

LANGUAGE AND
THOUGHT PATTERNS

Iɴ ʜɪs ᴀʀᴛɪᴄʟᴇ "*Mamesh*, a truly great *zach, l'maaseh*" (*Jewish Tribune*, Mar. 6, 2008), Rabbi Shmuel Ya'akov Klein has raised many fascinating ideas about the interrelationship between language and thought patterns. As he writes, "Paradoxical though it might at first seem, the essence of the human being is both a cause of his mode of speech AND a consequence of it. The manner in which we express ourselves – and even the tongue in which we do so – has a huge impact on the overall equation of Jewish life." In this article I would like to develop this theme through some observations I have made over the years on the nature of language.

The first point is that the very grammatical structures of a language both reflect and help mold the thought patterns of its speakers. It is only by studying different languages, and especially those with completely different patterns, that one can come to appreciate this. As an example, one might consider the different ways Indo-European and Semitic languages treat the relationship between the two nouns in the phrase "the life of man." In the former, it is the second word "life" that is treated as the absolute (nominative case) and the second is modified by being put in the genitive case (one of the few cases still surviving in English) as in the alternative form "the man's life," or, more strikingly, in the more clearly inflected Latin, "*hominis vita.*" This contrasts quite starkly with the way the latter view the relationship in that they consider the first word "man" as absolute and the second as dependent on it (*smichut*) as in "*chayyei ha'adam.*" How these different constructions affect the way speakers think is difficult to establish, but I suspect that they have an effect on the subconscious level.

Another difference between these two groups of languages is the way they treat verbs. In Indo-European languages, these have a well-developed tense structure using either suffixes as in Latin – *am-o*, I love; *am-ab-o*, I will love; *am-av-i*, I have loved, etc. – or by using auxiliary verbs, like be, do, have or will, as is done in English.

In Semitic languages like Arabic and Classical Hebrew, tenses as such do not exist and are replaced by the concept of aspect, i.e., a distinction is made between the perfect for completed actions, e.g., *shamar*, he guarded, usually past, and the imperfect for ongoing processes, e.g., *yishmor*, he will guard, usually future, though only context determines at what time the action takes place. This is the underlying reason for the apparently paradoxical effect of the *vav hahippuch* which appears not only to mean "and" but also changes the tense, e.g., *vayishmor*, and he guarded, as opposed to *ushemar*, and he will guard. This construction disappeared in the post-Biblical period and is not found in Mishnaic Hebrew though it is still used in Arabic to this day. Thus users of the latter tend to have a somewhat ambiguous concept of time, which might explain some of the problems speakers of the two types of language have in understanding one another.

This leads to another undeniable fact about spoken languages, that they tend to change in the course of time. The changes tend to be small, but some can be noticed even in a human lifetime.

However, over the centuries, these are cumulative and make texts in the older versions unintelligible to the untrained reader.

For modern English speakers, Anglo-Saxon, the form of the language current a thousand years ago, is in effect a foreign language. Not only has the vocabulary changed considerably, but it is a highly inflected language, more like present-day German, than English, where most inflections have been lost and auxiliary words are used to modify the sense of a word. Though it is much more similar to the current language, the Early Modern English of Shakespeare, which is only 400 years old, is still difficult to follow without notes to alert the reader to the changed meanings of words, e.g., the word "want" then meant "lack," whereas today it means "desire." Even in the last hundred years some constructions have dropped out of use and been replaced by others, lending even some relatively recent texts an archaic flavor, e.g., nobody today would write "I know not that…" but, instead, "I do not know that…" Many peculiarities of Modern English spelling are fossilized relics of these older layers of the language; for example, both the "k" and "gh" in the word "knight" were originally pronounced, as in the cognate German word "knecht," but have now become silent, making the word homophonous with "night".

Some changes are happening in our own time. One is the gradual blurring of the last remaining case inflections in pronouns, those for nouns having long been lost. Thus, all too often people say, or even write, such things as "to he who…" instead of "to him who…" or "the man who he admired" instead of "the man whom he admired." While this may be irritating to pedants, it is becoming progressively more common and will, no doubt, become the norm within a generation, or two at most. The speed of such changes can be surprising. It cannot be more than twenty years since the stress pattern of the word "kilometer" has been shifted from that of other measures of length like "centimeter" to that of measuring devices like "thermometer" despite the complete lack of any logic for such a change.

Similarly Latin changed into the Romance languages, French, Italian, Romanian, Spanish, etc., and Sanskrit into the many languages current in North India today, Bengali, Gujarati, Hindi, Punjabi, etc. This process of evolution can be seen since, in many cases, we have written texts from various periods from which we can see the different stages. By examining these, philologists have been able to work backwards and construct plausible proto-languages from which others, of which we know, have developed.

Though this theory of evolution of languages is fairly well developed, the precise details of any such reconstructions are open to challenge. Interestingly, the pioneer work in this field by the Brothers Grimm (of fairy tale fame) over two hundred years ago was probably what suggested, by analogy, to Charles Darwin for his theory of biological evolution that, however, rests on much shakier assumptions. In particular, the latter would appear to be inconsistent with the well-established Second Law of Thermodynamics, which states, in essence, that in the absence of outside controls, natural systems become more disorganized and random as time progresses, whereas Darwin's theory claims the reverse for biological systems.

The fact that, contrariwise, human society itself does become more organized as time progresses would seem to suggest that there is something "supernatural" in human beings. This might be seen as indicating that man is not merely a physical being constrained by the laws of nature and has a soul that is a spark of the Eternal – "In the likeness of G-d made He man."

The same sort of changes can be seen in Hebrew, where there are at least four different strata: Classical Hebrew (*Lashon Hakodesh*), Mishnaic Hebrew (*Lashon Chachamim*), Rabbinic Hebrew, and Modern Hebrew (*Ivrit*).

As I mentioned above, some constructions in Classical Hebrew had disappeared by Mishnaic times. In fact, the latter has a well-developed tense system probably developed under the influence of Aramaic and possibly ultimately from that of the Indo-European language, Greek, which was very influential at that transitional time. For example, we find *hu haya omer*, "he used to say," a construction that is not found in *Tanach*.

Similarly, Yiddish constructions crept into the usage of Rabbinic Hebrew. Modern Hebrew is an artificial construction, partly designed to make a break with what its protagonists saw as the "Golus mentality" of the Yiddish-speaking masses. Some classical phrases from previous strata were given new meanings in order to wean them from their traditional worldview, for example the phrase *avodah zarah*, which was always taken to refer to idolatry was given the meaning of "employing non-Jewish (Arab) workers." Thus one has to be particularly careful not to allow current usage to distort one's understanding of traditional texts. Perhaps this form of the language could be called *Lashon Mechullal*!

It is also clear that not only the grammar of Hebrew has changed under the influence of the vernacular, but also its pronunciation. Thus Ashkenazim, unlike those Jews who come from Arabic-speaking areas, cannot pronounce the gutturals *ayin* and *chet*, which are not found in the European languages and substitute *alef* and *chaf* respectively. Even where the sound, or a similar one, is found, the Hebrew tends to be assimilated to that of the vernacular. For example, one can easily distinguish a native French speaker from an English speaker by the way they pronounce the *tseirei*.

Similarly, Ashkenazim tend to stress the penultimate syllable, even though the Hebrew word should carry its stress on the final one, because that is the way most European languages allot stress. Something I have noticed recently is that English speakers (as opposed to Scots) tend not to pronounce the *reish* at the end of a syllable, since in Standard UK English the "r" is not pronounced there.

Many of the different pronunciations of Hebrew current in different communities can be explained by looking at the phonetic and phonological rules of the speakers' primary languages, and sound shifts that have taken place in the latter, but that would require a separate article to do it justice.

CHAPTER NINE:

MENSTRUAL CYCLE ANALYSIS: A PROBLEM IN PATTERN RECOGNITION

In THIS PAPER I describe a problem in Jewish religious law that involves the detection of various prescribed patterns in the menstrual cycles of a woman, which formed the basis of several student projects. It commences with a short description of the Jewish calendar followed by an introduction to the religious background. The various patterns described in the religio-legal literature are then listed, and the objectives of the program specified. Some of the problems in analyzing the data are presented, and an example of the required form of the output is given. The paper concludes with a discussion of how the problem might be used pedagogically as the basis of student programming projects at various levels.

INTRODUCTION

It is common knowledge that in the Jewish religion there are various dietary restrictions, such as the ban on the eating of pork. It is less well known that similar restrictions apply to many other aspects of life, one of the most significant of which concerns sexual relations. Like most religions, Judaism forbids incest,[1] though the precise nature of the prohibited degrees of relationship are slightly different from those of other faiths. These forbidden marriages are codified in terms of those women whom a man cannot marry and, since there is a degree of asymmetry, the corresponding relationships for a woman appear different but can easily be determined.[2] In addition, there is a categorical opposition to adultery or any extra-marital relationship. Even within marriage there are times related to the menstrual cycle of the wife when sexual relations are not permitted.

In Leviticus 18:19 it states, "You shall not approach a woman to have sexual relations with her when she is in a state of menstrual impurity," and in 20:18 the punishment of excision (a form of premature death) is given. This punishment, though not enforceable by the courts, is considered to be one of the most serious, second only to the death sentence, and emphasizes the seriousness with which this prohibition is viewed.

A woman who has experienced any bleeding from her womb is said to be in a state of *niddah*.[3] This is usually translated as menstrual impurity, though this is somewhat misleading since the bleeding merely initiates the state. Even after bleeding ceases, a woman remains *niddah* until she performs the prescribed purification by immersion in a *mikveh*, a specially constructed pool of naturally collected water. All sexual activity is forbidden until such an immersion is performed,[4] not merely while menstrual bleeding is experienced.

In view of the gravity of the offense, Jewish law proscribes sexual relations at those times when menstruation is expected to start so that a couple should not inadvertently transgress.[5]

As is well known, women have idiosyncratic patterns of menstruation though, as the word indicates, it tends to occur once a month. The pattern of occurrences is called *veset* (plural *vesatot*) in the literature. Since the various patterns are well defined, it occurred to me that it should be possible to design a computer program that can examine a table containing a woman's recorded dates on which menstruation commenced to determine whether any such patterns are present, and find the corresponding date on which abstinence from sexual relations is required.

As will become clear when the patterns are described, the problem of designing such a program can be of various levels of complexity, depending on how many of the more uncommon patterns are included. Thus the problem was used as the basis of projects for B.Sc.[6] and HND[7] students. Some of the simpler patterns could be used as programming exercises, especially if the complications of the Jewish calendar are excluded.

THE JEWISH CALENDAR

Before discussing *vesatot* we must note certain facts about the Jewish calendar, which is based on lunar months of 29 or 30 days each beginning on the new moon, called *Rosh Chodesh*. It is fitted to the solar year by adding an extra month seven times in a cycle of 19 years to ensure that the festivals whose dates are on the lunar months always fall in the appropriate seasons which depend on the Sun, unlike those of the Moslem religion which precess through them. The months are:

1.	*Nisan*	30 days
2.	*Iyar*	29 days
3.	*Sivan*	30 days
4.	*Tammuz*	29 days
5.	*Av*	30 days
6.	*Ellul*	29 days
7.	*Tishrei*	30 days
8.	*Marcheshvan*	29 or 30 days
9.	*Kislev*	29 or 30 days
10.	*Tevet*	29 days
11.	*Shevat*	30 days
12.	*Adar*	29 days

In a leap year an extra month is added called *Adar Rishon* after *Shevat* and consists of 30 days. There are then 13 months, the thirteenth, being the original *Adar*, consists of 29 days and is called *Adar Sheni*.

The first of *Tishrei* is the New Year, i.e., years are counted from *Tishrei*, whereas months are counted from *Nisan*.

The number of days in *Marcheshvan* and *Kislev* are fixed so that the following feast of Passover never begins on a Monday, Wednesday, or Friday. For the appropriate calendrical information for the years 5706–5780 (1945–2019), see Table 1.

Table 1: Year types 5706–5780 (1945–2019)					
Year	*Code*	*Year*	*Code*	*Year*	*Code*
06	+1	31	-2	56	-3
07	-2	32	-3	57	+1
08	+3	33	+1	58	-2
09	-3	34	-3	59	-3
10	-1	35	-2	60	+3
11	+2	36	+3	61	-1
12	-3	37	-1	62	-2
13	-3	38	+2	63	+3
14	+1	39	-3	64	-3
15	-2	40	-3	65	+1
16	-3	41	+1	66	-2
17	+3	42	-2	67	-3
18	-2	43	-3	68	+1
19	+1	44	+3	69	-2
20	-3	45	-2	70	-3
21	-2	46	+1	71	+3

22	+1	47	-3	72	-2
23	-3	48	-2	73	-1
24	-2	49	+1	74	+3
25	+3	50	-3	75	-2
26	-1	51	-2	76	+3
27	+3	52	+3	77	-1
28	-2	53	-1	78	-2
29	-3	54	-3	79	+3
30	+1	55	+2	80	-3 .

Key: (+) leap year (13 months); (–) ordinary year (12 months).

	Code		
	1	*2*	*3*
Days in *Marcheshvan*	29	29	30
Days in *Kislev*	29	30	30

It should be noted that on the Jewish calendar, a day commences at dusk. So when talking of Monday we mean the period from sunset on Sunday until sunset on Monday. Each day is considered as consisting of two *onot* (singular *onah*). An *onah* is either the night-time, from sunset to sunrise, or the day-time, from sunrise to sunset.

It is clear that calculating the number of days between two given dates is not as simple as on the Gregorian calendar, and a procedure to do so has to be included in any programs for finding *vesatot*. Similarly, a procedure for the inverse process, finding the date a given number of days after a given date, is needed. Either of these can be used as a programming example in its own right.

RULES FOR *VESATOT*

Before discussing the specific patterns described in *halachah*,

Jewish religious law, certain general rules for *veset* calculation must be clarified.[8]

Where menstruation is preceded by physical symptoms such as pre-menstrual tension on a regularly identifiable pattern, then a *veset haguf* is established.[9] However, by its nature it is not amenable to computer treatment and so was not included in this project.

There are two main computable systems of *veset*, the first based on the number of days between successive menstruations,[10] and the second based on days of the week or the (Jewish) month.[11]

Within these, there are two types, the fixed *veset* and the non-fixed *veset*, for which the application in practice varies. The fixed type is said to occur when a pattern has been noted on three successive occasions.[12] For example, if menstruation started on the 1st of *Nisan*, the 1st of *Iyar* and the 1st of *Sivan*, then a fixed *veset* for the first of the month is established. Other patterns are described below. Any other *veset* is non-fixed. If a fixed *veset* has been found, it supersedes any previous fixed *veset* of that type.[13] Should the next three observed menstruations not fit into the pattern predicted by it, it goes into abeyance but can be reactivated if it recurs once, provided it has not been superseded by some other fixed *veset*.[14]

A fixed *veset* is used to predict the next expected menstruation, i.e., a time when abstinence from sexual relations is required, until it goes into abeyance, or is superseded by another fixed *veset*. Thus, it is operative for at least three periods.[15] A non-fixed *veset*, on the other hand, is only used once.[16]

There is one further rule that applies to all *veset* determinations. Observations are only considered for pattern determination when they are on the same *onah*.[17] For example, if three successive menstruations commence on the first day of three successive months, *all* during the night, then a fixed *veset* is established for the first of the month by night. If, on the other hand, the last menstruation started during the day, no fixed *veset* is established, only a non-fixed one for the first of the month by day.

The generally accepted opinion is that, for the purposes of finding a fixed *veset*, only the time when menstruation starts is significant, i.e., it is the change from non-menstruation to menstruation that initiates the *niddah* state. This is referred to as *ma'yan satum*. Unless otherwise stated, we will only discuss this in what follows. There is a dissenting opinion that each *onah* on which menstrual bleeding takes place is as though it is the beginning of menstruation and has to be taken into account. This is called *ma'yan patuach*.[18] The practical difference can be seen from the following situation. If a woman starts to menstruate on the 6th of *Nisan*, the 6th of *Iyar* and the 4th of *Sivan*, and on the last occasion continues to menstruate for two more days, i.e., the 5th and 6th of *Sivan*, then on the *ma'yan satum* system, no fixed *veset* is established and she only has a non-fixed *veset* for the 4th of the month. However, on the *ma'yan patuach* system, she has a fixed *veset* for the 6th of the month and therefore can ignore the 4th of the month. A similar situation can happen on the interval system.

These principles are perhaps best understood by considering the following example, based on a list of intervals between successive menstruations, where all observations took place in the same *onah*. To avoid any complications we assume that the bleeding only lasted a short time and did not continue into the next *onah*. Table 2 could equally well apply to days of successive months with the appropriate change of wording.

Table 2: Menstruation patterns in interval system

Interval (*in days*)	Predicted Veset
28	Non-fixed *veset* of 28 days
28	Non-fixed *veset* of 28 days
29	Non-fixed *veset* of 29 days
	(one of 28 days cancelled)

Table 2: Menstruation patterns in interval system

29	Non-fixed *veset* of 29 days (one of 28 days still cancelled)
29	Fixed *veset* of 29 days found
27	Fixed *veset* of 29 days *and* non-fixed *veset* of 27 days
27	Fixed *veset* of 29 days *and* non-fixed *veset* of 27 days
28	Non-fixed *veset* of 28 days (one of 27 days cancelled, *and* fixed *veset* of 29 days in abeyance)
28	Non-fixed *veset* of 28 days (one of 27 days still cancelled, *and* fixed *veset* of 29 days still in abeyance)
29	Fixed *veset* of 29 days reactivated (non-fixed *veset* of 28 days cancelled)
28	Fixed *veset* of 29 days *and* non-fixed *veset* of 28 days
28	Fixed *veset* of 29 days *and* non-fixed *veset* of 28 days
28	Fixed *veset* 28 days (all previous *vesatot* cancelled)

There is an opinion that bans sexual relations not only on the expected *onah* but also on the *onah* preceding it.[19] This can be superimposed to any *veset*. We shall refer to this as the *Or Zarua* opinion.

Table 2 follows the rules previously stated. However, there is one opinion that a shorter-interval *veset* cannot cancel a longer one, and both have to be considered in the future[20] since, in this case, the expected day of menstruation has not been positively identified as one on which menstruation did not start. Thus, on the latter opinion, the table ends with a woman having two fixed *vesatot* of 28 and 29 days respectively. We shall refer to this as the *Beit Meir* opinion. Related to this is the opinion of the *Darkei Moshe*,[21] that when the most recent menstruation occurred before a date predicted as a result of the woman's previous pattern, the latter must also still be taken into account.

Non-fixed *Vesatot*

If a woman does not have a fixed *veset* of any type, then Jewish religious law requires abstinence from sexual relations on the same *onah* as the begining of her previous menstruation on the following days:

(i) the same number of days after her last menstruation as between it and the one before it, called a *non-fixed interval veset*[22]

(ii) the same day of the next (Jewish) month as her last menstruation, called a *non-fixed monthly veset*[23]

In the latter case, a problem arises when this last date was the 30th of a month and the next month only has 29 days. One opinion is that there is no corresponding day of abstinence, and another that abstinence is required on the last (29th) day of the next month and the day after it, which is the first of the following month.[24] For example, if a woman started to menstruate on the 30th of *Nisan* she would, according to the latter opinion, have to abstain from sexual relations on both the 29th of *Iyar* and the 1st of *Sivan* but, on the former, there would be no prohibited day until the 30th of *Sivan*.

There is one additional time of abstinence required in the absence of a fixed *veset*, the *onah benonit*,[25] average period. This consists of the thirtieth day after the start of the last menstruation or, according to the opinion of the *Sefer HaKreti*,[26] thirty days after it, i.e., the thirty-first day. The *onah benonit* has one extra stringency, according to many opinions, in that it consists of a full day and not only an *onah*.[27] So if the expected *onah* is by day, the *preceding* night is included, whereas if it is by night, then the *following* day *onah* is included, in accordance with the Jewish calendar.

Fixed *Vesatot* – Monthly System

There are several types of fixed *veset* that are based on days of the month mentioned in the *halachic* literature.

Fixed Monthly Veset[28]

The simplest fixed monthly *veset* is established when a woman starts to menstruate on the same day of three consecutive months, a pattern already described above. She must expect to continue this pattern and abstain from sexual relations on that day of the next and subsequent months. According to many opinions, more than one fixed monthly *veset* can operate concurrently.[29]

Veset Rosh Chodesh[30]

As explained above, months in the Jewish calendar consist of either 29 or 30 days, the first day being a minor holy day, *Rosh Chodesh*. When the previous month has 30 days, the thirtieth is also celebrated as *Rosh Chodesh* and for the purposes of *veset* calculation, the two days are treated as one according to some opinions.

For example, if a woman started to menstruate on the 1st of *Nisan,* the 30th of *Nisan* (which is considered to be the first day of *Rosh Chodesh Iyar*) and the 1st of *Sivan*, a *veset Rosh Chodesh* is established and she has to abstain from sexual relations on the 30th of *Sivan* and the 1st of *Tammuz*, both of which count as *Rosh Chodesh Tammuz*.

Veset Hasirug[31]

If a woman started to menstruate on the same day in three non-consecutive months but the number of intervening months is the same, then a *veset hasirug*, a "woven" *veset*, is established irrespective of whether she menstruated in those months on a different day or not.

For example, if a woman started to menstruate on the 4th of *Nisan*, 4th of *Tammuz*, and 4th of *Tishrei*, a *veset hasirug* for the 4th of every third month is established and she has to expect to menstruate next on the 4th of *Tevet*. This *veset* is established even if she menstruated at some other time in between, e.g., 23rd of *Iyar*.

As in (i), a *veset hasirug* can operate concurrently with another one, or a fixed monthly *veset*.[32]

Veset Hadilug[33]

If the dates on which a woman started to menstruate increase or decrease by constant amounts (*dilug*, jump, plural *dilugim*) each month, then a *veset hadilug*, a "jumping" *veset*, is established.

For example, if a woman started to menstruate on the 1st of *Nisan*, the 4th of *Iyar* and the 7th of *Sivan*, an increasing *veset hadilug* with jumps of three days is established, and she has to expect to menstruate next on the 10th of *Tammuz*.

Similarly, if a woman started to menstruate on the 25th of *Nisan*, the 20th of *Iyar* and the 15th of *Sivan*, a reducing *veset hadilug* with jumps of five days is established, and she has to expect to menstruate next on the 10th *Tammuz*.

Clearly a problem will arise when the jump predicts a date that cannot exist, like the 32nd of *Ellul*. According to some opinions,[34] this is treated as the 3rd of *Tishrei*. Similarly, the 4th of *Ellul* would have to be treated as the 27th of *Av*.

There is an opinion that a fixed *veset* can be established when the *dilugim* themselves increase or decrease by an equal amount three times.[35]

Veset Sirug Badilug[36]

Veset hasirug and *veset hadilug* can be combined to form a *veset sirug badilug*. For example, if a woman started to menstruate on the 1st *Nisan*, the 5th of *Sivan* and the 9th of *Av*, a *veset sirug badilug* is established, increasing the date by four with a gap of one month, and she has to expect to menstruate next on the 13th of *Tishrei*.

Veset Dilug Chalilah[37]

If a *dilug* pattern is repeated in blocks, then a *veset dilug chalilah*, a cyclic "jump" *veset*, is established. For example, if a woman started to menstruate on the 1st of *Nisan*, 2nd of *Iyar*, 3rd of *Sivan*, 1st of *Tammuz*, 2nd of *Av*, 3rd of *Ellul*, 1st of *Tishrei*, 2nd of *Marcheshvan* and 3rd of *Kislev*, then such a *veset dilug chalilah* is established and she must expect to menstruate on the 1st of *Tevet*, 2nd of *Shevat*, 3rd of *Adar*, 1st of *Nisan*, etc.

Fixed *Vesatot* – Interval System

The second system of *veset* determination is based on the intervals between successive menstruations. There are, however, several opinions regarding how these intervals are calculated for the purpose of determining regularity.

(i) The most commonly held view is that the interval is the number of days from the *start* of one menstruation until the *start* of the next one.[38]

(ii) Another opinion is that the interval is calculated from the termination of menstrual bleeding until the start of the next menstruation. The next menstruation is predicted as the same number of days after the *end* of bleeding.[39] Clearly if bleeding always lasts the same number of days, this will predict the same next expected menstruation as the first opinion.

(iii) A third opinion is the same as in the second, except where menstrual bleeding lasts for less than five days, the interval is counted only from the fifth day.[40] This is tied up with certain technical points in *halachah* not directly relevant to the problem of *vesatot*.

There is the *Dovid Tevele* opinion,[41] not accepted in practice, that all the above should be reckoned in *onot* rather than davs.

Usually, once a fixed *veset* is established, the *onah benonit* can be ignored. However, there is an opinion that where this predicts a menstruation later than that for the *onah benonit*, then the latter must also be taken into account.[42] This is parallel to the opinion that shorter intervals do not cancel longer ones (see above).

Whichever system is used for calculating intervals, one can have any of the following fixed *vesatot* that parallel the corresponding ones on the monthly system.

Fixed Interval *Veset*[43]

If a woman records four menstruations with three equal intervals between them, she must expect this pattern to continue and abstain from sexual relations that number of days after her last menstruation as described above.

Veset Hadilug[44]

If the intervals increase or decrease by a constant amount three times, then a *veset hadilug* is established. For example, a sequence of intervals of 29, 31, 33 days establishes a *veset hadilug* with jumps of two days, and the woman must expect to menstruate next after a further 35 days. There is an opinion that four intervals need be considered, i.e., three equal jumps.[45] With a decreasing jump in intervals, this *veset* must eventually break down when the predicted interval is negative. Finally, there is the opinion that a fixed *veset* can be established when the *dilugim* increase or decrease by an equal amount three times.[46]

Veset Dilug Chalilah[47]

As in the monthly system, this can be established when the intervals form a cyclic pattern. For example, a sequence of intervals of 27, 28, 29, 27, 28, 29, 27, 28, 29 days would establish such a pattern, and would predict that the next menstruation would occur 27 days later.

There is, for obvious reasons, no equivalent on the interval system to the *veset hasirug*.

Veset Hashavua[48]

There is one other computable *veset* that is established when a woman starts to menstruate on the same day of the week at regular intervals. This produces the same effect as a fixed interval *veset* but only requires three menstruations to become established, not four with three intervals. On this system no *veset hadilug* or *hasirug* is taken into account according to any opinion.

THE COMPUTER PROGRAM

The main objective of the program was to take a set of dates provided by a woman and determine any *vesatot* implied by it, giving a set of dates when abstinence from sexual relations would be required. Since there are conflicting opinions as to how some of the *vesatot* are computed and different communities follow different ones, it was hoped to cover all of them so that the program would be usable by all. The disadvantage of this approach is that the number of possibilities is quite large, yet only a limited number of them are relevant to any particular person. Thus, it could not be used by anyone not familiar with the *halachic* background and would be restricted in practice to rabbis expert in this field. This is perhaps not undesirable since the subject is complex and an error would have serious consequences.

Since the program was meant for those who were, in a computing sense, laymen, even if they were experts in the laws of *vesatot,* it was essential that the program be user-friendly. Various features were incorporated with this in mind.

The program was designed to

(i)   take a data file
(ii) add any new information and update the file
(iii) search the file for each *veset*

(iv) store any *veset* found together with the date of the next expected menstruation according to it

(v)   sort the dates into chronological order

The Data File

In order to avoid errors, it was decided to ask women to submit the dates on which menstruation began and compute the intervals as part of the program. A file was set up for each woman that could be added to each month as fresh data became available. All data was entered in response to simple prompts, and after each response the computer asked for verification. When all the data had been entered, it was displayed once more for checking before calculating the intervals. Having ensured that the data was correct, the intervals according to the various opinions described were computed.

In order to search for all types of *vesatot* described above, the following data was required for each menstruation:

(i)   day, month, and year of its start

(ii) the *onah* when it started, the day of the week on which it started, and the number of days it lasted.

For these purposes, the months were numbered as in section 2 and the years according to the Jewish reckoning.

The *onah* was coded as 0 for the night and 1 for the day.

The days of the week were numbered 1 for Sunday, 2 for Monday, etc. It was decided that since many women do not record this information, they should be asked to enter 0 if the day of the week was unavailable.

If the number of days that the menstrual period lasted had not been recorded, the woman was asked to enter 0. Thus, all the interval opinions then predict the same date.

Having entered the data, the intervals were calculated, and for these purposes a subroutine was called which made use of a data file containing the year types as included in the appendix.

Thus, an array was produced, each row of which contained the information relevant to one menstruation, the first six elements being the data provided, and the remainder the intervals as calculated according to the various opinions.

Table 3: Typical data file					
Day	Month	Year	*Onah*	Day of Week	Duration
8	12	46	1	2	5
5	13	46	1	2	5
2	1	46	1	6	4
30	1	46	0	7	5
27	2	46	1	5	6
27	3	46	0	6	7
26	4	46	1	7	5
24	5	46	1	6	5
21	6	46	1	5	6
22	7	47	1	7	5
19	8	47	0	6	5
15	9	47	0	4	4
10	10	47	1	1	5
6	11	47	0	3	5
1	12	47	1	2	5
29	12	47	1	2	6
2	2	47	1	6	5

A typical set of data might be as shown in Table 3. Since the years in the year-type file lie between 5706 and 5780, the first two digits have been omitted. Notice that when the month number changes from 12 (or 13) to 1, the year number is unaltered, whereas the latter changes after month 6.

The intervals and *dilugim* were calculated and, in order for the searches for patterns to be simpler, the *day* and *intervals* corresponding to a night *onah* start have been made negative. This produces the array shown in Table 4. The *onah*-based intervals could also have been included but were omitted since they are not accepted in any community in practice.

The Fixed *Veset* Searches

Each fixed *veset* has its particular rules as described in Section 3, and so a separate subroutine is needed for each one. Depending on how many possibilities are considered, the project can be made more or less difficult and therefore suited to courses of various levels.

1. At a relatively simple level, one might only include the non-fixed *vesatot* that are most common in practice. This would require subroutines for:

(i) finding the interval between two given dates on the Jewish calendar (to set up the data file); (ii) finding the date on the Jewish calendar a given number of days after a given date

2. At a slightly more sophisticated level, the *halachically* more significant patterns could be included. These would involve only considering *ma'yan satum* and ignoring the *Bet Meir* opinion. At this level, the *Or Zarua* opinion could be included with little extra complication.

From a programming point of view, the following are the simplest:

(iii) fixed monthly *veset* (iv) fixed interval *veset* (v) *veset hashavua* and possibly (vi) *veset Rosh Chodesh*. (The *Dovid Tevele* opinion could also be included.)

3. At a third level, one would include the *Beit Meir* and *Darkei Moshe* opinions.

4. At a still more sophisticated level, one would include the various *dilug* and *sirug* patterns.

Table 4: Extended data file

| Date | | | Onah | Day | Duration | Intervals | | | Dilugim | | | | |
D	M	Y				(i)	(ii)	(iii)	D	M	(i)	(ii)	(iii)
8	12	46	1	2	5	0	0	0	0	0	0	0	0
5	13	46	1	4	5	28	23	23	3	1	0	0	0
2	1	46	1	6	4	27	22	22	3	1	-1	-1	-1
30	1	46	0	7	5	29	25	24	28	0	2	3	2
27	2	46	1	5	6	28	23	23	-3	1	-1	-2	-1
27	3	46	0	6	7	30	24	24	0	1	2	1	1
26	4	46	1	7	5	30	23	23	-1	0	1	-1	-1
24	5	46	1	6	5	28	23	23	-2	1	-2	0	0
21	6	46	1	5	6	28	23	23	3	1	0	0	0
22	7	47	1	7	5	31	25	25	1	1	3	2	2
19	8	47	0	6	5	28	23	23	-3	1	3	2	2
15	9	47	0	4	4	27	22	22	-4	1	-1	-1	-1
10	10	47	1	1	5	26	22	21	-5	1	1	0	-1
6	11	47	0	5	5	26	21	21	-4	1	0	-1	0
1	12	47	1	2	5	26	21	21	-5	1	0	0	0
29	12	47	1	2	6	29	24	24	28	0	3	3	3
2	2	47	1	6	5	33	27	27	-27	2	4	3	3

5. Finally, everything could be run on the *ma'yan patuach* hypothesis as well as *ma'yan satum*.

Each subroutine would, if it finds a pattern, put a record in the results file. This would include the nature of the *veset*, the date and *onah* predicted by it. In the case of intervals, the number of days should be given, and in the case of *sirug* and *dilug* patterns, also the number of months or days respectively in the gaps.

The Results File

Having searched the data file with the subroutines of the appropriate level, the results file will contain a set of records. The final stage of the program is to sort these into chronological order and present the results in a suitable manner. A typical output of a level 2 program might be:

Abstinence from sexual relations is required on the following dates:

(i)   29th of *Iyar* by day: non-fixed interval, 29th day, *Or Zarua*
(ii) 1st of *Sivan* by night: non-fixed interval, 29th day
(iii) 1st of *Sivan* by day: non-fixed monthly, *Or Zarua*; *onah benonit*, *Or Zarua*
(iv) 2nd of *Sivan* by night: non-fixed monthly *onah benonit*
(v)   2nd of *Sivan* by day: *onah benonit*, full day; *onah benonit*, *Kreti*, *Or Zarua*
(vi) 3rd of *Sivan* by night: *onah benonit*, *Kreti*
(vii) 3rd of *Sivan* by day: *onah benonit*, *Kreti*, full day
(viii) 6th of *Sivan* by day: fixed interval, 35th day, *Or Zarua*
(ix) 7th of *Sivan* by night: fixed interval, 35th day

Notice that several of the dates are predicted by more than one *veset*. These have all been included in the printout to give a rabbi the full range of possibilities so that he can decide which are relevant to his community.

CONCLUSION

This problem has been used as a student project on the B.Sc. (Hons.) in Combined Studies and the HND in Mathematics, Statistics and Computing with reasonable success. It was found that for such students, a program at Level 3 was feasible, but Level 4 was too time-consuming. However, since further patterns can be added quite easily to a pre-existing program, it is hoped to eventually produce a complete Level 5 package.

ENDNOTES

1. Rabbi Joseph Karo, *Shulchan Aruch, Even haEzer*, chap. 15. The *Shulchan Aruch*, first published in Venice in 1565, is a digest of Jewish religious law, which, together with commentaries and navellae by later decisors, is the authoritative code for Jewish religious practice. An edition with the most important such additional material is that published by *Pe'er haTorah* (Jerusalem, 1958).
2. Cashdan, J. and Stern, M.D., 1987, *Math. Gazette*, 71 (456), 100–104.
3. Rabbi Joseph Karo, *Shulchan Aruch, Yoreh Deah*, chap. 183.
4. *Ibid.*, chap. 197, paragraph 1.
5. *Ibid.*, chap. 184.
6. Jacobs, J. 1986, Finding Patterns in Tables of Menstruation Dates. B.Sc. (Hons.) Combined Studies dissertation, Manchester Polytechnic.
7. Ormesher, A.M. 1987, Translation of a Program to Find Patterns in Tables of Menstruation Dates. HND in Mathematics, Statistics and Computing dissertation, Manchester Polytechnic.
8. Rabbi Joseph Karo, *Shulchan Aruch, Yoreh Deah*, chaps 184–191 (abbreviated YD). All references, unless otherwise specified, are henceforth to paragraphs in these chapters or works based on them. A commentary/compendium on these and related chapters is *Badei haShulchan* (abbreviated BS) by Rabbi F. Cohen (New York: Rabbi Jacob Joseph Press, 1980). This consists, in addition to the text, of explanatory notes (numbered), glosses discussing the underlying *halachic* arguments and references both to the earlier works on which the *Shulchan Aruch* is based and later authorities. In view of its comprehensive nature, references are, where possible, given to it rather than to the primary sources.
9. YD, 189.19.
10. YD, 189.2.
11. YD, 189.6.
12. YD 189.2.
13. YD, 189.15.
14. *Ibid.*
15. YD, 189.2.
16. *Ibid.*
17. YD, 189.13.

18. BS, gloss *Vekivan* to YD, 184.6.
19. BS, 17 to YD, 184.2.
20. BS, 106 to YD, 189.13.
21. *Ibid.*
22. YD, 189.5.
23. YD, 189.2.
24. BS, gloss *Chosheshet* to YD, 189.13.
25. YD, 189.1.
26. BS, 8 to YD, 189.1.
27. BS, 7 to YD, 189.1.
28. YD, 189.6.
29. YD, 189.32.
30. BS, 48 to YD, 189.6.
31. YD, 189.9.
32. YD, 189.32.
33. YD, 189.7.
34. BS, gloss *Ad* to YD, 189.7.
35. BS, 61 to YD, 189.7.
36. BS, gloss *Beechad* to YD, 189.9.
37. YD, 189.8.
38. YD, 184.1.
39. BS 1.1 to YD, 184.1.
40. Rabbi Y. Farkash, 1989, *Machsheret Tarah* (New York: Moznaim Press).
41. BS, 92 to YD, 189.13.
42. BS, 25 to YD, 186.3.
43. YD, 189.2.
44. YD, 189.5.
45. BS, gloss *Kegon* to YD, 189.5.
46. BS, gloss *Shebechol* to YD, 189.5.
47. BS, gloss *Raatah* to YD, 189.8.
48. YD, 189.6.

CANTILLATION SIGNS
(*TA'AMEI HAMIKRA*)

Sᴉɴᴄᴇ ᴍᴀɴʏ ʀᴇᴀᴅᴇʀs may not be entirely familiar with the full significance of the traditional cantillation signs, as found in our printed editions of the Torah, I shall briefly outline them first. They are part of the Torah *shebe'al peh* and have three purposes. Firstly, they act as punctuation signs, and secondly, they indicate where the syllable is stressed. Finally, they are a form of musical notation with which the text is to be chanted, but this aspect will not concern us here. Like the vowel signs, they are part of the Torah *shebe'al peh*, without which the written text would, in effect, be unintelligible.

The signs are divided into two groups: the conjunctives, which join a word to the next, and the disjunctives, which separate them. The latter are subdivided into four levels of disjunction analogous to full stop, semicolon, and comma in English. Because of the differing musical expressions, there are several symbols with the same effect as punctuation marks. There are various rules for particular situations, but these are beyond the scope of this work.

The punctuation aspect of the cantillation signs can significantly alter the meaning of the text. This has been noted in many places by the commentators. Similarly, they can avoid a serious misreading of the text by preventing the misplacement of the stress on a word that would radically alter its meaning.

This summary only includes cantillation signs found in the *Shema*. There are several not used in the *Shema*, quite apart from the completely different system which is used in *Iyov*, *Mishlei*, and *Tehillim*. The reader is referred to Mordechai Breuer's *Ta'amei HaMikra* (Chorev, Jerusalem, 1989) for a fuller treatment of these matters. Since not everyone is familiar with them, it is apposite to list them here briefly in their various categories.

Disjunctives
In decreasing power of separation, these are:

(i)   *kaizerim* ("emperors"),
      sof pasuk (also called silluk) אַ (equivalent to a full stop),
      etnachta אַ (main subdivision of a verse)

(ii) *melakhim* ("kings")
      segol אֶ, zakef katan אֶ, zakef gadol אֶ, tippecha אַ

(iii) *mishnim* ("viceroys")
      revia' אֶ, zarka אֶ, pashta אֶ, yetiv אֶ, tevir אֶ

(iv) *shelishim* ("officers")
      gershayim אֶ, azla אֶ (known as an azla geresh when not
      preceded by a kadma)

Conjunctives (which link words)

munach אֶ, *merekha* אֶ, *mahpakh* אֶ, *darga* אֶ, *kadma* אֶ

Within each category, the *te'amim* have equivalent power, the choice of which one is to be used in any particular situation being determined by rules associated with where the words appear in a verse, and their musical expression, neither of which concerns us here.

In addition, there are three other symbols that appear in our text that have some relevance to its punctuation and/or pronunciation. The first is the *makkaf*, hyphen, א־א, which joins two words so that they are regarded to a certain extent as if they were one word. The second is the *pesik*, a vertical line between two words, א ׀ א, which signifies a short pause between the words, irrespective of any other cantillation on them. The third is the *meteg* (also called *ge'ayah*), א, which indicates a secondary stress within the word.

In general, the cantillation marks are placed on the stressed syllable, except for the *segol*, *zarka* and *pashta*, which are always placed on the final syllable, and the *yetiv*, which always precedes the word. Where the stress is not on the last syllable, the *pashta*, and in many texts also the *zarka* and *segol*, are placed on that syllable as well.

The reader will notice that the same symbol is used with more than one meaning: *sof pasuk* and *meteg*, *pashta* and *kadma*, and *yetiv* and *mahpakh*. The first pair can be distinguished since the *sof pasuk* must appear on the final or penultimate syllable, whereas the *meteg* can never do so. Also, a word with a *silluk* is always followed by the punctuation mark :. The *pashta* is always at the end of the word (אא), whereas the *kadma* is at the beginning of the stressed syllable, even in monosyllabic words (אא). Similarly the *yetiv* is to the right of the vowel of the first syllable (א) whereas the *mahpakh* is always to the left of the vowel of the stressed syllable (א).

APPENDIX 2

GEMATRIA SYSTEMS

Eᴀᴄʜ ʟᴇᴛᴛᴇʀ ɪɴ the Hebrew alphabet represents a number, thus any word has a corresponding numerical value known as its *gematria*. There are also several derived systems of which only the *mispar katan*, where powers of ten are discarded, has been used in this work. For a further discussion of these and related matters, the reader is referred to Matityahu Glazerson's *Letters of Fire* (Feldheim, 1984).

letter	א	ב	ג	ד	ה	ו	ז	ח	ט
gematria	1	2	3	4	5	6	7	8	9
mispar katan	1	2	3	4	5	6	7	8	9

letter	י	כ	ל	מ	נ	ס	ע	פ	צ
gematria	10	20	30	40	50	60	70	80	90
mispar katan	1	2	3	4	5	6	7	8	9

letter	ק	ר	שׁ	ת
gematria	100	200	300	400
mispar katan	1	2	3	4

In some systems, the final letters are given values that continue the sequence, whereas in others they take the same *gematria* as their medial form. In the former, their *gematriot* are:

letter	ך	ם	ן	ף	ץ
gematria	500	600	700	800	900
mispar katan	5	6	7	8	9

PREVIOUSLY PUBLISHED WORKS

1967		1
1.	Optimal Quadrature Formulae	Comp. J. 9.4, Feb.
1985		**11**
2.	A Remarkable Approximation to Pi	Math. Gaz., 69.449, Oct.
3.	A Matter of Conception...and Misconception	J. Tel., 4th Oct.
4.	Halacha and the Chemist	J. Tel., 18th Oct.
5.	Forbidden to Limit Family	J. Tel., 1st Nov.
6.	Modern Trend of Small Families	J. Tel., 8th Nov.
7.	Doctors Not Trained in Ethics	J. Tel., 15th Nov.
8.	Rabbi is Wrong!	J. Tel., 22nd Nov
9.	Conforming to the Norm	J. Tel., 29th Nov.
10.	Calculations before Calculators	Math. Gaz., 69.450, Dec
11.	A Question of Ambiguity	J. Tel., 6th Dec
12.	Jews – an Endangered Species	J. Tel., 13th Dec.
1986		**38**
13.	Realizing Hitler's Dream...Voluntarily	J. Tel., 3rd Jan.

14	A Wife's Birth Right (in "Rabbi Wachman Answers")	J. Tel., 3rd Jan.
15.	When Girls Become Second-Class Men	J. Tel., 10th Jan.
16.	Woman of Work – or Worth?	J. Tel., 24th Jan.
17.	Corrupt Poison of Feminists	J. Tel., 31st Jan.
18.	Haunted by Spectre of the Vanishing Jew	J. Tel., 7th Feb.
19.	Low Birthrate	J. Chron., 7th Feb.
20.	Family Planning – A Torah Perspective	Private pub., 12th Feb.
21.	Don't Just Talk about the Problem	J. Tel., 14th Feb.
22.	Keeping British Jewry Alive	J. Tel., 21st Feb.
23.	Women Not Dishonest	J. Tel., 28th Feb.
24.	Manipulated by the Media	J. Tel., 7th Mar.
25.	New London Synagogue	J. Chron., 7th Mar.
26.	Appalling Attitude to Sex	J. Tel., 21st Mar.
27.	Across the Religious Divide	J. Chron., 21st Mar.
28.	How to Deal with the Gabbled Kaddish	J. Tel., 28th Mar.
29.	Unworthy Motives for Birth Control	J. Tel., 5th Apr.
30.	New London's Theology	J. Chron., 11th Apr.
31.	Travesty of Truth	J. Tel., 23rd Apr.
32.	One Way to Cross the Religious Divide	J. Chron., 2nd May
33.	Birth Control in Halacha	J. Chron., 16th May
34.	We Want More – But it's Never Enough	J. Tel., 23rd May
35.	Birth Control Propaganda	J. Trib., 29th May
36.	Birth Control: the Dangers	J. Chron., 30th May
37.	Squaring the Circle – an Esoteric Tradition?	Cat. & Anc. Hist. 8.2, Jul
38.	Let Good Sense Prevail	J. Gaz., 4th July
39.	Let's Disagree in an Amicable Manner	J. Tel., 22nd Aug.
40.	Seder Selichos leYom haKippurim keMinhag Adass Yeshurun	Private pub., Oct.
41.	Mrs W's Feminist Prejudice	J. Tel., 7th Nov.
42.	Case for a New Girls' School	J. Tel., 14th Nov.
43.	Divine Solution to Israel's Problems	J. Tel., 21st Nov.

44.	Partial Fractions: a Problem in Rigid Thought Patterns	Math. Gaz., 70.454, Dec.
45.	Domestic Central Heating: a Student Modelling Exercise	Teach. Math., 5.3, Dec.
46.	Kahane: Two Facts the Left Should Know	J. Tel., 19th Dec.
47.	Every Child a Unique Blessing	J. Gaz., 19th Dec.
48.	Rabbi Goren and Reform	J. Chron., 24th Dec.
49.	But is there Any Other Solution?	J. Tel., 31st Dec.
50.	Conservative "Judaism" – Kosher or Kosher-style?	J. Trib., 31st Dec.

1987		**25**
51.	Don't Knock Reform but…	J. Gaz., 2nd Jan.
52.	AIDS	J. Tel., 9th Jan.
53.	'Justifiable' Attack	J. Gaz., 9th Jan.
54.	Secular Zionism's Answer?	J. Tel., 30th Jan.
55.	How Could Israel Remain Jewish Under the P.L.O.?	J. Tel., 13th Feb.
56.	Why the Mechanic Kicked the Car – a Teaching Aid for Transfer Functions	Math. Gaz., 71.455, Mar.
57.	Keeping It in the Family…	J. Tel., 27th Mar.
58.	A Mathematical Notation for Family Relations (with J. Cashdan)	Inter., 22.1, Apr.
59.	Depressing Story	J. Gaz., 20th May
60.	Forbidden Marriages from a Woman's Angle (with J. Cashdan)	Math. Gaz., 71.456, June
61.	Finding the Largest Reshut haYachid	Niv haMidr. 20, June
62.	T.S. Screening	J. Chron., 17th July
63.	The Impending Schism in Anglo-Jewry	J. Trib., 23rd July
64.	Vital to have Large Families	J. Gaz., 24th July
65.	Tay Sachs: to Screen or Not	J. Chron., 31st July
66.	Some Reflections on the Shema	J. Trib., 6th Aug.
67.	Schism in Anglo-Jewry	J. Trib., 6th Aug.
68.	Let's Help Each Other	J. Chron., 7th Aug.

69.	Consanguinity of Witnesses: a Mathematical Analysis	Teach. Math., 6.2, Sep.
70.	Shul Tickets	J. Chron., 18th Sep.
71.	A Time to Speak…	J. Trib., 22nd Sep.
72.	Anti-Zionism at Israeli Yeshivot	J. Chron., 6th Nov.
73.	Kaddish Yosom – The Orphan Kaddish	J. Trib., 12th Nov.
74.	Searching for God and Faith after the Holocaust	J. Chron., 27th Nov.
75.	A King Extolled with Praises	J. Trib., 24th Dec.
1988		**21**
76.	Women and the Tallit	J. Chron., 29th Jan.
77.	Pronounciation of the Shem	J. Trib., 25th Feb.
78.	Volumes of Some Depth – An A-level Miniproject	Teach. Math., 6.4 Mar.
79.	Public Danger	J. Trib., 31st Mar.
80.	Modesty Forbids	J. Tel., 13th May
81.	Holiness in the Home	J. Chron., 10th June
82.	Fundamentals of Jewish Belief	J. Chron., 1st July
83.	Torah from Heaven	J. Chron., 5th Aug.
84.	Non-Orthodox Conversions – A Halachic Analysis	J. Trad., Aug.
85.	Misod Chachomim Unevonim	J. Trib., 8th Sep.
86.	Shock Over a Pregnant 16-year-old	J. Tel., 16th Sep.
87.	Recognition of Rabbis	J. Chron., 23rd Sep.
88.	Pitfalls of Ignorance	J. Trib., 23rd Sep.
89.	Buses to Work – A Modelling Week Problem	Teach. Math., 7.3, Oct.
90.	The Kiddush Widow, part 1	J. Trib., 24th Nov.
91.	ibid., part 2	J. Trib., 1st Dec.
92.	Who is a Convert?	J. Trib., 1st Dec.
93.	A Time to Speak	J. Trad., Dec.
94.	Satisfying One's Client – Volumes of Some Depth Reconsidered	Teach. Math., 7.4, Dec.
95.	The Law of Return – An Orthodox View	J. Echo, 16th Dec.

146.	Mathematical Motivation through Matrimony	Math. Mag., 63.4, Oct.
147.	Should All Conversions be made Conditional?	J. Press, 12th Oct.
148.	Dates for Ramadan	Math. Rev., 1.2, Nov.
149.	Preserving the Belfast community	J. Chron., 9th Nov.
1991		**14**
150.	Sunrise, Sunset – a Modelling Exercise in Iteration (with N.S. Ellis)	Teach. Math., 9.4, Mar.
151.	Reform Conversions Without Mikvah Challenged	J. Chron., 1st Mar.
152.	Three into Four Won't Go	Math. Rev., 1.4, Apr.
153.	Conversion Questions	J. Chron., 5th Apr.
154.	Mastery of Words…or Mastery through Words	J. Trib., 16th May
155.	Ugly Face of Liberal Intolerance	J. Tel., 24th May
156.	It's a Long, Long Time from June to September	Teach. Math., 10.1, June
157.	Know How to Answer an Apikoros	J. Trib., 13th June
158.	Fundamentalism or Torah Judaism?	J. Trib., 5th Sep.
159.	Sacks and Dialogue	J. Chron., 20th Sep.
160.	Conflict between Religious and National Traditions in Iran: A Group Case Study (with L.A.M. Nejad)	Teach. Math., 10.3, Oct.
161.	Evidence of Knowledge of the Decimal Notation in Fourth Century Babylonia	Theta, 5.2, Dec.
162.	'Approval' was Given for Intermarriage	J. Tel., 20th Dec.
163.	Let's not Rewrite History	J. Tel., 27th Dec.
1992		**15**
164.	A "Hidden" Value of Pi	Yis.Yis., 1.11, Jan.
165.	They should not Exploit Public Ignorance	J. Tel., 10th Jan.
166.	Giving a Rabbi his Title	J. Tel., 17th Jan.
167.	Reform Movement is 'Changing the Facts'	J. Tel., 24th Jan.

168.	Discrete Avoidance of Marital Indiscretion	Math. Rev., 2.3, Feb
169.	Teaching the Need for Model Verification: a Simple Example (with R. Saunders)	Teach. Math., 11.1, Apr.
170.	A Firm Line on Current Affairs (with M. Rycraft)	Math. Rev., 2.4, Apr.
171.	A Response to the Missionary Menace	Le'ela 33, Apr.
172.	Torah from Heaven	J. Chron., 12th June
173.	Entrance Policy	J. Chron., 24th July
174.	Young Children in Shul	J. Trib., 30th July
175.	Career or Carer? The Dilemma of the Modern Orthodox Jewish Woman	J. Press, 31st July
176.	Leap Years	Yis.Yis.1.12, Aug.
177.	A Closer Look at the Shema	J. Trad., Sep.
178.	Correcting the Figures	J. Trib., 17th Sep.
1993		**8**
179.	How Chazal Approached the Missionary Menace: A Lesson for our Times	J. Trad., Mar.
180.	Liberal Marriages	J. Chron., 14th May
181.	Liberal Marriages and Halachah	J. Chron., 18th June
182.	Kara Lashemesh Vayizrach Or	Niv haMidr. 24, July
183.	Inclusivism – A Model for Communal Harmony?	J. Trad., Aug.
184.	'Third Sex' Idea Poses Problems	J. Chron., 20th Aug.
185.	Seder Hadlakat Ner Chanukah im Maoz Tzur Hamurchevet	Private pub.
186.	Can Inclusivism Preserve the Jewish Community	J. Trib., 2nd Dec.
1994		**28**
187.	Masorti Marriage Controversy	J. Chron., 7th Jan.
188.	Requirements for Conversion	J. Chron., 21st Jan

1995		18
215.	Jewish Mothers 'Not Funny'	J. Gaz., 6th Jan.
216.	The Fight for the Soul of the Manchester Kehilla	Yated, 11th Feb.
217.	Torah from Heaven	J. Chron., 24th Mar.
218.	A Doctrine of Deceit	Yated, 7th Apr.
219.	Masorti Revisionism Refuted: Reclaiming Chief Rabbi Hertz as an Orthodox Jew	Le'ela 39, Apr.
220.	B'sha'ah Tovah: The Jewish Woman's Clinical and Halachic Guide to Pregnancy and Childbirth (review)	Le'ela 39, Apr.
221.	How are they Getting There? (with M. Rycraft)	Int. J. Math. Ed. 26.1, Apr.
222.	To Silence the "Prosecutor"	Yated, 26th May
223.	Aliyos for Reform Ministers and Bishops	J. Trib., 22nd June
224.	Aliyos and Reform Clergymen	J. Trib., 29th June
225.	Falling Birth and Marriage Rates	J. Chron., 4th Aug.
226.	Points to Ponder in the Shema	Yated, 11th Aug.
227.	School was Right to Bar 'Masorti Child'	J. Tel., 8th Sep.
228.	Masorti's Campaign to Mislead	J. Tel., 29th Sep.
229.	This Phone Call Should Have Been Kept Secret	J. Tel., 27th Oct.
230.	To Clear the Air	J. Trib., 10th Nov.
231.	The Invalidity of Masorti Marriage	J. Trib., 23rd Nov.
232.	HaShir Lo Tam	Amudim, Dec.
1996		10
233.	No Way to Treat Chief Rabbi	Fin.Tim., 30th Jan.
234.	Masorti Assault on Leeds Community	J. Trib., 16th May
235.	Masorti in Leeds	J. Trib., 27th June
236.	This Birthrate is NOT Declining	J. Tel., 2nd Aug.
237.	Conversion: the Painful Facts	J. Chron., 16th Aug.
238.	Writing, and Not Writing, to the Press	J. Trib., 12th Sep.

239.	To Write, or not to Write?	J. Trib., 26th Sep.
240.	Acceptance of the Yoke of Mitzvot	J. Chron., 27th Sep.
241.	Letter Writing	J. Trib., 24th Oct.
242.	Why Reform Converts are not Jews	J. Tel., 8th Nov.

1997   **15**

243.	Torah-true Jews don't Write to London Paper	J. Tel., 3rd Jan.
244.	Orthodox Concern for Progressives	J. Chron., 4th Apr.
245.	When the Davening Finished too Late	HaMaor, 30.2, Apr.
246.	Reaching Solution to Conversion Rift	J. Chron., 25th Apr.
247.	Dear Chaim (no. 1)	J. Trib., 2nd May
248.	Can Members of Reform Still be Assumed to be Jews?	J. Trib., 8th May
249.	Let's Concentrate on Unity Instead of this Infighting	J. Tel., 23rd May
250.	Reform and Masorti 'separate Religions'	J. Tel., 11th July
251.	Eating Preferences of Anglo-Jews	J. Chron., 18th July
252.	Reform and Masorti 'Not Forms of Judaism'	J. Tel., 25th July
253.	Without Basic Beliefs can it be Judaism?	J. Tel., 29th Aug.
254.	Masorti and Reform 'separate Religions'	J. Tel., 12th Sep.
255.	Which Groups can be called Jewish?	J. Tel., 26th Sep.
256.	Why have Reform and Masorti Stayed Silent?	J. Tel., 10th Oct.
257.	Why Jews Treat Others as Separate Religions	J. Tel., 7th Nov.

1998   **10**

258.	Orthodoxy's View of Limmud	J. Chron, 2nd Jan.
259.	The United Synagogue and Limmud	J. Trib., 22nd Jan.
260.	'Suicide' for Orthodox	J. Tel., 23rd Jan.
261.	Some Tips on being a Sheliach Tzibur (Dear Chaim no.2)	J. Trib., 19th Mar.
262.	Dear Chaim (no.3)	J. Trib., 4th June

289.	Couples Living Together 'Need not be Bad Thing'	J. Tel., 27th Aug.
290.	Rejected Convert	J. Tel., 3rd Sep.
291.	For Everything there is a Time	HaMaor 33.1, Sep.
292.	Can British Reform Still Be Considered A Jewish Movement?	Yated, 24th Sep.
293.	Halachic Answers to Agunot's Plight	J. Chron., 15th Oct.
294.	Avoid Action that may Divide the Community	Lon. J. News, 29th Oct.
295.	Putting the Misguided Right over Halacha…	J. Tel., 5th Nov.
296.	Misconceptions of the Agunot Issue	Lon. J. News, 5th Nov.
297.	Making a Stern Stand on the 'Jacobs Affair'	Lon. J. News, 3rd Dec.
298.	Manchester Siyum Marks Completion of Seder Moed (with Rabbi Y.M. Rosenbaum)	J. Trib., 9th Dec.
299.	Husband's Rights in Get Cases	J. Chron., 10th Dec.
2000		**29**
300.	Rise in Reform Conversions	J. Chron., 25th Feb.
301.	Tell us the Reform Marriage Figures	J. Tel., 25th Feb.
302.	Reinterpreting Marriage Statistics	Lon. J. News, 25th Feb.
303.	Dividing the Jewish People – the Reform Way	Yated, 3rd Mar.
304.	How Accurate are Conversion Figures?	J. Tel., 10th Mar.
305.	Conversion Figures are 'Propaganda'	Lon. J. News, 10th Mar.
306.	Reform Marriages	J. Tel., 17th Mar.
307.	FEEDBACK	Yated, 31st Mar.
308.	Reform Converts 'Can Switch to Orthodoxy'	J. Tel., 31st Mar.
309.	Is Reform Really a Legitimate Religion?	Lon. J. News, 31st Mar.
310.	Not Being a Cohen is no Disaster	J. Tel., 19th Apr.
311.	Blame Husbands not the Rabbis	J. Tel., 28th Apr.
312.	Cookery Comment Insensitive	J. Tel., 28th Apr.

313.	Reform Figures are so Misleading	Lon. J. News, 28th Apr.
314.	Rabbis don't have Unlimited Authority	J. Tel., 12th May
315.	No TV? It's not Racist	J. Tel., 19th May
316.	Kashrut Conflicts	Lon. J. News, 19th May
317.	Those Who Shun TV have a Point	Sal.Adv., 25th May
318.	Comparisons are Misleading	J. Tel., 26th May
319.	Do Unto Others…	J. Tel., 16th June
320.	Agunot: Conflict Between Courts	J. Chron., 16th June
321.	Conservative Argument not Quite what it Seems	J. Tel., 30th June
322.	How do Liberals Define Judaism?	J. Tel., 21st July
323.	Missionary Avoided the Vital Question	J. Tel., 18th Aug.
324.	What Really Constitutes Judaism?	J. Tel., 15th Sep.
325.	A Man does not Even Know his Time	HaMaor 34.1, Oct.
326.	What is not Judaism	J. Tel., 13th Oct.
327.	Murder	
328.	Measured Response to the Riots	Lon. J .News, 24th Nov.
2001		**33**
329.	A Book for Purim	Yated, 2nd Mar.
3309.	Keep Mouths Shut and Identities Open	J. Tel., 20th Apr.
331.	More about Chazarat Hashatz	HaModia, 11th May
332.	Where is Masorti's Claimed Tolerance?	Lon. J. News, 18th May
333.	Wild Stories	Metro, 25th May
334.	More on Chazarat Hashatz	HaModia, 1st June
335.	Attitudes that Prolong Conflict	J. Chron., 8th June
336.	How Palestinians Might have Acted	J. Chron., 29th June
337.	Palestinians Must Bring Pressure for Peace	Metro, 12th July
338.	Orthodox English Demographics	Yated, 27th July
339.	Births are Down – or are They?	J. Tel., 27th July
340.	Chassunos and Timekeeping	J. Trib., 2nd Aug.
341.	No Warning	Metro, 6th Aug.
342.	Positive Visions for the Middle East	Times, 18th Aug.

343.	Chassunos	J. Trib., 23rd Aug.
344.	Double Standards	J. Post, 28th Aug.
345.	Double Standards in the Middle East	Lon. J. News, 31st Aug.
346.	Racist Crimes against the Jewish People	D. Tel., 5th Sep.
347.	More about Chuppa Timing	HaModia, 7th Sep.
348	Media Bias against Israel and Jews	Yated, 7th Sep.
349.	The Durban fiasco	J. Post, 7th Sep.
350.	Absurd Charge	J. Press, 12 Sep
351.	Why no Tefillin During Selichos	HaModia, 14th Sep.
352.	Neturei Karta Horrified Me	J. Tel., 14th Sep.
353.	Terror in USA and Peace Prospects	J. Chron., 21st Sep.
354.	L'Dovid HaShem Ori	J. Trib., 21st Sep.
355.	Calling Palestine by its Name	Guard., 27th Sep.
356.	Correct Pronunciation in Tefillah	J. Trib., 1st Nov.
357.	Wedding Expenses	J. Trib., 29th Nov.
358.	Correct Pronunciation in Tefillah	J. Trib., 6th Dec.
359.	Marked Target	J. Post, 16th Dec.
360.	Correct Pronunciation in Tefillah	J. Trib., 20th Dec.
361.	Parents should Oppose Lavish Weddings	HaModia, 28th Dec.

2002		**19**
362.	Pronunciation of Tefillah	J. Trib., 17th Jan.
363.	New Directions?	J. Chron., 29th Mar.
364.	A Truly Modest Wedding Proposal	J. Chron., 21st June
365.	Some Guidelines	J. Trib., 17th July
366.	The British Did It	J. Post, 23rd July
367.	No Guarantee of Safety	Metro, 26th July
368.	Cheering the Attack	J. Post, 2nd Aug.
369.	Disloyalty's Due	J. Post, 8th Aug.
370.	Conservatives: The Deserters	J. Trib., 15th Aug.
371.	Agree to a Timetable	HaModia, 16th Aug.
372.	Fair Game	J. Post, 21st Aug.

373.	Zeman Tefillah Lechud Uzeman Tzedokoh Lechud	Yated, 30th Aug.
374.	Food for the Media	J. Post, 4th Sep.
375.	Davening & Charity – Each in their Own Time	Voice, Sep.
376.	The Government and Faith Schools	J. Trib., 21st Nov.
377.	Right to Refuse	J. Chron., 29th Nov.
378.	Unrealistic Remedies	J. Tel., 13th Dec.
379.	Myth about Palestinians	J. Tel., 20th Dec.
380.	Bero Mezakeh Abba	Yated, 27th Dec.

2003		42
381.	Future is Here	J. Tel., 28th Feb.
382.	Why Wait for Latecomers?	J. Trib., 8th May
383.	Memory and Massacres	J. Chron., 9th May
384.	Malign Intent?	J. Post, 15th May
385.	Royal Answers	J. Tel., 16th May
386.	Don't Encourage Latecomers	HaModia, 16th May
387.	Case of Racism	J. Post, 9th June
388.	Cruel Methods of Killing Animals	Ind., 12th June
389.	Theater of the Absurd	J. Post, 17th June
390.	Late Maariv	J. Trib., 19th June
391.	Children at Early Maarivs	HaModia, 20th June
392.	…Commitment	J. Post, 1st July
393.	Gay and Lesbian Unions in Synagogue	Lon. J. News, 4th July
394.	Is the Chief Rabbi being Straight about Gays?	J. Chron., 11th July
395.	'Coming Out' is Offensive	J. Tel., 11th July
396.	Failure of Reason	J. Post, 23rd July
397.	Big Slump	J. Tel., 1st Aug.
398.	Gay and Lesbian Unions in Synagogue	Lon. J. News, 1st Aug.
399.	Middle East Myths	Ind., 1st Aug.
400.	Masorti Movement like Salt Beef Jews	Lon. J. News, 8th Aug.
401.	Mosque Incitement	J. Post, 8th Aug.

402.	The Jacobs Affair	J. Trib., 21st Aug.
403.	Honor the Sefer Torah	Voice, Sep.
404.	More on Tachanun for our Times	HaModia, 19th Sep.
405.	Scandal in Bournemouth	J. Post, 29th Sep.
406.	Avoid the Deniers	J. Press, 1st Oct.
407.	Masorti 'Beefing'	J. Tel., 10th Oct.
408.	Jews for Hamas?	J. Post, 12th Oct.
409.	Dangerous Demands	J. Tel., 31st Oct.
410.	Fashion Style Change in Shul	J. Tel., 7th Nov.
411.	Time Waits for No Man	J. Trib., 13th Nov.
412.	Captive Columnist	J. Post, 2nd Dec.
413.	On Ostentatious Weddings	HaModia, 5th Dec.
414.	The Jews for Jacobs 40 Years On	Yated, 5th Dec.
415.	Abortion Dilemmas	Ind., 8th Dec.
416.	What Semites?	J. Post, 9th Dec.
417.	Time Waits for No Man (follow-up letter)	J. Trib., 11th Dec.
418.	Converts	J. Tel., 12th Dec.
419.	Sodomy, Homosexual Desire and the Bible	Lon. J. News, 19th Dec.
420.	New Religions?	J. Post, 24th Dec.
421.	The BBC can be so Surprising	J. Tel., 24th Dec.
422.	New Jews or non-Jews?	J. Post, 29th Dec.
2004		**59**
423.	A Letter from Martin Stern, England	Yated, 9th Jan.
424.	'Arabic' Numerals	D. Tel., 13th Jan.
425.	What a Wedding!	J. Trib., 15th Jan.
426.	More on Chasunas	HaModia, 23rd Jan.
477.	Israeli Envoy's Protest at a Work of 'Art'	Lon. J. News, 23rd Jan.
428.	Romain's Way with Reform Conversions	Lon. J. News, 6th Feb.
429.	A Spade? Surely Not!	J. Post, 9th Feb.
430.	No Tail-waggers	J. Tel., 20th Feb.
431.	History of Hatred	Ind., 1st Mar.

462.	Merits and Defects of Zionism and Zionists	J. Chron., 20th Aug.
463.	The Obscenity of Sudan	J. News., 20th Aug.
464.	New Attitudes Needed to Break Middle East Deadlock	Guard., 25th Aug.
465.	Rabbi Dunner and the Stern group (2004)	J. Chron., 27th Aug.
466.	…What's a War Crime	J. Post, 2nd Sep.
467.	Headline Pointing in Wrong Direction	B. Tel., 10th Sep.
468.	Wall a Proven Protector	Scot., 22nd Sep.
469.	Loss of Community	Times, 27th Sep.
470.	Clive's 'Ignorant Attack' on Charedi	J. News., 1st Oct.
471.	Law Series is a Positive Expose	J. Tel., 6th Oct.
472.	One Day, or Two?	J. Post, 12th Oct.
473.	Are Anti-Zionists Anti-Semites?	J. News, 15th Oct.
474.	Humpty Dumpty Already Did It	J. Post, 17th Oct.
475.	Hebrew…as She is Spoken	J. News, 29th Oct.
476.	Coining a Phrase	Metro, 16th Nov.
477.	Separate the Denominations	Ha'aretz, 23rd Nov.
478.	The Origins of Specious	J. News, 3rd Dec.
479.	Technicalities, that's All	J. Post, 13th Dec.
480.	Belmarsh Alternative	Ind., 28th Dec.
481.	Female Mohel	J. Tel., 31st Dec.
2005		**50**
482.	Who's to Blame for Disasters	J. Post, 16th Jan.
483.	Go Gently	D. Tel., 17th Jan.
484.	Moat will Stop Demolition	Guard., 18th Jan.
485.	Danger to Pedestrians	J. Trib., 27th Jan.
486.	Jacobs's Views	J. Chron., 28th Jan.
487.	Studying History Teaches you to Think	D. Tel., 29th Jan.
488.	Secular Humanism	Scot., 7th Feb.
489.	Muslim Boycott of Holocaust Event	J. News, 11th Feb.
490.	Live in the Real World	Ir. Ind., 11th Mar.

491.	'Marrying Out'	J. Post, 17th Mar.
492.	Mayor's Jewish Roots (Purim spoof)	J. News, 24th Mar.
493.	Tachanun – a Case of Religious Coercion?	J. Trib., 31st Mar.
494.	Teacher's Case Tests Scales of Justice	J. News, 31st Mar.
495.	People of Israel	J. Post, 8th Apr.
496.	Tachanun Clarification	J. Trib., 14th Apr.
497.	Beth Din Right	J. Chron., 15th Apr.
498.	Pride and Prejudice	Scot., 11th May
499.	Convert Confusion	J. News, 16th June
500.	Sagal Case: Where is the Unlegislated Chesed?	J. Chron., 17th June
501.	One Rule for Them…	Scot., 21st June
502.	Gerus Crisis	J. Trib., 30th June
503.	The Denial of our Heritage will do Nothing to Prevent Terrorism	Scot., 14th July
504.	Pure Polemic	J. Post, 14th July
505.	Gerus in Halacha	J. Trib., 14th July
506.	Soldiers 'Legitimate' Target for Stern Gang	B. Tel., 18th July
507.	Misleading	B. Tel., 20th July
508.	BBC's Blind Spot	J. Press, 20th July
509.	Heaven Awaits all the Righteous	Ind., 21st July
510.	Our Defenders of the Faith	J. News., 21st July
511.	Terrorists' Targets	Scot., 25th July
512.	Would a Jewish PM have to Convert?	J. News., 28th July
513.	No Real Choice	J. Post, 4th Aug.
514.	No UN Protests	Her., 4th Aug.
515.	Return of Old Prejudices	Scot., 5th Aug.
516.	Ban would Negate Human Rights	Ind., 9th Aug.
517.	Effective Solution	Scot., 29th Aug.
518.	Is Peace Possible?	J. Post, 29th Aug.
519.	Reassurance Still Needed	J. Chron., 2nd Sep.
520.	Why School Barred Convert Children	J. Tel., 2nd Sep.

521.	When a Convert Marries a Cohen	J. News, 15th Sep.
522.	Caveat Emptor	J. Post, 16th Sep.
523.	When a Convert Marries a Cohen	J. News, 6th Oct.
524.	Unity not Uniformity	J. Post, 17th Oct.
525.	Taste of Selwyn	J. Tel., 4th Nov.
526.	A Little Bit of Background Puts a New Slant on the Story	Hen. Times, 17th Nov.
527.	Elections?	J. Trib., 1st Dec.
528.	Solution to Fowl Tasting Chicken	Sal. Adv., 1st Dec.
529.	Keep Out of Danger	J. Tel., 9th Dec.
530.	Not Forms of Judaism	J. Tel., 16th Dec.
531.	Disappointing Coverage	J. Tel., 23rd Dec.

2006		**73**
532.	Jacobs Vote	J. Trib., 12th Jan.
533.	Brian Gordon and Dr. Louis Jacobs	J. News, 12th Jan.
534.	Adherents of Judaism	J. Tel., 20th Jan.
535.	Kings and Countries	S. Her., 22nd Jan.
536.	Mufti Sought Hitler's Help	Scot., 6th Feb.
537.	Islamophobia is the New Anti-Semitism	Obs., 12th Feb.
538.	Suspension of Disbelief	J. Post, 1st Mar.
539.	Palestinians and Israelis	Scot., 2nd Mar.
540.	Starry Nights	J. Chron., 3rd Mar.
541.	Caterpillar Vote Disquiet	CofE News., 3rd Mar.
542.	…oh Really?	J. Post, 7th Mar.
543.	Subliminal Implants	D. Tel., 9th Mar.
544.	Reinforcing Conversions	J. Chron., 10th Mar.
545.	Israel's Actions in Context	Tab., 11th Mar.
546.	Disproportionate Vehemence	J. Post, 13th Mar.
547.	Pronunciation	Scot., 13th Mar.
548.	Age-old Tastes	J. Tel., 24th Mar.
549.	Parasites	Scot., 24th Mar.
550.	Labour's Loans Row is a Fuss about Nothing	Metro, 24th Mar.

580.	Doubts about Evolution	Ir. Ind., 12th Sep.
581.	Aveilim – Seeking Understanding	J. Trib., 14th Sep.
582.	Conflict Unresolved	B. Tel., 16th Sep.
583.	Darfur and Lebanon: a Morality Tale	Ir. Ex., 18th Sep.
584.	How the West Ignore Darfur	Ir. Ind., 19th Sep.
585.	Bus Attack	M.E.N., 21st Sep.
586.	Israel and Resolution 242	Ind., 9th Oct.
587.	Wrong Word	Metro, 9th Oct.
588.	Blaming Israel: if only Darfur Could Do It	Ir. Ex., 12th Oct.
589.	Arba Minim and New Yekkish Shul	J. Trib., 19th Oct.
590.	Slow Daveners	J. Press, 25th Oct.
591.	About Small-Town German Jews	Yated, 25th Oct.
592.	No Risk from Quota	J. News, 26th Oct.
593.	Hiding Behind a Muslim Veil	Ir. Ind, 27th Oct.
594.	Should We Defend the Muslim Veil?	J. News, 2nd Nov.
595.	Veils for Men	J. Tel., 3rd Nov.
596.	Veiled Allusion	J. Post, 12th Nov.
597.	Children in Shul	HaModia, 15th Nov.
598.	Author Jacobson	J. Tel., 17th Nov.
599.	Dying? No Revivifying	J. Post, 1st Dec.
600.	To Fly El Al, or Not	J. Post, 13th Dec.
601.	…Too Much for the Satmars	J. Post, 14th Dec.
602.	Maintaining Status Quo	J. Trib., 14th Dec.
603.	Responding to Extremist Views	Times, 23rd Dec.
604.	Dangerous Emissions	Scot., 29th Dec.

2007		**27**
605.	Origin of Concentration Camps	Ir. Times, 1st Feb.
606.	Diversionary Tactic	J. Post, 11th Feb.
607.	Points of View	M.E.N., 20th Mar.
608.	Worrying Fact	J. Tel., 23rd Mar.
609.	Doubts over Darwin Theory	J. Tel., 27th Apr.
610.	Price of Freedom	Scot., 7th May

611.	Too Simplistic	Scot., 22nd May
612.	…Except When it Doesn't	J. Post, 30th July
613.	Charedi Births	J. Chron., 10th Aug.
614.	Absurd Claim	J. Tel., 17th Aug.
615.	Sorting Things Out	J. Post, 19th Aug.
616.	Points of View	M.E.N., 23rd Aug.
617.	Comparing Indian and Palestine Partition	J. News, 23rd Aug.
618.	Arab Neglect	J. Tel., 24th Aug.
619.	Not-so-Jewish State	J. Chron., 31st Aug.
620.	Saving the Jews: Rewriting History is Nothing New	Ir. Ex, 12th Sep.
621.	Casual Labor	J. Post, 12th Oct.
622.	Treatment No Entry	Scot., 30th Oct.
623.	Contradictory Voices	Scot., 15th Nov.
624.	Squeeze on Gaza breaks Geneva rules	Ind., 23rd Nov.
625.	Faulty Logic	J. Post, 29th Nov.
626.	One Man's Free Speech…	Scot., 1st Dec.
627.	Bernard Misunderstood Rabbi Answer	J. Tel., 7th Dec.
628.	Conversion Concerns	J. Post, 18th Dec.
629.	JFS	J. News, 21st Dec.
630.	Candle Custom	J. Tel., 28th Dec.
631.	Halacha on Smoking	J. Post, 31st Dec.
2008		**62**
632.	Why Write It?	J. Tel., 4th Jan.
633.	If Only…	J. Tel., 11th Jan.
634.	For the Record	J. Post, 20th Jan.
635.	When Wedding Guests do not Want to Wash	J. Tel., 25th Jan.
636.	Idolatry? Oh No	J. Post, 29th Jan.
637.	Party to Folly	J. Post, 4th Mar.
638.	Growing Chareidi Community	J. Trib., 6th Mar.
639.	Higher Birthrate	J. Tel., 7th Mar.

640.	'Who is a Jew' Case	J. News, 13th Mar.
641.	Why a Fuss about their Marriages	J. Tel., 14th Mar.
642.	Why the Reform Movement is Backing the Chief in the JFS Case	J. Chron., 14th Mar.
643.	Purim and the Persian Kings	Guard., 25 Mar.
644.	Purim Gifts	J. Trib., 27th Mar.
645.	Religious Tyranny	J. Tel., 28th Mar.
646.	Live in Peace	M.E.N., 8th Apr.
647.	Language and Thought Patterns	J. Trib., 10th Apr.
648.	Are our Schools Becoming Jew-ish	J. News, 10th Apr.
649.	Tolerate fans exuberance'	Scot., 21st May
650.	Who's to Blame for the Conversion Crisis?	J. News, 26th June
651.	The Debate over the Israeli conversion row continues	J. Chron., 27th June
652.	Trouser women	J. Tel., 4th July
653.	Poland and the Jews	Times, 2nd Aug.
654.	For health tap into pure water	B. Tel., 7th Aug.
655.	Jewish issues in secular courts	J. News, 7th Aug.
656.	Forbidden love	J. Tel., 8th Aug.
657.	An inspiration to us all	M.E.N., 9th Aug.
658.	Poland's role in the Holocaust	Week, 9th Aug.
659.	Junior fasters	J. Tel., 22nd Aug.
660.	Hubcap horror	M.E.N., 27th Aug.
661.	Synagogue changes	J. Tel., 19th Sep
662.	Evolution is not proven	Scot., 22nd Sep.
663.	The problem with evolution	J. Press, 24th Sep.
664.	Seats in Shul	J. Tel., 17th Oct.
665.	Points of view	M.E.N., 23rd Oct.
666.	Simchat Schochet	J. News, 23rd Oct.
667.	Wrong razor	J. Tel., 24th Oct.
668.	Synagogue seats	J. Tel., 31st Oct.
669.	Super-pious seating	J.Post, 3rd Nov.

670.	Story not creditworthy	J.Trib., 6th Nov.
671.	Wasted food at simchas was so appalling	J. Tel., 7th Nov.
672.	Light that died with Kennedy rekindled	Ind., 7th Nov.
673.	TV Licensing's tactics	D. Tel., 11th Nov.
674.	Mormon mumbo-jumbo	J. Post, 12th Nov.
675.	Seriousness of silence in shul	J. News, 13th Nov.
676.	Treife option	J. Tel., 14th Nov.
677.	The Missing hekesh	J. Trib., 20th Nov.
678.	Cheaper meat	J. Tel., 21st Nov.
679.	Ribis and credit cards	J. Trib., 27th Nov.
680.	Military targets in the Middle East	Ind. 28th Nov.
681.	Non-kosher meat	J. Tel., 28th Nov.
682.	Hekkesh debate continues	J. Trib., 4th Dec.
683.	What happened to hekesh	Yat. US, 5th Dec.
684.	Points of view	M.E.N., 8th Dec.
685.	Congestion delays Manchester buses	Fin.Tim., 9th Dec.
686.	Bedtime yawn	J. Post, 10th Dec.
687.	Hekkesh: summing up	J. Trib., 18th Dec.
688.	More on Hekesh	Yat. US, 19th Dec.
689.	Bedroom TV	J. Tel., 24th Dec.
690.	Jewish standards	J. Post, 30th Dec.
691.	Mass murder	Ir. Ind., 31st Dec.
692.	In hindsight	J. Tel., 31st Dec.
693.	Mileil and milra	J. Trib., 31st Dec.

In addition, there are a large number of contributions on topics of Jewish interest on the Mail Jewish website, which can be accessed at http://mail-jewish.org

KEY

Amudim	pub. by HaKibbutz HaDati, Tel Aviv
Aus. J. News	Australian Jewish News, Melbourne

B. Tel.	The Belfast Telegraph, Belfast
Bir. J. Rec.	Birmingham Jewish Recorder, Birmingham
Cat. & Anc. Hist.	Catastrophism and Ancient History, A Journal of Interdisciplinary Study, Los Angeles
CofE News.	Church of England Newspaper, London
Comp. J.	The Computer Journal pub. by The British Computer Society
D. Tel.	The Daily Telegraph, London
Fin. Tim.	Financial Times, London
Guard.	The Guardian, London
Ha'aretz	Tel Aviv
HaMaor	pub. by The Federation of Synagogues, London
HaModia	Jerusalem
Hen. Times	The Hendon and Finchley Times (et al.) pub. by Newsquest Media Group, London
Her.	The Herald, Glasgow
Ind.	The Independent, London
Int. J. Math. Ed.	International Journal of Mathematical Education in Science and Technology, pub. by The Center for Advancement of Mathematical Education in Technology, University of Technology, Loughborough
Inter.	Intercom, pub. by The Association of Orthodox Jewish Scientists, New York
Ir. Ex.	Irish Examiner, Cork
Ir. Ind.	Irish Independent, Dublin
Ir. Times	Irish Times, Dublin
J. Chron.	Jewish Chronicle, London
J. Echo	Jewish Echo, Glasgow

J. Gaz.	Jewish Gazette, Leeds & Manchester
J. News	Jewish News, London
J. Post	Jerusalem Post, Jerusalem
J. Press	Jewish Press, New York
J. Tel.	Jewish Telegraph, Glasgow, Leeds, Liverpool & Manchester
J. Trad.	Jewish Tradition, Johannesburg
J. Trib.	Jewish Tribune, London
J. Zeit.	Judische Zeitung, Zurich
Le'ela	pub. by The Office of the Chief Rabbi and Jews' College, London
Lon. J. News	London Jewish News, London
Math. Gaz.	Mathematical Gazette, pub. by The Mathematical Association, Leicester
Math. Mag.	Mathematics Magazine, pub. by The Mathematical Association of America, Santa Clara, California
Math. Rev.	Mathematics Review
M.E.N.	Manchester Evening News, Manchester
Metro	Metro, London et al.
Niv haMidr.	Niv haMidrashia, pub. by The Friends of the Midrashia in Israel, Tel Aviv
Obs.	The Observer, London
Sal. Adv.	Salford Advertiser, Salford
Scot.	The Scotsman, Edinburgh
S. Her.	The Sunday Herald, Glasgow
S. Tel	The Sunday Telegraph, London
Tab.	The Tablet, London
Teach. Math.	Teaching Mathematics and its Applications,

Theta	pub. by Crewe & Alsager College of Higher Education, Crewe
Times	The Times, London
Week	The Week, London
Voice	The Voice of the Community, pub. by The Manchester Beth Din, Manchester
Yated	Yated Ne'eman, Jerusalem
Yat. US	Yated Ne'eman (US edition), Monsey, NY
Yis. Yis.	Yismach Yisroel, Manchester

ABOUT THE AUTHOR

Martin Stern studied mathematics at Cambridge University, where he received a bachelor of arts degree and continued his research in Oxford, receiving his master of arts degree. He took up a post as Lecturer in Mathematics at the John Dalton College of Technology, later named Manchester Metropolitan University.

Beginning in 1985, the author became involved in defending Torah Judaism in the more secular Anglo-Jewish press, and developed an interest in liturgical and social problems affecting the Jewish community. He was particularly active in the largely successful campaign to combat the attempts of the Masorti (Conservative) movement to establish itself in Manchester. In more recent years he has used his epistolary skills to defend Israel against its detractors, both in the more secular Anglo-Jewish and general non-Jewish press.

He is well known for his forthright approach, and refusal to bow, to political correctness of any kind – something that has led, on occasion, to abuse by those who cannot tolerate independent thought.